More praise for *Great Customer Connections*

"In this book Gallagher enables people to manage complex and ever-changing situations with easy-to-grasp ideas and techniques. His work has literally transformed how we at the university have been working with parents, students, and others—and now some of our staff who were struggling have become stars."

   —Dr. Adam Weinberg, Dean of the College, Colgate University

"Gallagher has nailed the essence of serving others with practical ideas that work. Make great connections with your customers today!"

   —John G. Miller, author of *QBQ! The Question Behind the Question* and *Flipping the Switch*

GREAT CUSTOMER CONNECTIONS

Simple Psychological Techniques That Guarantee Exceptional Service

Richard S. Gallagher

◆**AMACOM** **AMERICAN MANAGEMENT ASSOCIATION**

New York ■ Atlanta ■ Brussels ■ Chicago ■ Mexico City ■ San Francisco
Shanghai ■ Tokyo ■ Toronto ■ Washington, D.C.

This publication is designed to provide accurate and authoritative information in regard to the subject matter covered. It is sold with the understanding that the publisher is not engaged in rendering legal, accounting, or other professional service. If legal advice or other expert assistance is required, the services of a competent professional person should be sought.

Library of Congress Cataloging-in-Publication Data

Gallagher, Richard S.
    Great customer connections : simple psychological techniques that guarantee exceptional service / Richard S. Gallagher.
        p.   cm.
    Includes bibliographical references and index.
    ISBN 10: 0-8144-7308-3 (pbk.)
    ISBN 13: 978-0-8144-7308-5
    1. Customer services.   2. Customer services—Psychological aspects.
3. Customer relations.   4. Customer relations—Psychological aspects.
I. Title.

HF5415.5.G348   2006
658.8'12—dc22

                                                        2005033220

Printing number

10   9   8   7   6   5   4   3   2   1

*To my wife, **Colleen**—and to all who share the pleasure of serving others.*

C O N T E N T S

Preface   xi
Acknowledgments   xv

1   The New Science of Customer Service   1

A New Way of Looking at Customers   2
Beyond Attitude   4
What This Book Will Cover   8

2   The Inner Game of Customer Contact   11

The Science of How We Give Off "Vibes"   12
Beyond "Vibes"—Tapping into the Inner Game of Customer Contact   14
Your New Mind-Set: Becoming a Neutral Observer   25

3   The First Thirty Seconds   29

The Opening Greeting: Getting Beyond "Hello"   30
The Turning Point: Your First Response   34
The Art of Active Listening   37
Creating Great Customer Experiences in Thirty Seconds   44

4 Getting the Message Across 45

Why We Don't Communicate Customer Information Well 46
How to Deliver the Message: The Staging Technique 48
How Staging Works 49
It's Never Just the Situation 59

5 Getting into Your Customer's Head 61

The *Jeopardy!* Technique—Putting Things in the Form of a Question 62
When the Customer Is Always Wrong—Using the "I" Technique 67
Role Reversal: Speaking Like a Customer 71
The Ultimate Goal: Think Like a Customer 73

6 Respect and Empathy: More Than a Feeling 75

Looking at Respect 76
Understanding Empathy 82
Moving from Personal Feelings to Professional Skills 88

7 How to (Almost) Never Say No 89

How to Stop Saying No: Doing the Can-Can 90
The Can-Can in Detail 94
Beyond the Can-Can 102
The Can-Can Way of Life 104

8 How to Become a Human Bomb Squad 107

Understanding Why We Get Angry 108
Defusing a Crisis: The Triple-A Approach 110
Putting the Triple-A Technique to Work 118
Angry and Abusive Are Two Different Things 122
The Paradox of Angry Customers 125

9 Managing Specific Customer Personalities   127

Your Personality   128
Customer Personalities: Four Key Types   129
How to Say the Same Thing in Four Different Languages   136
Personality and You   138

10 Wrapping Things Up   141

The Talkaholic   142
The Strong, Silent Type   146
The Nonlinear Thinker   148
The Needy Novice   151
The Verbal Receipt   154

11 The Tough Cases   157

Case 1: Oops!   158
Case 2: The Stakes Are High   162
Case 3: Mr. Angry   164
Case 4: Painting the Town Red   168
Case 5: Too Close to Your Customer   170
It's All in the Fundamentals   173

12 Pulling It All Together   175

The Core in Common   176
In Closing: The "A" Word   178

Appendix A. Coaching for Peak Customer Experiences   181

The Case for Coaching   182
Strength-Based Coaching   184
Customer Skills as Coaching Skills   188
Effective Coaching: Some Closing Thoughts   193

Appendix B. From Customer Service to Real Life   197

The Chatty Coworker   198
When Your Friends Hit a Sour Note   200
That *Was* a Nice Vase   203
Home (Not So) Sweet Home   206
When Customer Skills Save Lives   210
Postscript: How to Be a Better Customer   212

Appendix C. Customer Skills for Great Customer Connections   215

I.   Before the Transaction Starts   215
II.   At the Beginning of a Transaction   216
III. Basic Customer Communications   218
IV.   Showing Respect and Empathy   220
V.   Preventing and Defusing Confrontations   221
VI.   Managing Specific Customer Personalities   222
VII. Wrapping Things Up   223

Notes   227
Index   231
About the Author   239

This book will change the way that you communicate with customers. Perhaps more important, it will also change the way that you look at customer situations—from an art to a science.

Many people feel that the skills of good service should be obvious: Smile. Be nice to people. Think good thoughts. But in reality, good service goes against human nature. The reason that clerks often greet you with the phrase, "We're closing in five minutes," dates back to prehistoric times, when people wanted a piece of that juicy brontosaurus we just hunted for dinner—and we would instinctively, for the sake of our own survival, respond with all the things we can't, won't, and don't do. We are biologically programmed to protect ourselves first, rather than serve others.

If we fast-forward to the present day, this same human nature governs how we instinctively respond when people confront us with their problems. The things that feel the most natural to say often fail us when we are face-to-face with a customer. And even the nicest people in the world often feel helpless and powerless when confronted with difficult customer situations such as unrealistic expectations, unsolvable problems, and angry words.

That's where this book comes in. It teaches you a set of simple—but extremely powerful—techniques that will dramatically change the way customers react to you. They are all based around established principles of behavioral psychology but are surprisingly easy to put into practice. Their secret lies in the fact that they almost all run counter to human nature—but when you put them in action, they give you the power to handle interpersonal situations like you never have before.

There is a lot in common between these communications skills and physical skills. Exercise goes against our human nature to lead sedentary lives, but it can make a big change in our health and long-term survival. When we are injured, physical therapists coach us to do things that do not feel right at first but eventually restore our strength and range of motion. In much the same way, learning and practicing these communication skills may feel different for most people at first, but they will make powerful changes in the way that you relate to others—with a potentially major impact on your career, your interpersonal relationships, and your life.

There is no such thing as a college degree in customer service. My degree happens to be in engineering, with a dual major in psychology. My fraternity brothers at Cornell University in the 1970s joked that I would grow up to design bridges that would talk people out of jumping off of them, but in reality I spent much of my career doing something that drew heavily from both fields—managing customer support call center operations for software companies. There are few more interesting behavioral science laboratories than a customer contact center, and it was here that I observed firsthand the impact of changing how we communicate.

Since then, I have been fascinated by the mechanics of how people interact with each other. As a veteran of more than twenty-five thousand customer transactions and over a quarter century of management experience, I have been equally fascinated by the remarkable results that certain interpersonal techniques have when you learn and practice them. The teams I have managed and the thousands of people I have trained were able to consistently transform their service quality—and their own self-confidence—by following the techniques in this book. These methods have a track record that includes worst-to-first turnarounds in customer rankings; near-zero turnover levels; and even one campus where, amazingly, one hundred trained student employees had *no* customer complaints for an entire semester. These techniques really work, and you can literally and figuratively take the results to the bank.

This book examines the psychology behind what happens at each stage of a customer transaction and, perhaps more important, puts this psychology to work with specific, named techniques that you can use right away in your own customer situations. The book also explores deeper issues such as how to coach other people to use these skills, how to manage the most difficult situations, and how to extend these skills beyond customer service into other areas of your life. Above all, we put forth the concept that you can make nearly any customer situation go extremely well, with no need to change your basic personality, by simply fine-tuning the mechanics of what you say and think. Communications skills with customers are exactly that—skills—that you can learn and practice.

My greatest pet peeve in life is hearing customer service described in terms of being quote-unquote "nice people" with a "good attitude." In reality, there is a great deal of science behind what happens in great customer experiences. By following this science, we all have the power to become supremely confident in our interactions with other human beings. My wish for you is to start seeing customer service in a completely new light—as a set of professional skills, much like those of being a doctor, an athlete, or a craftsperson—and use these skills to benefit your life, as well as the lives of those you serve.

A C K N O W L E D G M E N T S

I t would not be physically possible to thank each of the people who have played a role in the ideas, concepts, and life experiences that form the contents of this book—however, particular credit is due to the following people:

- First and foremost, to all of my students in the many communications skills and leadership courses that I have taught over the years. I never stop learning from you, and your energy and enthusiasm for solving real-life customer problems continually inspire me.

- To the many good friends and professional colleagues who have shared their insights and supported my work. In particular, I would like to thank Professor Susan Hecht for nurturing a long and satisfying writing career, Lou Crain for my first experience managing a worldwide customer support operation, Fredrick R. "Dick" Kippola and Katie Spallone for sharing their expertise on retail customer situations, Rene Palmer for inspiring an excellent customer case study, retired police officer Janice Pack for her insight on how people respond in crisis situations, trainer and facilitator extraordinaire Beth Van Dine for her observations on strength-based coaching, and many others who are too numerous to name.

- To Diana Finch, my literary agent, who probably set a world land speed record for responding to a book proposal (approximately four hours), and shepherded this project to one of the world's great publishing houses in this field.

- To Ellen Kadin, my editor at AMACOM Books, Associate Editor Erika Spelman, and all the professional staff at AMACOM who were involved in the production of this book. It is an honor and a pleasure to work with all of you.

- Finally, and most importantly, to my wife, Colleen. One of my greatest rewards for learning good communication skills in the workplace was meeting you over thirty years ago. I love you.

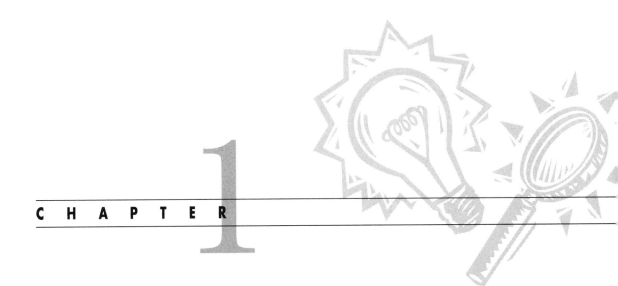

THE NEW SCIENCE OF CUSTOMER SERVICE

There are basically two types of books about customer service: One type talks about how to be a nicer person, and the other presents stirring war stories about doing great things for customers. This book is neither of these.

This book looks at customer service in a way that most people have never looked at it before: as a science, based on known principles of behavioral psychology, that will help you become supremely confident in the way that you interact with people—even in difficult situations. When you master these skills—which is easier than you think—you gain a whole new set of powers that let you:

- Instantly connect with people from the moment you speak to them

- Discuss delicate situations with grace and tact

- Defuse angry people and turn them into allies

- Make people feel special and important

- Speak in each customer's own unique language

- Control the transaction and bring it to a smooth, productive ending

And when you manage teams of people who work with the public and coach people on these skills, the benefits are even greater— including dramatic improvements in performance, higher morale, lower turnover, and customers who flock to your business. These skills will help your bottom line soar, but they go much deeper than that: These skills create an environment where both you and your employees come to work with a smile on your faces every day and leave for home with one as well. As someone who has watched this approach work time after time, in real-world customer contact teams all over the world, the results are nothing short of magical.

The price for all of these benefits? Simply learning and practicing some simple, verbal techniques that will quickly become a natural part of how you communicate with people. These techniques can replace our human nature with a new set of skills based around the best knowledge that modern behavioral science has to offer. These skills will do more than help you treat people better: They will change your life. Read on, and start taking a fresh new look at the relationship between you and your customers.

A NEW WAY OF LOOKING AT CUSTOMERS

Customer service, like many things in life, is often seen as a morality play. There are good people in it, and bad people. The good people are nice, have great attitudes, and go the extra mile to please you. The bad people are surly, indifferent, and undercook your breakfast. And much of what passes for customer service skills training consists of urging you to be a good person rather than a bad person.

Like any stereotype, there is a grain of truth in this view of the world. There are people who naturally interact well with customers, and those who naturally do not. Nevertheless, I would like to introduce a very different view—one that will dramatically change the way you interact with customers, both now and in the future. This view is based on science rather than feelings. And, more important, this view has been proven over and over again to work.

Your Car Is Gone—Can I Help You?

"What do you say to someone after you've just towed their car away?"

As a trainer, I often pose this question to people in the audience—and then usually encourage a couple of brave volunteers to role-play the situation. Invariably, the situation turns out the same way every time: The first person tries to explain why he or she had to tow the car away, the second person gets angrier and angrier—even in role play—and even the nicest people quickly become like deer frozen in the headlights.

Next, we start looking at the seemingly impossible task of wording this situation in ways that benefit the customer. After some hemming and hawing, the ideas start to flow from the audience: "Your car is in a safe place." "Even though it unfortunately was towed away, I can help you get your car back." "I get frustrated when things like this happen to me." Before long, people are seeing this situation with a new set of eyes—and when we role-play it again, the person whose car has been towed now finds it very hard to stay angry. ■

Many people look at customer service as a matter of how to be nice to people. To me, it is also the science of how you tell people that you have just towed their car away—in a way that most effectively reunites them with their car, while preserving dignity and good feelings on both sides. Put on a larger scale, customer service is the science of how to communicate in any customer situation, in a way that produces the most positive outcome for everyone. This book introduces the liberating idea that you don't need to change your personality to create excellent customer experiences, but rather can take a fresh look at the mechanics of what you say—in short, by replacing smile training with specific verbal skills.

Nearly every interaction between you and a customer has the potential to go very well, or very badly. And as often as not, the reason has little to do with courtesy or attitude but a great deal to do with behavioral psychology. For example, the way that we encouraged people to respond in the previous situation wasn't advice that we simply made up—it involved known communications techniques whose results are extremely powerful. The reality of the situation remains exactly the same either way: The person's car has been towed, and he or she still must pay to retrieve it. But by simply changing the "script" of what you say and do within this reality, you achieve a very different outcome.

This is one small example of a broad range of structured communications skills, which in total create a different kind of customer experience from what we are normally accustomed to. Most of these skills share one important thing in common—they are at odds with how we are instinctively programmed to react to someone else's problems. This means that changing the dynamics of a customer situation requires changing your normal reactions, by using specific communications techniques that you learn and practice.

These techniques may make sense to you intellectually, but they will probably feel strange when you first start to use them in real life—much like learning a new golf grip or signing your name with the wrong hand. However, with time and practice, these techniques will become an instinctive part of who you are and how you respond to people—which, in turn, will dramatically change the interactions between you and your customers.

BEYOND ATTITUDE

If you are reading this book, chances are that you—or the people you manage—are among the majority of working adults who serve the public in some capacity. Many of you will spend this day taking our dinner orders, solving our technical problems, handling our complaints, or saving our lives—and then get up tomorrow and do it all over again.

This means that you are no stranger to the term *customer service* and probably have the same image of customer service as most people—that you should smile, be courteous, say "please" and "thank you," and treat customers like they are always right. Deep down inside, you may even believe that excellent customer service is primarily the domain of perky, happy people who always get up on the right side of bed and never have a bad-hair day, but not you.

You could refer to this image as the "attitude" school of customer service—and there is some truth to it, because nice people do tend to provide better customer experiences than unpleasant ones. However, in my own experience of managing real-world customer support operations and training thousands of people in communications skills, this isn't enough. Nor, surprisingly, is it even the most important thing. Being nice will not carry you through a situation where someone is loudly demanding something you cannot give him or her. Smiling won't defuse a tense situation where you have to deliver bad news to someone. And courtesy won't help you take back control of the conversation when someone is overbearing. But the good news is that you *can* handle these situations differently, with the help of a little applied psychology.

In the attitude school of customer service, managers routinely urge their employees to be nice to people, develop slogans to encourage good service, bring in motivational speakers who talk about having a

FROM GOOD SERVICE TO "WOW" SERVICE

"A few weeks from now, you are all going to see customers in a completely new light." These were my first words at an all-hands meeting of a customer support call center that I had just joined as its new manager—a team of talented, dedicated people providing twenty-four-hour technical support for a mission-critical software product.

Soon after this meeting, we had the first of several training sessions designed to change the way they responded to the customer situations that they identified as being the most difficult—such as what to say when they could not give someone an on-the-spot answer, how to defuse an irate client, or what to do when someone was talking too much. We also looked in detail at the mechanics of how we did things like greet customers, close transactions, and execute when situations happened. We role-played real-life examples of these situations as a team and followed up with one-on-one coaching over a period of several weeks.

At first, many people found it too easy to revert to human nature and handled situations the way that they always did. But when we started to coach these skills with people individually, things began to change—gradually at first, and then one by one the lights started to come on for everyone on the team. Within a few weeks there was a real change in the air, and from there the results were nothing short of amazing: near-perfect annual customer satisfaction ratings from our clients, best-of-class rankings in industry benchmarks—and a fresh new spirit that was reflected in near-zero turnover for nearly two years.

great attitude, and criticize people when they do not handle customers well. Does this sound like your workplace? If so, you have lots of company, because this scenario follows our human nature. However, with the approach we used in the accompanying sidebar, none of these things happened:

- Instead of being asked to change their attitudes, people were taught techniques that changed the mechanics of what they said and did.

- Instead of being focused on "treating customers better," the focus was on developing life skills that benefited both their work and their personal life.

- Instead of simply being told what to do by an instructor, they actively role-played situations, performed team exercises, and had one-on-one follow-up coaching.

- Instead of being criticized when they made mistakes back on the floor, these situations became positive and nonjudgmental teaching moments.

More important, instead of following human nature, we followed several timeless principles of behavioral psychology. Although some people refer to customer interactions as a "soft skill," in reality there is a great deal of hard science behind what happens during the interaction between you and a customer:

- When you deliver bad news to customers, they often react badly.

However, when you rephrase bad news in a specific way—with a formal introduction, a detailed explanation, and a choice of words that speaks from within their frame of reference—they almost *never* get upset with you.

- When you tell customers that they did something wrong, they will usually become defensive. However, if you instead "model" their behavior from your own perspective, by talking about what *you* would or wouldn't do, they almost always "get it" and don't feel threatened.

- When you try to ignore an overly talkative person, it fuels the person to talk even more. However, when you actively and enthusiastically engage this person with the right kinds of questions, you can usually take control of the conversation very quickly.

These are just three examples among a wealth of predictable "moments of truth" that occur at known points in the life cycle of a customer transaction. Throughout this book, we will look in detail at how to understand and manage these situations, as well as the many others that occur across the life cycle of a customer service transaction. These skills are part of a growing evolution in the psychology of how we interact with customers—one that steps away from simply telling you to be nice, and moves toward specific verbal skills and techniques that you can use in real-world customer situations.

There is a strong parallel between this evolution and one that has gone on for a long time in professional sports, because competitive teams have a strong incentive to understand the behavioral psychology of what makes them win. Once upon a time, the popular image of a sports coach was that of a short-tempered taskmaster who exhorted people to win at all costs, and yelled at them when they messed up. Today, the most successful coaches are often master tacticians and, more important, master *technicians*.

Winning: It's All in the Mechanics

New York Yankees skipper Joe Torre isn't big on motivational speeches. He rarely raises his voice and hates team meetings. Nevertheless, literally hundreds of times per year, he meets one-on-one with his players—to get into their heads, to discuss scenarios, and to talk through the mechanics of how they play. In his book *Joe Torre's Ground Rules for*

Winners, Torre summarizes his philosophy as "winning is a by-product" and feels that by keeping his focus on the skill sets of his players, the winning will take care of itself. The results of his coaching style speak for themselves, with his Yankees being perennial division and World Series champions since the mid-1990s.[1]

On a broader scale, a typical baseball coach from a generation ago might walk out to the mound and tell a struggling pitcher to pitch better—or else. Today, that same coach is more likely to walk out to the mound and say things like, "How is your arm strength? Your fastball is dropping about a foot closer to the plate than it usually does. What do you think about switching to a four-seam fastball for this batter?" The way that Joe Torre describes his management style, he would be unlikely to scream at a player to play better—but he would be very likely to pull him aside at regular intervals and discuss the mechanics of how he functions at the plate and on the field. ∎

My goal in this book is not to teach you how to be more polite but to teach you when to use a four-seam fastball. And we will do it by learning structured communications skills that will get the response you want from customers and coaching skills that will get the response you want from people on your team—with no need to change your personality in the process. When you nail the mechanics of both of these skill sets, the good feelings that we call "attitude" invariably follow as a by-product.

Let's bring some of these principles around to the real world, and look at an actual situation that I recently experienced with a particular service provider. I had inadvertently applied a payment to the wrong account number and needed to get the charge reversed. Here is what transpired:

Agent: Welcome to XYZ Corporation, where we promise to help you in ten minutes or less, guaranteed.

Me: Hi, I'm having a problem with a charge that needs to be reversed.

Agent: I'm sorry, sir, but our computers are down. You'll have to call us back later.

Me: Can't you take the information and follow up on it?

Agent: No, sir.

Me: So you aren't guaranteeing to help me in ten minutes or less?

Agent: Sir, you don't understand; our computers are down.

Some people may look at this transaction as a case of an indifferent attitude on the part of the agent. Others may look at it as a case of a customer who doesn't understand that there is a problem beyond the agent's control. Still others may chuckle at the irony between this company's scripted greeting and the reality of the situation. However, I see it as a perfect example of a transaction chock-full of interactions that—if worded differently—would create very different feelings, and a very different outcome.

Up to this point, we have frequently mentioned a simple two-word reason why these transactions are so common: *human nature*. In this book, we will explore new ways to communicate that transcend human nature, based on known principles of behavioral psychology. At first, many of them will feel like wearing a T-shirt backward. However, with time—and, more important, practice—they will become a natural part of who you are and how you communicate.

Now, let's return to this transaction and break down the mechanics of what happened in a little more detail:

Review the dialogue in Table 1-1 and then take a moment and mentally play back the responses in the right-hand column in your mind. How would you feel if you were that person's customer? I suspect that many people would feel much better speaking with the person in the far-right column, even if they are not happy about the situation itself.

However, I also want to point out something even more important—at a quick glance, many people would interpret the person in that column as simply being "nicer" about the problem. I am here to tell you that there are specific techniques, at each point in the life cycle of this transaction, that go beyond attitude and become innate skills. Nearly any person can sound like the person in the right-hand column, no matter who he or she is or what his or her personality is, by learning and practicing a specific set of techniques—which, in time, become your natural way of communicating.

WHAT THIS BOOK WILL COVER

This book is based around the premise that excellent customer experiences fundamentally have their roots in what we say to people. In the chapters that follow, we will look in detail at specific techniques to use at each stage of a customer transaction. Starting from when a customer first approaches, we will examine the crucial first thirty seconds of the encounter, and then move forward to those issues that form the

Table 1-1. Human nature vs. customer skills.

Situation	Human nature	Customer skills
Customer introduces problem.	Focus on your problems: "I'm sorry, sir, our computers are down."	Focus on the customer's expectations: "I certainly understand. Normally we can straighten this out right here on the phone."
You can't give customer what he or she wants.	Tell the customer what to do: "You'll have to call us back later."	Give the customer options worded to his or her benefit: "If you can send the request from our website, we can process it as soon as our computers are up. Would you like to do that, or would it be easier to call us back later?"
Saying no.	Just say no: "No, sir."	Anticipate the customer's reaction: "I wish that there was a way that we could do this, because I hate to see you have to call back again."
The customer questions your response.	Defend yourself: "Sir, you don't understand; our computers are down."	Speak from the customer's voice: "It's really frustrating when we can't help people in a situation like this."

groundwork of a customer transaction: how to communicate effectively, deliver information, get into a customer's mind-set, and look at some surprising ways to show respect and empathy.

Next, we look in detail at the tough issues of working with customers: preventing confrontations from starting by managing expectations, defusing angry situations, understanding specific personalities, and handling people who take up large amounts of time. The approaches we use here may surprise you as well: For example, you will learn how to strike the word *no* from your vocabulary (really!), how to calm down an angry person without ever needing to defend yourself, and how to quickly "smoke out" different customer types and speak their language. These approaches are based on solid behavioral research, as well as extensive experience in the real world, and you will be amazed at how well they will work with your own customers.

Finally, we move on to the advanced course: a novel and effective strategy for coaching other people with these customer skills; advice on how to apply these skills in some of the toughest real-life situations imaginable; and, perhaps most important, an insightful look at how these skills can change all the relationships in your life, inside and outside of work.

This book is designed to teach you interpersonal and leadership skills that will last for a lifetime, and change your perceptions about how you deal with people—and in my experience, there is no limit to where these skills can take you. Read on, and you will learn that excellent customer skills are not the domain of a few people who are so-called naturals at it, but can become strong career and life skills for *any* person who learns and practices these techniques.

THE INNER GAME OF CUSTOMER CONTACT

A recent movie portrayed a futuristic world where police could predict who would become a criminal in the future—and then used this information to get these people off the streets ahead of time. In one scene, a fugitive is being chased down. When he is finally caught, the authorities tell him, "You are under arrest for crimes that you have not yet committed."[1]

In a sense, the same kind of process often happens at the beginning of a customer transaction. Your basic stance toward customer situations—combined with cues that individual customers give off, such as clothing, hairstyle, or facial expression—forms an internal mental image in your mind, before they even say a word about what they want or need from you. This mental image often predetermines your reactions, which in turn affect how well the transaction ultimately goes. They are essentially convicted of crimes they have not yet committed—or conversely, given the benefit of your goodwill—before a word is ever spoken between the two of you.

Therefore, while a large part of this book concerns what you say to people, here we are focusing on what you *think*—in other words, your basic mind-set toward a customer. This mind-set has a subtle but important effect on the words you choose, your tone of voice, and your body language, which in turn affect how a customer reacts to you. By using some proven mental imaging techniques, derived from powerful techniques in modern psychology, you can start to create a noticeable difference in your customer interactions before you even open your mouth to speak!

THE SCIENCE OF HOW WE GIVE OFF "VIBES"

Most of us like to think of ourselves as having a consistent personality and, for that matter, a nice one. According to one recent survey, nearly 90 percent of people view themselves as having an above-average level of politeness.[2] But in reality, we all take on many different roles depending on the circumstances. To your boss, you may be a cooperative team player. To the people whom you buy things from, you may be a tough negotiator who is as hard as nails. And to the people you bowl with every Thursday, you are a fun-loving person. Each of these people sees a different side of you and, in fact, might never imagine your having the persona that you show to other people. In all of these cases, whether we realize it or not, we are choosing an emotional state that governs how we react to situations. Some laypeople refer to this as giving off "vibes"—and psychologists have long taught that these "vibes" strongly influence your behavior.

Unfortunately, the basic nature of a customer transaction—with its inherent challenges and potential for confrontation—often leads us to choose a mental image of customers that does not benefit either the situation or ourselves. We may subconsciously react to someone's displeasure, bristle at how she speaks or dresses, or replay the difficulties of past customer situations before a word is ever spoken. But when we become aware of this natural tendency, and adopt the right mind-set for a customer situation, we can make things go much better for both customers and ourselves.

First, be aware that this process is naturally influenced by your own biases toward other people. When we interact with another person, we often choose our vibes in response to that person's vibes, and vice versa. Based on your own life experiences, you may feel that specific people are too rebellious, too square, or look too much like your crabby uncle. When they are "too" something, it triggers an automatic pattern recognition process, as part of what psychologists refer to as *social cognition.*[3] It springs from an innate learning process that keeps us from having to relearn our responses to specific people: when someone seems to fit a certain profile, for example, we mentally put on the "crabby uncle" tape, which preprograms a different set of behaviors and responses than, say, the "friend down the street" tape.

Like many behaviors, social cognition has its roots as a survival trait. Those ancestors who learned that a rustle in the bushes could mean a predator, or that a scowling person was more likely to bop them on the head, were much more likely to survive and pass these pattern recognition skills along to future generations. Moreover, there are strong biological pressures to sustain these stereotypes. If you see a tough-looking group of people on a nearby street corner, little or nothing is lost by avoiding them, even if they are completely harmless. But if you walk past them anyway and guess wrong, you could end up threatened—or even dead. As a result, we tend strongly toward the negative option of self-protective behavior, even when it excludes many less-threatening situations.[4]

This explains why, when you walk into a store, the first thing you sometimes hear is "We're closing in ten minutes." More often than not, statements like this are purely the result of our natural self-protective instinct kicking in. In this case, the store clerk may be responding to perhaps a 5 percent chance that you would not leave by closing time—and, more important, the much smaller chance that you would argue with him about it. As a result of being primed to respond to unpleasant but low-probability events, much of our innate behavior resembles that of a bad psychic who is constantly foretelling the future but guessing wrong most of the time. In the process, we often lose those moments that let us build great service and strong customer relationships, as we continue to build these protective walls without even thinking.

In addition to our own learning, many psychologists feel that we are all born with an innate process of recognizing friend versus foe, based on inherited past experience. Carl Jung referred to this process as a *collective unconscious* of traits that we inherit from the genetic experiences of all of the ancestors who came before us.[5] At a practical level, it means that people whose neurobiology made them more cautious about situations were less likely to be eaten by predators, leaving them alive to pass their genetics on to subsequent generations. Put in today's terms, this means that the way you respond to an upset customer may have as much to do with your historical predecessors outrunning a hungry bear as it does with your modern social skills.

All of these things combine to form the science of how we give off vibes to other people, and in turn react to these vibes from others. Perhaps, most important, this process encompasses more than just an animal instinct—it is also a skill that can be learned and refined to our benefit. In fields such as law enforcement and the military, for example, the science of threat assessment involves learning to read everything from facial expressions to the characteristics of a crowd to judge the level of danger and react appropriately. Conversely, we can also learn to rise above our normal reactions: a good example is when professional actors get into a mind-set that lets them react with specific emotions like joy, anger, or passion even when it's the fourteenth take, and they personally would rather be doing their taxes.

Putting these skills in the context of customer situations, most of us tend to behave a little like the cops—in other words, we develop a hypervigilance to potential threats that may be appropriate for a hostile crowd, but doesn't help our interests in serving customers. Our goal here is to help you react more like the actors—by looking at techniques to change your basic mind-set toward a customer, and thereby change the emotional stance that you take toward a customer, before the transaction even begins.

BEYOND "VIBES"—TAPPING INTO THE INNER GAME OF CUSTOMER CONTACT

Human nature often works against us when someone confronts us with a problem or complaint, because we are inherently programmed to identify friends and foes, or good versus bad situations, and we tend to respond to both things in ways that protect our so-called turf. But the good news is that you can change this mind-set, with the help of a little psychology. And when you do, you will observe a very noticeable difference in the way that customers interact with you.

In this section, we will break down the three most common things that go wrong when you first encounter a customer. All of them are essentially errors in judgment, which create bad feelings even before a transaction begins. What all three share in common is a tendency to create a mental image that is frequently incorrect—and, more to the point, not helpful to either you or the customer. These three key errors are:

1. *Negative expectation*—thinking and acting under the assumption that a customer has ill intentions toward you

2. *Stereotyping*—forming a judgment about how a customer will act based on external appearances such as what he or she looks like, dresses like, or says

3. *Personalization*—making an incorrect presumption that a customer's feelings are directed toward you personally

For most of us, these feelings are universal to some degree; and because of this, they are often hard to recognize within ourselves, because they feel so natural in real life. But they can be recognized—and changed—with practice. Here, we will look at some specific techniques that you can use to prevent these errors in judgment in order to create a different outcome with your customers in the future.

Negative Expectation

How many times have you walked into a store and had a conversation that goes something like this?

You: I'd like to rent a copy of the movie *Dangerous Customers.*

Clerk: We're normally out of stock on that title.

You: No, you aren't. I just saw it on the shelf.

Clerk: Well, OK then. Just remember that you'll have to return it by Monday, or there will be a $10 per day late fee.

You: No problem, I plan to return it on Sunday.

Clerk: We close at 3 P.M. on Sundays.

What you are seeing here is an example of a mind-set known as *negative expectation*—that is, the unspoken presumption of bad intentions from the other person, which in turn leads us to focus almost exclusively on protecting ourselves.

Negative expectation is almost universal in the world of customer interactions. As we mentioned earlier, most of us wake up every morning secure in the belief that we are nice people. But then we go to work, and as we interact with people, we find—almost without knowing it—that we tend naturally to respond to nearly everything in ways that defend or protect ourselves, rather than in ways that speak to the interests of a customer. This, in turn, often creates bad feelings in the minds of the people whom we serve.

The phenomenon of negative expectation is so well known in fields such as psychology and medicine that there is even a clinical term for it: the *nocebo* effect. This term, taken from the Latin term for "I will harm," is the opposite of the well-known *placebo* effect, where people expect to benefit from a dummy treatment. With negative expectation, people expect that they will *not* benefit and imagine problems so clearly in their own minds that they react accordingly. This effect explains why patients in research studies who get harmless sugar pills instead of medication often report experiencing severe (and totally imaginary) side effects—and, more important, why many people react negatively to others in what should otherwise be harmless customer situations.[6]

In the previous example where you were trying to rent a movie, it would be easy to interpret the clerk's responses as having something against you—to the point where you may wonder if he actually wants your business! Ironically, this person is probably not reacting to you personally at all. Instead, he is probably reacting to the last customer who brought in a tape late and argued with him—or a boss who yelled at him for not enforcing store policies—or a gang of kids who kept him from closing on time two months ago. In any event, you are now the beneficiary of a normal human urge toward self-protection, fueled by past experience.

Negative expectation is unique in the sense that it often remains hidden from our consciousness as we are doing it. You rarely notice it when you are the person working with customers. When you are on the receiving end of it, however, it is immediately obvious and often perceived as a bad attitude. More accurately, it is a mind-set we enter when we focus on our own interests—and the key to dealing with it lies in recognizing and changing this mind-set, before a customer even shows up.

Dealing with Negative Expectation: Unconditional Positive Regard

The late Carl Rogers was one of the great psychology researchers of the twentieth century. He is credited by many with coming up with one of the first unified approaches to personality and psychotherapy. He was also a genuinely kind and gentle man, and perhaps his greatest research discovery sprung from his own personal nature: the idea that the effectiveness of psychotherapy depended in large part on how much empathy people felt from their psychotherapists, and not just the techniques used.

A cornerstone of Dr. Rogers's approach to therapy was a principle known as *unconditional positive regard*. In practice, this approach meant turning therapy sessions into a judgment-free zone where a person experienced unconditional empathy for whatever he or she was feeling, and a genuine effort on the part of the therapist to see the person's perspective. In his classic book *On Becoming a Person*, Rogers explained the principle: "When someone understands how it feels and seems to be me, without wanting to analyze and judge me, then I can blossom and grow."[7]

Unconditional positive regard is probably best explained by example, so let's compare it with the normal way of thinking in some typical customer interactions. As you can see from Table 2-1, unconditional positive regard has two components:

1. You frame your thoughts in terms of the customer's reality rather than your own.

2. You genuinely accept the customer's behavior for what it is, within the bounds of fairness.

Table 2-1. Using unconditional positive regard.

Situation	Negative expectation	Unconditional positive regard
A customer is holding up the line.	"She is going to waste everyone's time."	"This person needs a little more time."
You are busy with someone, and another customer tries to get your attention.	"This person is butting in, and I need to straighten him out."	"This situation seems to be very important to him."
A customer picks through every item on the shelf.	"Can't this woman make up her mind?"	"She really wants to make sure that what she purchases is right for her."
A customer is speaking with his friends, and you can hear him from across the store.	"Uh-oh, another loudmouth."	"This person is very expressive with his friends."

BE NICE TO YOUR SHOPLIFTERS

One longtime retail clothing store manager in my native upstate New York has an interesting strategy for dealing with merchandise theft—to kill people with kindness. She explained, "When we see someone who looks a little suspicious to us—like a potential shoplifter—the first thing that we do is engage them. We welcome them warmly to our store and ask if there is anything we can do to help them." She goes on to point out that this kind of attention not only helps them treat all of their customers with respect but makes the bad guys feel conspicuous—with the result that more of their merchandise stays on the shelves.

Of course, underneath their pleasant exterior, she and her staff are still prepared to deal with people who cross the line. "We are very friendly and helpful—but if someone actually tries to steal from us, we don't hesitate to detain them and call the police." However, by putting this unconditional positive regard into practice, they both substantially reduce the number of people who shoplift in the first place and give a good experience to the vast majority of honest customers who enter their store.

Perhaps, most important, unconditional positive regard affects what you think rather than what you do. This is a subtle but very important point. For example, in the case of the person who is interrupting you with another customer, it does not necessarily mean that you drop what you are doing and help him. Rather, it just means that you respect his frame of mind—which, in turn, will make a noticeable difference in your body language, your tone of voice, and the words that you choose, even if you decide to ask him to wait. It is a mental image that will change your vibes. Unconditional positive regard is not just a vague sense of thinking nice thoughts about people. Rather, it is a mind-set that you actively develop over time, which changes the way you look at customers and their problems.

At this point, some perceptive people may be thinking: "How can I practice unconditional positive regard when so many customers behave badly? Every day I deal with people who try to 'game the system' by returning merchandise that they have already worn. Or they damage something in the store and ask for a discount. Or they just plain treat our staff rudely. Sometimes I even have a gut feeling that someone is going to try to shoplift from our store, and it turns out to be correct! How can I feel positive in situations like these?"

My response would be to break these situations into two component parts: the periods of time (a) *before* and (b) *after* a customer actually does or says something bad. My experience is that people react during time (a) in ways that they should reserve for time (b). In other words:

- Because *some* people have returned used merchandise in the past, you emotionally stiffen up when *anyone* returns merchandise.

- Because *some* people have mishandled your merchandise in the past, you react disapprovingly when *anyone* claims that merchandise is damaged and requests a discount.

- Because *some* people have been rude to your staff in the past, you feel stiff and defensive with *everyone*.

This reality that some people, in fact, do bad things, but that most do not should guide your personal mind-set of unconditional positive regard. It means that you still do what you must do, but you don't presume as much as you once did. You still have carte blanche to set limits, enforce rules, and defend your interests *when you need to*, while being consciously aware to keep these concerns separate from your normal, everyday dealings with customers.

To sum this point up in one neat package, our actions and our demeanor invariably reflect what we are feeling inside. Dealing with negative expectation is one of the most important things that you can do for that all-important first impression on customers, and it starts with a conscious decision to assume the best about every person with whom we interact. By developing a sense of unconditional positive regard, we will often find that customers suddenly become more polite, less demanding, and easier to work with—even though the only thing that has changed is ourselves.

Stereotyping

The word *stereotype* is defined in the dictionary as "a standardized mental picture . . . that represents an oversimplified opinion, prejudiced attitude, or uncritical judgment."[8] The word itself springs from a French term for a printing plate that gets cast once and used over and over again. It is a practice that no one approves of, but everyone does.

Stereotyping springs from the same kinds of social cognition skills we discussed earlier—in other words, the ability to recognize patterns of behavior in people and react to them. In some ways, it is a useful and adaptive trait. Because of past assumptions that toddlers have a tendency to wander into the path of oncoming traffic, you spring to the alert when young children are near a road. Similarly, when you see a person in a wheelchair, you may instinctively hold open the door for him or her. In cases like these, stereotyping can be beneficial. Nevertheless, this same trait gets us into trouble when we apply it to other segments of the population—for example, if we presume that women are emotional, college professors are absentminded, or Latin Americans are excitable—and then react accordingly.

Few of us need to look very far to find examples of stereotyping in our own life. Here are just a few examples from my own personal experience:

- An acquaintance of mine once visited a computer store and could not get the sales staff to pay any attention to her. However, when younger customers came in, the sales staff would eagerly help them. As she put it, "As far as they were concerned, I was a middle-aged soccer mom who knew nothing about computers." In reality, she was a noted science fiction author who probably knew more about computers than the store's entire staff combined—and as a result of how she was treated, she left without buying from them.

- One of my first jobs was working the night shift at a campus computer center. One evening, a man showed up wearing work clothes and a tool belt, asking to come in and fix someone's computer. I politely told him that we normally scheduled service calls during the day and asked him to come back later—at which point a coworker quietly pulled me aside and informed me that he was a well-known physics professor who was stopping by after hours to look at his girlfriend's system. (All turned out well: He did get to fix her computer, later hired me for one of my first jobs as a software developer, and years later went on to win the Nobel Prize!)

- One day at a car dealership, several customers were waiting for assistance. One, a scruffy-looking teenager, had his questions impatiently answered by salespeople so that they could rush on to prospects that looked more promising. That teenager was me, over thirty years ago. I had been sent to the dealership by my parents, who were on sabbatical in Europe, to get information about having a new car shipped to them there, and I was probably the most qualified buyer in the showroom.

In all of these cases, the people involved followed their normal human instincts:

- The salespeople at the computer store were probably following past experience about who tended to know little about computers and would therefore be less likely to make a purchase and earn the salespeople a commission. So, they shied away from a situation that they felt would be an unproductive use of their time, even though *this* woman was quite different.

- I observed someone who appeared to be a repairman, based on the way he was dressed—and so I instinctively followed our rules for working with repair people, without asking more questions to understand why *this* person was there.

- The car dealership undoubtedly had a profile of teenage customers as people who had no money and took up their time with unproductive joyrides—not realizing that *this* teenager was a serious new-car buyer.

While at one level, our stereotyping skills can help us to quickly use our judgment in customer situations—such as helping an elderly person to the car with his or her groceries—it can also lead to forming wrong impressions about people. At a darker level, it can lead to the kinds of racial or social profiling that undermines a civilized society. There are still, sadly, too many news stories that surface where people receive poor service because of their race, ethnicity, gender, or other difference. While these incidents move beyond the issue of service quality and diminish us as a society, they also serve as a worst-case example of where human nature can lead us astray in a customer transaction.

Dealing with Stereotyping: Reframing

Stereotyping has its roots in statements that you tell yourself about a customer, based on the person's external appearance, which in turn cause you to form emotions about the customer before you even interact with him or her. These statements may be true ("This person speaks more loudly than I am normally comfortable with") or incorrect ("These kind of people are all the same"), but in either case, they can strongly influence your behavior toward the customer in front of you.

The pull of stereotyping draws on faulty assumptions that surround our own prejudices. However, there is a simple technique that you can use on demand, in any customer situation, to help change your stereotypes about people. I call it *reframing*, and it can be summed up in one basic principle:

Think of one unique thing that you respect about each customer, and picture it clearly in your mind.

The operative phrase here is "one unique thing." You don't have to suddenly become enthralled with each one of your customers. You just have to think of one positive thing that you could possibly respect about this person, which in turn can help you approach the customer with a fresh and positive mental image, as shown in Table 2-2.

No matter who you are dealing with, there is at least one small thing that you can respect about the person. Even someone who works for the Internal Revenue Service probably has good math skills! And when you can develop a habit of finding these things, you will not only find your customer relationships improving but also the way you feel about yourself and your job.

As with unconditional positive regard, reframing may sound at first like a simplistic process of thinking nice thoughts. However, in reality,

Table 2-2. Using reframing.

What you observe	Stereotyping	Reframing
A man is dressed in grubby work clothes and a cowboy hat.	"He's probably a crude, sexist redneck."	"This person probably works very hard."
A woman speaks English with a thick accent.	"Another ignorant foreigner who's going to take up my time."	"This person is bilingual and adventurous enough to live in a different culture."
A rowdy group of teenagers comes into your store.	"These punks are nothing but trouble."	"These kids have boundless energy and fellowship with each other."
An elderly man shuffles in using a walker.	"These old codgers take forever to shop and dicker over everything."	"This man has a lifetime of experience and is trying to stay independent."

there is some powerful psychology behind this technique, which has led to a revolution in treating emotional problems. Rethinking and reprogramming your reactions to people and situations has become a key component of cognitive-behavioral psychotherapy, one of the more popular approaches in use today for treating mood disorders. When you apply it to customers, this simple but powerful technique can make a real change in your interactions with people. Try it, and see what happens when you see—and treat—people in a whole new light.

Personalization

Years ago, I discovered that one of the worst things I could do was to tell my wife that she looked cute.

It was honestly meant as a compliment, but her response was quick and to the point. "Years ago, you used to call me beautiful—now I'm 'cute.' I must be getting older and less attractive. I probably should be wearing nicer clothes than I do. Or maybe I just don't measure up any more to those young hotties that you see on television."

Every one of these statements had two things in common. First, they had no connection whatsoever with reality. I still happen to feel that my wife is one of the most attractive people who walk the face of the earth. (And I also happen to think she is cute—although I will probably never, ever tell her that!) But the other thing that these statements had in common was her taking a neutral event and filtering it through a negative lens of personal responsibility. We all experience these feelings, and experts refer to this phenomenon as *personalization.*

Personalization is a nearly automatic process of observing other people, and presuming feelings toward you from what you see. It is like being a bad translator who consistently puts the wrong meanings to what people say—and yet it is a nearly universal trait that colors our dealings with customers and each other. Table 2-3 shows some examples of how we personalize what we observe from customers before we even interact with them.

The common denominator in each of these cases is that you are taking something that you observe objectively and translating it into something else that is directed at you personally. In each of these cases, what you think is probably *not* a correct assumption.

Table 2-3. Examples of personalization.

What you see (reality)	What you think (personalization)
A customer is scowling as she enters the store.	"She dislikes me personally and is going to give me a hard time."
A younger customer has a baseball cap pulled over his eyes and is wearing a tattoo.	"He thinks I'm an authority figure and is probably going to challenge me."
An older customer is taking a long time in front of a counter that you are waiting to restock.	"He knows I am in a rush and is trying to hold me up on purpose."
A young woman says nothing as you greet her.	"She thinks she is superior to me."

- The first customer is much more likely to be scowling because of something that is bothering her, and not because of someone like you whom she has never met.

- The second customer has a look and dress that fits his social crowd, but that doesn't mean that he won't be polite and cooperative if you treat him with respect.

- The third customer probably cannot move quickly and, in all likelihood, has no idea that he is inconveniencing you.

- The fourth customer may suffer from social anxiety and be very uncomfortable speaking to others in public.

Why do we tend to personalize so many things? Because of a trait that we see clearly in almost any three-year-old, which is that our world revolves around us. More accurately, our own creativity and intelligence lead us to imagine any possible scenario that might involve a challenge or threat to us and then prepare to defend ourselves against it. A problem occurs when this tendency to personalize leads us to react in ways that are not accurate and do not help either the customer or us.

One of the reasons that personalization is rampant in customer service is that we often handle people with problems—and people with problems are no fun. But people with broken legs are no fun either, and doctors and nurses in an emergency room learn early in their careers to handle these situations with a combination of compassion and objective professional detachment. In much the same way, we all can learn to recognize our own tendency toward personalization and understand and manage it as part of our professional skills with customers.

Dealing with Personalization: Reattribution

In his landmark *Feeling Good* book series, Dr. David Burns describes personalization as one of several key errors in thinking that make us unhappy. Dr. Burns, a pioneer of cognitive-behavioral psychotherapy, teaches people to deal with this and other errors of thinking by writing down their automatic thoughts—and then examining the fallacies of these statements and writing down more accurate thoughts to replace them. For example, if a customer scowls and you automatically think, "This customer doesn't like me," you might replace this potentially self-fulfilling prophesy with a more accurate thought, such as, "This customer is probably having a hard time with something that I can help him with."[9]

Burns refers to this process as *reattribution*, and the idea behind it is similar to the reframing approach discussed previously for attacking stereotypes. In both cases, you substitute your instinctive thoughts with more rational ones to change both your mood and your reactions. You can also apply a similar approach to your feelings about what will happen and how you will respond—for example, instead of presuming, "This customer is going to give me a hard time," you can instead tell yourself, "If I do my best to treat this customer as my friend, he will probably like me. And in those cases where they don't act nice toward me, I can still treat them professionally and know that I am doing my best."

A key difference between reframing and reattribution is that, rather than simply envisioning good traits about a customer, you actively seek reasons to disprove that this customer has something personally against you or means ill toward you. Once again, it involves taking the automatic thoughts and assumptions that human nature hands us and replacing them with better ones that serve both your interests *and* the customer's much better.

YOUR NEW MIND-SET: BECOMING A NEUTRAL OBSERVER

These specific techniques all revolve around a larger issue—namely, what is your basic mind-set toward customers when they walk in the door?

The popular image of customer service involves nice people doing nice things for other nice people, who always appreciate it. But in reality, people generally seek out a service transaction when they are having problems. They tend to be dissatisfied about something, which may range from a trivial merchandise complaint to a life-or-death health-care concern. They may be upset, demanding, or even rude. And in any event, they are not likely to be happy when they first approach you. This is why the mental game of customer service ultimately revolves around a liberating thought: observing rather than reacting to what you see.

If you look closely at the three techniques in this chapter, you will see some common threads among each of them:

- They all deal with that point in time before you—or a customer—has said a word.

- They all involve thinking past our natural self-protective instincts.

- They change the way you will ultimately interact with these customers by changing the mental image you have beforehand.

These points, in turn, tie in with a larger truth about customer service: Customers are not always happy people. However, with practice, we can ultimately learn to see them with the professional detachment that, in turn, can change our emotional and even physical reactions to a customer situation. Psychologists have taught us for many years that we respond to our own mental images, in any situation, and can change these mental images. In customer situations, developing your own sense of being a neutral observer can have a truly powerful impact on your interpersonal skills with customers.

Being a neutral observer is not the same as being cold and detached. In fact, quite the contrary, it often removes the emotional baggage that stands between you and being warm, sincere, and genuine with each of your customers. For example, as a young man working on a computer help desk, I noticed that customer behavior would personally upset many of my colleagues—and me too, at first. But eventually I learned to start seeing my work as that of a sociologist studying the tribal behavior of early computer users—and, therefore, came to view their anger, frustration, and technical missteps as a *normal* and *expected* part of my workday, to which I could then apply my professional skills to make them whole once again.

In much the same way, you too can make your life much easier with customers, by using techniques that don't even require saying a word. When you change your mind-set, things change with your customers—often in a big way—and the good news is that this mind-set doesn't require an attitude or personality change, but rather a few simple techniques that are easy for anyone to learn. With a little practice, your creative imagination can eventually become one of the most powerful tools in your everyday dealings with people.

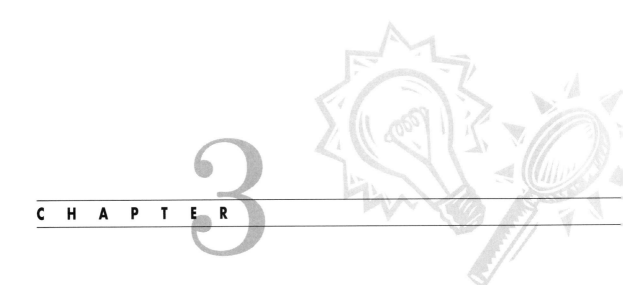

CHAPTER 3

THE FIRST THIRTY SECONDS

We live in a society that judges us on first impressions. Common wisdom holds that when you interview for a job, go on a date, or—as I did for this book—send a proposal to an editor, you have only thirty seconds to gain the trust and interest of the other person. Exactly the same thing is true when you interact with customers: The first thirty seconds that you spend with this person will determine, in large part, how well the rest of the transaction will go.

Chapter 2 discussed what psychologists refer to as *social cognition*—the innate process of judging whether someone is a friend or foe, as a survival instinct, and preparing to react accordingly. What you and a customer perceive at first glace affects how you relate to each other, but what you say when you first open your mouth is even more important. This is because the opening exchange in a customer transaction—in other words, what happens in those first thirty seconds—will give a customer important cues for what is to follow, and will set the tone for the entire transaction. This chapter will explore specific behavioral techniques for creating a good transaction right from the start, including the opening greeting, your first response, and the subtle art of active listening.

Aside from making a good first impression, learning how to deliver a good opening is perhaps the simplest way to make a major upgrade to your interpersonal skills. This is one area where our natural social cognition works in your favor, because once customers make that initial decision that they like you, it becomes much easier for them to trust all the other things that you do and say from there. This means that if you want to really change the way you deal with people, it isn't quite as daunting a challenge as it might seem. Good customer relations is a process that involves skills at all stages of a transaction—but the good news is that you can get there quickly and easily, just by learning how to handle the first thirty seconds.

THE OPENING GREETING: GETTING BEYOND "HELLO"

What is the worst greeting that you've ever received as a customer yourself? Here are some of my favorites:

- "Can I have your serial number please?"

- "Are you the next person in line?"

- "Sorry, we don't open for another five minutes."

- "It's our lunch hour—you'll have to come back."

- "I'm busy with other people right now."

Chances are, the last time that you were a customer and things went bad, they went bad right from the start. When someone didn't care, wasn't competent, or put his interests ahead of yours, he probably telegraphed those feelings right from the moment he started speaking with you—and in all likelihood, you probably reacted in kind. This is why we need to pay careful attention to the opening words that we choose with a customer.

Companies understand the importance of this first impression so much that many of them carefully script what their employees first say to greet a customer. Although this doesn't always produce the desired results (particularly when a bored, unhappy employee mouths these scripted greetings by rote), it still underscores the importance that organizations often place on your very first words to a customer.

Whether your greetings are scripted or fashioned from your own words, the following three guidelines will help you make a strong opening impression:

1. *Sincere*—Say something that feels right for you and sounds good to the customer. A simple greeting that you *do* mean is far superior to a flowery one that you *don't* mean.

2. *Appropriate*—There are norms in any transaction for what a customer *expects* to hear, based on the situation and, more important, its context. When you are working with a group of rugged, tough cowboys, a good opening greeting would not be "Good evening, sir. What can I do to assist you?" Similarly, if you are the concierge at a fine hotel, greeting your customers with, "Yo! Whaddya need?" probably isn't endearing. However, if you are on the staff of a teen hangout, this same phrase might actually be perfectly acceptable to say.

3. *Benefits the Customer*—This guideline automatically eliminates most of the "bad" greetings mentioned previously. A simple rule of thumb here is that if it doesn't somehow benefit the customer, it cannot be the *first* thing that you say.

One thing that you will notice these guidelines *don't* do is prescribe that you should say "X" to a customer. Unless your greeting process is scripted by your employer, the specific words that you say should flow from your best judgment of the situation—as long as they are *sincere, appropriate,* and *benefit the customer*. Conversely, what often goes wrong with a typical opening greeting is that human nature pulls us in directions that work against these guidelines:

- Instead of being sincere, we mouth a catchphrase greeting with obvious disinterest—or worse, we don't directly acknowledge customers until they say something.

- Instead of being appropriate, we use impersonal customer-service-speak that creates distance between us and a customer, because it's easier to just say what we've been taught ("Next person in line please") instead of tailoring our greeting to the situation ("Thanks for waiting! What can I do for you this afternoon?").

- Instead of saying something that benefits the customer, we give in to our natural instinct for self-protection and lead

NAME, RANK, SERIAL NUMBER? I LOVE IT!

Suppose that you manage a service center where your customers are required to provide several pieces of information before someone can assist them. For example, you have to locate their customer records, make sure that they have a valid service contract, and assess what their product type and problem is so that you can direct them to the right person—all told, probably requiring one to two minutes of their time. Believe it or not, depending on how you choose to handle this "intake" process, it can end up being a very positive experience for the vast majority of your customers.

How can you accomplish this? Through a very carefully executed process, involving the following steps:

1. *Ask for the customer's name.* Welcome the customer warmly and then—before anything else—ask him or her, "May I have your name?"

2. *Use the customer's name frequently.* Make use of this name regularly within the transaction, starting right away: "Thank you, Mr. Jones!"

3. *Lead with a benefit to the customer.* Before you ask for your information, start by asking the customer how you can benefit him or her with an opening question like: "What can we do to assist you today?"

4. *Use a light touch.* If this person shows up on your records as being a first-time customer, introduce what is to follow with a touch of humor: "I just have a few nosey questions to ask you, and then we'll be glad to put you in touch with the right person."

5. *Keep focusing on benefits.* Before asking your questions, first explain why: "We just need to gather some information from you to update our records, so that we can track your issue and make sure that you are getting the assistance you need."

The result of this scripted approach—combined with the talents of the people handling the transaction—will be not only a lack of customer resistance but also a great first impression that customers go out of their way to compliment.

with the kinds of openings outlined at the beginning of this section, which focus either on our needs ("Can I have your serial number please?") or our constraints ("It's our lunch hour—you'll have to come back!").

Let's look at some examples in Table 3-1 of how using these three guidelines can change your opening greeting. In each of these questions, the common denominator is not a vague matter of being nicer—rather, it is a process of refocusing your opening statements toward the interests and feelings of the customer. Perhaps more important, there is nothing quote-unquote "wrong" with most of the statements in the left column—we hear most of them every day in the course of

Table 3-1. Improving your opening greeting.

Typical opening greeting:	Better opening greeting:
"Can I help you?" There is nothing really wrong with this statement, but it is such a widespread formality that it is often perceived as a meaningless catchphrase. Instead, consider personalizing this statement to make it your own.	"Welcome! Is there anything special I can help you find?"
"Next?" This opening benefits you—"If you want service, you need to come to me"—instead of the customer.	"It's your turn. What can I do for you?"
"Welcome to The Gift Shoppe" Here again, this is a perfectly acceptable greeting that can—especially with the wrong tone of voice—sound tired and uninterested. This is an opportunity to engage customers with something sincere that compliments them and your store.	"You have good taste in dollhouses. That model is one of our best sellers."
"We aren't open yet." This statement is technically correct but crosses the boundary from disinterest to rudeness. A better greeting should leave customers feeling that you are glad they chose your establishment.	"Make yourselves comfortable! We'll be able to seat you in just a few minutes."
"May I have your contract ID number?" Questions like this may be necessary but when asked *first* make it sound like the customer is less important than your procedures. Address the customer's agenda first and then explain the benefits of your questions.	"We'll be happy to help you. I'd like to get some information so that I can get you the right kind of assistance. May I ask you a couple of quick questions?"

dealing with people, and they are all technically correct. But using these three guidelines to craft your own unique greetings, in a way that best fits the situation, will make an important difference in how people respond to you.

The science of coming up with a good opening underscores an even more basic principle behind many of the approaches in this book, which is to understand the mind-set of the customer in front of you and to respond from his or her perspective rather than your own. By doing this first, right up front, you establish a relationship, in much the same way that we establish relationships in other areas of our lives—namely, by showing an interest in the other person and his or her agenda.

THE TURNING POINT: YOUR FIRST RESPONSE

Sometimes, it can seem that customer problems are like patients in different rooms of a hospital. One person may have a simple question such as, "How much does this product cost?" while the next one is furious because the same product spewed motor oil all over everyone at his family reunion. This uncertainty about what might happen next—and how you should respond to it—is often one of the most uncomfortable things about serving the public.

Much of this discomfort happens because we all have a sense of closure. We want neatly packaged problems that we can resolve immediately, and preferably involving as little inconvenience as possible. Therefore, when people have problems we cannot solve—or requests that we are unable to accommodate—we often freeze when it comes to what to say. And far too often, we then follow the path of least resistance to focus on things that can defend us, rather than on things that will help the customer feel better—which ironically makes the situation worse.

The solution to this discomfort is to have a simple rule that guides the first thing that we say in response to any customer—a rule that helps us say something that will connect with a customer right away, and then set the stage for the rest of the transaction to go well. This rule involves doing something that is obvious in theory but often counterintuitive in practice:

Address the customer's agenda—preferably using his or her own words.

The reason this is obvious in theory—and easy to learn and practice—is that it lets customers themselves guide us on what to say in response. Conversely, the reason it is counterintuitive in practice is that, instinctively, we prefer to respond to people by talking about our favorite person: ourselves. But in terms of how they affect customers, the difference between "me first" and "you first" responses are strik-ing—let's compare some examples in Table 3-2.

Much like the customer-focused greetings that were discussed in the last section, a customer-focused response shifts our reply from our feelings to the customer's feelings—with a corresponding difference in results. And you might have noticed another difference between these statements: The self-focused statements rely heavily on the "royal we" (We don't, my department does not, and so forth), while the customer-focused statements imply personal ownership of the situation by using "I" phrases, like "I'm sorry" or "I can try." By linking this sense of "I" with the customer's own phrases—such as mentioning the shirt, the disk drives, or the order—you send a powerful message to customers that you heard them, understand them, and will do what you can to help them.

This practice of addressing the customer's agenda becomes partic-ularly important when the person is upset or feels wronged about something. For those of us who serve the public, these situations tend to be the most uncomfortable ones we deal with. This is because we often feel confronted personally and then are at a loss for what to say. We may not yet be able to agree with their claims or accede to their demands. Moreover, it becomes very tempting to revert to self-protection by retreating behind a wall of policy. In cases like these, a planned response aimed at the customer's concerns can substantially change the mood that follows.

Phrases like the ones in Table 3-2 work well because they make you aware of, and responsive to, what customers are feeling. They work because they take the focus off of you and move it toward the customer, which in turn serves as part of a more fundamental mind-

Table 3-2. Self-focused vs. customer-focused responses.

Situation	Self-focused response	Customer-focused response
I'd like to return this shirt.	We don't take returns on merchandise.	I'm sorry this shirt wasn't acceptable.
How do I install this disk drive on my computer?	My department can't help you with that.	I know who the expert on disk drives here is.
Your company fouled up my order.	We almost never make mistakes like that.	I can try to straighten this order out right now.

set that helps you consistently give an appropriate first response. In this broader sense, we introduce a concept that you can use to guide the first thing that you say to any customer. This concept is:

Feelings are never wrong.

A customer may be wrong about whose fault a situation is. He or she may be wrong about what your responsibilities are to resolve the situation. However, the customer's feelings are *never* wrong—by definition, they represent what he or she is honestly feeling. For example, when a customer drops his cellular phone in the bathtub and ruins it, it may not be your responsibility to replace it, but he is still going to feel upset—and, for that matter, probably *should* feel upset. And even if you cannot replace his phone, you can still share his feelings by acknowledging them.

This fact that feelings are never wrong gives you a solid foothold for what to say in awkward customer situations—because you can always agree with customers' feelings, even when you don't agree with their facts. When you address these feelings first, it will make the negotiating process that follows much easier and more cordial on both sides.

One note of caution: The concerns that we mentioned earlier about using catchphrases and formalities in your opening greeting become even more important in your first response. Your goal is to quickly create a bond of warmth and empathy with a customer—and even when the words are technically correct, common formalities will not get you there. This is the reason that when you are trying to tell someone that you understand, perhaps the worst phrase you can use is "I understand."

I Understand, Sir

I once had the pleasure of teaching a workshop via videoconference for agents at a large, offshore call center. These agents were a polite, intelligent group of people whose native language was not English but who were being taught how to work with U.S. customers to solve their technical problems.

Over the course of a week, working with several groups, one question came up over and over again. The agents said, "We have been taught to use the phrase 'I understand how you feel' when a customer is angry—but every time we use it, the customer always get angrier! How come this phrase doesn't work?"

The answer I gave them—and will give you—is that North American customers expect to have their feelings acknowledged *in detail*. Specifically, they need to hear enough detail about what *they* told *you* to make them feel that you heard them. Therefore, the solution to this problem is disarmingly simple—use key phrases from the customer's own words in your response.

Over the course of this training program, we explored this point over and over in role-playing exercises. If a customer was complaining that a product did not work on his or her daughter's birthday, the word *birthday* had to be somewhere in their response. If a customer mentioned that a problem was affecting his or her deadline, the customer had to say *deadline*—early and often. The results of this simple intervention were astounding: In follow-up call monitoring, a high percentage of these agents suddenly were connecting with customers in a way that they never had before. ■

Perhaps the best way to sum up the mechanics of your first response is not only to focus on a customer's issues—often, using the customer's own words and phrases to help you—but to put a little of yourself into your response as well. By speaking to a customer in much the same way that you would address a good friend, in your own personal style, you take the first step in developing standard responses that are unique, personalized, and yet extremely effective. In the process, you will break down an important barrier in both your customer relationships and your own personal comfort zone in any situation.

THE ART OF ACTIVE LISTENING

Once you get past the opening greeting and initial response, your next priority is listening to customers in a way that they feel heard and understood.

Listening to customers is not a passive process. Rather, it is a very engaged process of giving the customer the time and space to communicate, showing your interest and comprehension, and seeking understanding and closure. Here we will look at the mechanics of how we listen to customers and provide a framework for how you can listen to people in a way that always connects with them.

As a trainer, I've always taken a unique tack in teaching people the basics of active listening: I put them in a situation where they naturally become engaged and interested in listening to each other and then have *them* teach *me* what made this situation a good experience. I break the students into pairs and have them ask each other the following three questions—with no pens, no paper, but just listening to each other:

1. Assuming that money and time were no object, describe your all-time dream vacation. Where would you go? What would you like to do? How long would you spend there?

2. After a long trial for culinary indiscretions, you have just been condemned—to a lifetime of chain-restaurant fast food. You will never again eat a meal that isn't packaged in little cardboard containers. However, given the severity of the sentence, the judge has allowed you one last meal of your choice. Describe it in detail.

3. You are on a daylong train or airplane trip to attend a conference. What person—past or present—would you most like to have as a seatmate for the trip, and why?

Over the next several minutes, I then observe how people in the group react to each other as they ask these questions. Without fail, everyone is having a good time—they are all smiling, laughing, and having a lot of fun asking each other these questions. If I were a customer of one of these people, I would be having a very good customer experience! Then as we reassemble the full group and people share detailed, entertaining stories of what their partners said, it's clear that people were really *listening* to each other.

So what made this a good example of active listening for everyone? I always ask the class to answer this question for themselves—and here is a summary of some of the key points people share with me:

- *Interest and Feedback.* No one sat staring blankly while the other person spoke—instead, everyone enthusiastically chimed in with his or her thoughts about the other person's dream vacation, last meal, or favorite travel partner.

- *Gathering Information.* The people doing the listening asked questions to clarify the other person's thinking, which in turn demonstrated their interest. "How long would you stay in Bora Bora? What kind of dessert would you have with your fettuccini Alfredo? What kinds of things would you and Abe Lincoln talk about?"

- *Keeping Things Light.* This exercise wasn't a dour recitation of tax codes, but a lively, interactive session with lots of smiling and laughter.

- *Eye Contact and Body Language.* The partners were very engaged with each other and telegraphed their interest with their physical reactions.

Now, all you have to do is behave exactly the same way with your customers, and they, too, will have a great first impression of you! And the good news is that it's easier than you might think to translate that "good friends" experience to other people, even customers whom you've never met. Let's take a look at each of these areas in detail and learn how to do this:

Showing Interest and Giving Feedback

Showing interest, and sharing this interest with your customer, represent the key to active listening. But many people mistakenly view interest as a feeling that you have (or don't have), as opposed to a skill that you learn and practice. This is why learning the mechanics of showing interest, in any situation, is one of the most powerful things you can learn in working with the public.

In the class exercise previously described, I intentionally chose a scenario in which most people are naturally interested. "But," you're thinking, "I work at a slag heap. It's a job. I'll never be passionate about slag heaps. How can I show interest to *my* customers?" The answer lies in focusing on what your customer wants—and, more important, conveying your interest in it. Here are two techniques that you can use to make this happen:

1. *Paraphrase the customer.* The Merriam-Webster dictionary defines the word *paraphrase* as "a restatement of a text, passage, or work giving the meaning in another form."[1] Paraphrasing makes a very powerful impact on customers, because it involves taking *their* ideas and putting them in *your* words—which, in turn, shows customers that you not only heard what they said but accept and understand it.

Dr. Carl Rogers, the psychologist mentioned in Chapter 2, made the art of paraphrasing and repeating back what clients expressed to him a cornerstone of his therapy work—so much so that graduate students in the field used to joke that if one of his patients were ever to jump out a window, Dr. Rogers would probably jump right after him! But he did this for an important reason: Using his client's own words sends a powerful message of acceptance and understanding, serving, as he elegantly put it, "(to) clarify not only the meaning of which the client is aware, but even those just below the level of awareness."[2]

So now, let's go back to the slag heap. Even when your customers are people who want to truck several tons of slag away, you can still show a great deal of interest—the easy way—by paraphrasing what they say. Let's take a look:

Without paraphrasing:

Customer: I'm here to haul another load of slag.

You: OK.

Customer: We're really busy this month back at the plant.

You: I see.

Customer: Where should I load from?

You: Over there.

With paraphrasing:

Customer: I'm here to haul another load of slag.

You: So you've got another load going out, Tom?

Customer: Yes, we're really busy this month back at the plant.

You: Sounds like they've really got you guys jumping.

Customer: Yeah, this is the fifth load I've had to bring in this week.

You: That's a lot of slag!

Customer: I'll say. By the way, where should I load from?

You: Let's see . . . today, the best spot to load from might be over there, where you'll have a clear path to load it.

With almost no extra effort, you have now suddenly become the most knowledgeable and likable person at the slag heap! And you've done it by using a very simple communications technique of using words that the customer handed to you. In much the same way, para-

phrasing anything that a customer says will build respect and cooperation, in a way that will make the transaction easier for both you *and*
the customer.

> **2.** *Show your expertise*. The practice of *showing your exper-
> tise* is another potent technique that deserves special mention.
> By knowing your product or service very well—no matter how
> humble it is—and sharing this expertise with others, you dem-
> onstrate a level of interest that builds trust, demonstrates com-
> petence, and helps customers feel that they are dealing with
> the right person.
>
> Just one small step beyond expertise lies a sense of passion
> for what you do. You can't force passion, but you can build
> expertise, and expertise often leads to success, which in turn
> leads to passion. Don't think that these feelings are limited to
> Hollywood stars and multimillion-dollar entrepreneurs—I have
> known trash collectors who were excited and professional
> about their work, and technical experts with Ph.D.s who were
> bored and jaded. No matter what your profession is, you can
> always find ways to stand out and shine about what you do, and
> this in turn will make an indelible impression on customers.

Gathering Information

When friends gather to talk about something, they normally don't just
sit silently and nod in acknowledgment at each other. More often than
not, their responses include questions that clarify the other person's
statements. These questions aren't simply an attempt to gather information but are an important part of how we show interest in each
other. More important, many people feel these questions serve as a
basis for how we continually evolve our views about other people and
the world around us.

Perhaps the single biggest difference between a *friends* interaction and a *customer* interaction is that with friends there is often a
more engaged effort to ask questions and gather information. This
means that when you use the same approach with a customer, and *ask
more questions*, you suddenly increase the level of acceptance and
understanding that a customer feels. It is a simple and powerful way
to change the dynamics of a customer transaction in its early stages.

Asking the right questions is an art unto itself, and one that is so important that we devote an entire section to it later in Chapter 5 of this book. But to summarize the benefits here, asking the right questions in the opening seconds of a transaction gives you important data that help you to understand customers and solve their problems, *and* it demonstrates a level of interest that goes far beyond what is shown by many people who work with the public.

Keeping Things Light

Picture two doctors: One is always smiling and joking. The other is dour and serious. Which one are you more likely to allow to get near you with sharp instruments in the exam room? Studies have shown that a physician's bedside manner relates strongly to a patient's overall satisfaction with his or her medical care—and, surprisingly, it even correlates with how often these doctors are sued for malpractice![3] In much the same way, setting a light, upbeat tone in your own work can make a big difference in customer satisfaction.

Some of the key components of having a light touch include:

- *Using warm, upbeat responses.* Most situations lend themselves to responses—often planned and rehearsed in advance—that break the ice and put people at ease. Phrases such as, "That's right!" or "You've come to the right place!" or "I love tackling problems like this" have it all over the plain old "Yes" that most people use.

- *Using humor where it's appropriate.* I once asked a real estate lawyer if he would like to be paid on the spot. His immediate reply was, "My mother taught me to never refuse money from anyone." It's never good to laugh at a customer—or to crack so many jokes that you aren't taking people seriously—but when it is appropriate and feels right to you, a little humor can go a long way.

- *Reassuring people.* Anything that you can say to make people feel like their requests are normal, natural, and not a problem works very well—especially in situations where they are uncomfortable or embarrassed to begin with.

Above all, in creating a lighthearted mood with customers, the important thing is to be true to who you are. If you are normally bubbly

SERVICE WITH A SMILE

One of my greatest pet peeves is the belief that good customer service revolves around "having a good smile"—both because it trivializes the skills needed to handle difficult situations and because of my real-life experience that people can give truly excellent service even when they don't naturally have an incandescent 100-watt grin. But I am going to grudgingly give them this much credit: Done properly, your facial language can make a tangible difference in how you sound to people—even in situations like telephone service, where people cannot see your face.

Try an experiment sometime. Go somewhere where you can call your own answering machine or voice mail (or that of a cooperative partner). But before you do this, look into a mirror and scowl with as much anger as you can muster. Think of something that really upsets you, and let it all hang out in your facial expressions. Then pick up a telephone and leave a message on the answering machine. Next, make the same call again, but this time smile with as much sincerity as you can, and then pick up the phone and leave another message. Now listen to both of them. Can you tell any difference?

and outgoing, you should try to be yourself with customers. And if you are quiet and pensive, you should *also* be yourself with customers. Keeping a happy atmosphere is a matter of being genuine rather than forced, and shy courtesy can be every bit as effective as gregarious laughter. But in either case, look critically at the normal levity and good humor you share with those you care about, and find ways to share the same good vibe with your customers.

Understanding the Importance of Eye Contact and Body Language

Finally, in situations where you are face-to-face with a customer, your physical presence and body stance can speak volumes about how you feel—which, in turn, makes it an important component in active listening.

Just for fun, the next time you are with good friends, pay close attention to how they relate to you physically. There is a good chance that they will make regular eye contact with you, lean toward you when you speak, and maintain an open posture. Then observe the behavior of people who serve you as a customer. In all likelihood, you will see a very different picture—little or no eye contact; greater physical distance; and a closed, more defensive posture.

With customers, the way you manage your personal space can have an influence on the way that they first react to you. Here is how to keep your physical presence in synch with the process of listening to a customer:

- Follow the customer's lead in terms of eye contact and physical space.

- Lean slightly forward as a customer is speaking.

- Be aware of a natural tendency to physically "close up" around strangers—by hunching your shoulders, crossing your arms, and lowering your head—and learn to notice and counteract it.

In recognition of the important role of body language and physical space, some businesses coach and train people about their effective use—for example, one upscale department store chain even has its clerks physically come out from behind the counter to hand purchases to customers. At a personal level, developing effective body language can help you stand out as a service expert in your own career.

CREATING GREAT CUSTOMER EXPERIENCES IN THIRTY SECONDS

The techniques presented in this chapter all revolve around one simple but life-changing idea: When you first encounter a customer, a good relationship with him or her is almost always less than thirty seconds away. And, more important, you can practically ensure this good relationship just by making simple changes in three specific areas: your opening greeting, your first response, and your ability to actively listen to people.

The beauty and simplicity of managing the first thirty seconds of a customer transaction is that a lot of what you say in these situations can be rehearsed and practiced ahead of time—and, more important, integrated with your own personality and communications skills to produce a style that is uniquely, comfortably yours. Done well, it represents an important step toward not only putting customers at ease but also building your own confidence level in managing any customer situation. From there, you will find yourself making a real change in how people respond and interact with you—right from the start.

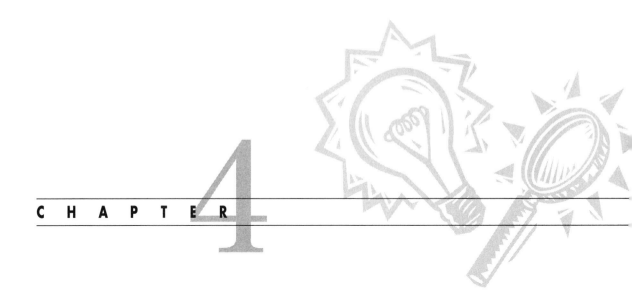

GETTING THE MESSAGE ACROSS

Every time you interact with a customer, it is fundamentally a transfer of information. Whether it is as trivial as what time the movie starts or as critical as the results of someone's medical test, sharing information is the basic currency of any customer transaction. Nevertheless, the way this information is delivered will make all the difference in the world to you; to your organization; and, most important, to your customers. It represents the central moment of truth in the encounter between you and a customer.

This chapter will teach you how to frame this information so that customers respect you, cooperate with you, and leave satisfied—even when the information itself isn't what the customer wanted to hear in the first place.

More important, you will learn that it is the communication process, and almost never the situation, that drives a customer's reaction. If you were fortunate enough to have a career that consisted of telling people that they have won a million dollars, you might think that delivering information to people is easy. But if you are telling people that their car won't be fixed for another two hours, that their flight has been delayed, or that their child is being sent home from school, human nature and good intentions will often fail you—and you may think, mistakenly, that there is nothing that can be done about making these transactions go better.

The good news is that with the right approach, you can deliver these and other messages with a highly predictable level of success. This chapter discusses an extremely powerful set of techniques for delivering any kind of information to customers successfully, particularly when the news is unpleasant. Used properly, it will virtually guarantee that a customer will not respond with hostility toward you personally, even when he or she is not happy with the situation itself.

WHY WE DON'T COMMUNICATE CUSTOMER INFORMATION WELL

When you were growing up, did you ever attend a play for children? If so, you probably remember what happened when the villain on stage was about to do something horrible—every child in the audience was calling out, in unison, trying to get the attention of the hero. And, of course, the hero stayed true to the script and didn't respond to you, which caused you to scream all the louder.

The reason that you and the other children were yelling is fundamental to understanding how we communicate information to a customer. When children want to share information, they say the first thing that comes to their minds, with little or no processing beforehand. This is because it is an important survival trait—we need this communication reflex to tell people to run from an approaching wild animal, to get out of the way of an oncoming train, or to avoid other dangers. That is why humans develop this skill first, to ensure that we stick around to develop the more subtle skills.

Out of the Mouths of Babes

I remember one real-life example of this phenomenon very well. As a young man in my late teens, I could have stood to lose a few pounds—and, at one point, started to grow a neatly trimmed beard. Most of my friends and neighbors either said nothing or commented that I looked nice. But one day as I was going out to the mailbox, a very young tyke who was playing across the street looked at me, smiled, and said to no one in particular, "Hey, fatso's growing a beard." There was no malice or forethought involved, just simple observation of reality as he perceived it. ■

In time, as we grow up and learn to socialize with other people, we learn to frame messages in the context of the situation. This is why young children will make very blunt comments about what they see and hear (as in one cartoon where a child blithely told his parents' guests, "We're trying something new tonight. Dad said that we're having stuffed shirts for dinner."), while a grown man isn't likely to greet a blind date with the observation that her dress is ugly. Instead, he probably gets to know her as a person, shows her a good time, and perhaps builds a relationship—and only then, if ever, would he consider sharing his feelings about the dress.

So now we come full circle to what happens when we deliver information to a customer. The short, impersonal transactions we typically have with customers rarely give us the feedback—or the motivation—of how to "package" information for them, the way that our other communications eventually become socialized. So when a customer's delivery is late, we simply say that it is late. When someone's favorite meal is sold out, we just say that it's sold out. When a situation exceeds our ability to respond to it, we state first and foremost that it isn't our job. We essentially revert to the grown-up equivalent of "We're having stuffed shirts for dinner," because we have not been socialized to do better.

Another factor in how we communicate information to customers is self-protection: When people confront us with a problem, we tend to distance ourselves from responsibility for it in order to avoid negative consequences. Whether the stimulus was a neighborhood bully, an angry parent, or the school principal, most of us grew up learning to respond with statements like, "It's not my fault!" or "That was Debbie's job," or a hasty excuse. Years later, when you are behind the counter of a store and a customer is upset about not being able to return a piece of sale merchandise, we respond similarly with statements like, "Sorry, that's our policy." (We'll discuss what else you could say in this situation a little later in this chapter.)

Psychologist B. F. Skinner envisioned this phenomenon many years ago, in describing the principle of *operant conditioning*. This principle describes how we move toward behaviors that tend to reward us, and move away from behaviors that tend to punish us—for example, the way that touching a hot stove burner as a child teaches us not to put our hand near those burners again. As we accumulate good and bad experiences over a lifetime, our reactions to these experiences form a strong influence on our future behavior.[1]

Monkey Don't See, Monkey Do

A well-known story among trainers involves five apes in a cage. A researcher dangles a banana at the top of a staircase within the cage, and as soon as one of the apes starts to climb the stairs to get the banana, all of the apes are sprayed with ice-cold water.

Later, one of the apes is replaced by a new ape, and as soon as he starts for the stairs to get the banana, he is immediately assaulted by the other apes. This process continues until each of the original five apes is replaced by a new ape—at which point they still assault any ape who goes near the stairs but now have no idea why they are doing it except "that's the way we've always done things around here." ■

In much the same way as these apes learn to avoid being doused with ice water, we learn at an early age to avoid confrontation with other people by setting limits—and to do it as quickly and bluntly as possible. This tendency is innate, and not just a function of one's attitude. This is why, if we look critically at the customer transactions we experience ourselves, we encounter so many situations where service employees don't seem to hold our interests at heart. And the irony is, even though these responses often cause us to react badly and escalate the problem, they still have their roots in the avoidance of temporary pain.

When I teach workshops with customer service teams, I see the same phenomenon over and over again—when we role-play by having people confront them with a problem that they cannot solve, their innate response is usually words to the effect of "I can't help you" or "that's our policy"—and the customer gets angrier and angrier, even in role play. The fact that these customer service agents are often experienced professionals and very well-meaning people speaks volumes for how we are genetically hardwired to deal with these situations. To change these customer interactions, you can't just change your attitude. You must change your programming.

HOW TO DELIVER THE MESSAGE: THE STAGING TECHNIQUE

We often mistakenly feel that customer reactions are governed solely by the situation. But there is a technique that lets you deliver any kind of information while still keeping the customer in dialogue and maintaining a good relationship. We call this technique *staging*, because it involves communicating a message by using specific, predictable stages. It borrows from the same kinds of communications strategies used by professionals who deal regularly with crisis situations, such as paramedics and police officers.[2]

Staging is remarkably effective because it follows an important principle of psychology known as *systematic desensitization*, a form of behavioral conditioning first used as psychotherapy in the late 1950s by the late Dr. Joseph Wolpe.[3] His approach was to gradually expose people to things that they feared, in stages, where the steps were small enough that they never experienced overwhelming anxiety—and in a high percentage of cases, his patients recovered from their phobias. The success of this method revolutionized modern-day treatment for anxiety disorders.

The staging technique works in a very similar manner, by giving information to people in stages rather that all at once. And, much like its psychotherapeutic cousin, it serves as a powerful technique for delivering difficult messages. Done well, it not only allows people to absorb the information you are providing but also makes you an ally of the person with whom you are communicating.

HOW STAGING WORKS

The late actor Orson Welles once said, "I want to give the audience a hint of a scene. No more than that."[4] In much the same manner, staging helps you "hint" at a situation in a way that prepares the customer for what you are about to say and lays the groundwork for both of you to discuss the issue productively. It takes our normal urge to simply blurt out bad news and replaces it with a structured communications process that we learn and practice. It involves three steps, as follows:

Step 1. Introduce what you are going to say *before* you say it.

Step 2. Explain what you are saying *as* you say it.

Step 3. Empathize with the customer—whatever his or her response is—*after* you say it.

This technique is best explained by example. Let's say that you take your television set in for a repair, because of what seems like a minor problem with the picture quality. Later that day, you call to check on the status of your television. First, let's see what happens when the people who answer you *don't* use staging.

Without staging:

You: I'm calling to check on my television set.

Them: Yes, sir, we've looked at it. The repair is going to cost $1,000.

This is, unfortunately, how most people would deliver this message. But how are you, as a customer, going to react to this statement? Probably with a great deal of anger and frustration. You will probably feel that they "dumped" this information on you, with little concern for your feelings. But there is a better way to handle this: Now, let's try the same situation again *with* staging.

With staging:

You: I'm calling to check on my television set.

Them: (*Step 1—Introduce*) Yes, we have looked at your television. Since this was what seemed to be a minor issue with the picture quality, we were hoping that we could take care of it easily, as an adjustment. Unfortunately, it turned out to be something more serious than that.

You: What was the problem?

Them: (*Step 2—Explain*) I'm going to explain what we found. Since you have a wide-screen plasma television, it uses a relatively expensive display monitor. It turned out that the problem we found with your picture was related to a structural problem with the display itself, rather than a simple tuning issue. Unfortunately, replacing the display itself is a fairly expensive process.

You: I see. How much do you think that this will cost?

Them: I just checked, and replacing the display would run about $1,000 including parts and labor.

You: Wow, that is expensive! That is almost half as much as the television itself cost!

Them: (*Step 3—Empathize*) You're right; that is a lot of money. I certainly don't blame you for being frustrated, and we will be happy to do whatever you like. You could actually keep using the set in its current condition for a while longer, or perhaps look at some newer models, if you aren't comfortable with doing the repair. Would you like to touch base about some options when you stop by the store again?

You: Sure, that would be good.

In both cases, you are not going to be happy about the situation. But in the second case, you are much less likely to get angry with the person you are speaking with, because he or she has used a structured communications technique that accomplishes several important objectives. In just a few short sentences, that person has:

- Cushioned the blow of the bad news by preparing you for it

- Demonstrated an interest in making this situation as good as possible

- Provided you with data that helps you understand the situation

- Shown that he or she is willing to spend time with you about this matter

- Expressed a genuine concern for your feelings

At a deeper level, the experience of these two service professionals becomes vastly different as well. In the case of the first person answering this call, he or she probably thinks, "What a lousy job I have. It isn't my fault that people's television sets break down, and it isn't my fault that the repairs are expensive. But these people are always taking out their frustrations on me." Conversely, the second person might say, "I have a great job. Even when I have difficult news to deliver to customers, I know exactly what to tell them. These customers treat me with respect, and I really enjoy dealing with them." It is the same situation, but with radically different results.

Be aware that staging is not human nature, so it does not come naturally to most people. In fact, if you have never used it before, it will feel like wearing a T-shirt backward at first. At the same time, when you learn, practice, and become good at it, staging will create a dramatic difference in the way that people react to you. When I do role-playing exercises on this technique with students in my training courses, people notice an amazing thing—when they are staging, the person they are role-playing with *cannot stay angry*. It is at that point when the lights start to come on for people, and they realize that they aren't simply at the mercy of a customer situation.

Now let's take a more detailed look at the component parts of the staging process.

Step 1: Introduce

Suppose that a customer comes in with a broken stereo that he or she wants fixed. You look at the receipt and see that the customer's ninety-day warranty expired two weeks ago. Unfortunately, there is nothing that you can do to change this fact. The manufacturer's rules are quite firm on this, and you could not get the stereo fixed for free even if you wanted to.

What is the first thing that you should say to this customer? If you are like the vast majority of people, your innate response is to say that the warranty has expired. In fact, every fiber of your being will probably be screaming to say this first. *Don't do it*. Instead, find a statement—any statement—that allows you to *introduce* what you are about to say first.

By introducing your message first, you have an opportunity to prepare the customer for what is to follow while establishing yourself as an ally. The best introductions take one of the following four forms:

1. *Relate to the situation.* "I can't blame you for being frustrated, since this broke down less than four months after you bought it."

2. *Share information.* "I'd like to explain how the warranty coverage is structured on this equipment."

3. *Seek common ground.* "This is a very nice stereo. I have a unit very similar to this."

4. *Prepare the customer for bad news.* "I was hoping that this would be a covered repair."

The specific things that you can say to introduce a situation will be unique to your own workplace and personality, and most people develop their own comfortable style of introduction with time and practice. However, the most important thing—and a central reason that we call this technique *staging*—is that you should set the stage for what information is to follow by introducing it first.

Step 2: Explain

We are intrinsically programmed to say as little as possible when a customer has a problem, because this is human nature when we are confronted by someone. Moreover, in today's metrics-driven work environment, we have institutionalized this value and turned it into a high art—nowadays, many customer service environments such as call centers measure their representatives on time goals such as talk time and transaction productivity.

This makes the second step, explaining the message, seem almost counterintuitive. In this step, you finally deliver the information to the customer—and at the same time provide details about the situation. But even a small amount of explanation will make a substantial difference in how a customer reacts to you, which in turn will govern how long the transaction ultimately takes. You must learn to see this step as a small investment of time that will reap much larger rewards in your overall productivity with customers.

As with the first step of introduction, the fact that you are providing these details is perhaps even more important than the details themselves. This step not only provides the customer with facts but also gives the person time and space to absorb the situation. More important, this explanation demonstrates your level of interest to the customer, because it runs counter to our innate response to dump bad news and then withdraw. You instead are moving toward the customer and his or her situation—albeit very briefly—but the fact that you are doing it at all changes the dynamics of the situation and helps the customer see you as an ally instead of an adversary.

Let's return to the previous example of a customer whose stereo is out of warranty to compare the impact of describing this situation with and without an explanation.

Without explanation:

You: Sir, your warranty has expired.

With explanation:

You: These stereo units, like many consumer electronics nowadays, have a warranty period of ninety days. Naturally, most people want to be able to use their equipment for more than three months, so we also have some repair options for units that are out of warranty, like yours is.

You may be thinking to yourself, "How could I be glib enough to come up with an explanation like that when I am being confronted by a customer? These situations sometimes feel like they are coming at me at 80 miles an hour." The answer is twofold. First, it is a good idea to prepare and rehearse strong explanations for the most common situations that you encounter in your business. Second, and more important, you can use one or more of these options to help guide your response when you are in a new or unique situation:

- *Provide information.* "I'm going to explain what we're seeing on these X-rays."

- *Show your concern for the situation.* "I feel bad that your flight was cancelled. Let's see what we can do here."

- *Demonstrate your competency.* "I've had a lot of experience with this problem, and I think I know exactly what happened here."

- *Provide options.* "Even though we can't do this for free, we do have a couple of options that might save you money."

- *Anticipate and counteract objections.* "I realize that you've had a bad experience with this equipment. Here is why I feel you won't have the same problems with a replacement unit."

A good explanation has the obvious benefit of giving the customer information, but it also has the equally important benefit of putting the customer at ease, and giving the person perspective on the situation. Have you ever been on an airline flight and been reassured by the captain's calm discussion of the sights over the intercom? In a customer transaction, explaining the situation often has the same effect on customers as this pilot's in-flight talk—it builds trust and confidence, making it much easier for customers to accept the situation and move toward a sense of closure.

Step 3: Empathize

The third step of staging is perhaps the most critical one of all. Delivering difficult news to customers will frequently result in an emotional response. Your innate reaction to these responses will be to defend yourself or your company. But by acknowledging the customer's emotions instead, you set the stage for resolving the issue as a partner with him or her, and bringing the transaction to a successful close.

As we discussed in Chapter 3, *feelings are never wrong.* Even when a customer is saying something that you don't agree with—such as that your company is lousy or that your products are shoddy—you can always agree with the person's feelings.

Let's continue with our example of the customer with the broken stereo. Be honest and ask yourself how many of your own customer transactions have gone like the following one:

Customer: This must be a pretty rotten, low-quality piece of equipment to break down after only three and a half months.

You: Sir, I'm afraid this only has a ninety-day warranty. There is nothing I can do about it.

Now, how did the person react? It is unlikely that the customer said, "Silly me, you're absolutely right! The warranty has obviously expired. I'm sorry to have troubled you." A more common scenario is that the customer pouts, complains, threatens to write letters to your management, and continues to stand there while you wish you could crawl under the counter—because you responded in a way that was factually correct but completely ignored the customer's feelings. And the customer isn't going to let you forget it, so the transaction often continues until both of you are exhausted and upset.

Now, let's try this again, but this time let's try to empathize with each and every one of the customer's feelings.

Customer: This must be a pretty rotten, low-quality piece of equipment to break down after only three and a half months.

You: I don't blame you at all for being frustrated. That is a very short period of time.

Customer: And you are a rotten store for selling such junk.

You: I can certainly understand how you feel that way. I don't want you to be upset with our store, so I'd like to see what options we still have to help you.

Customer: OK, what can we do from here?

What you are seeing here is a process that ultimately leads the customer to cooperate with you so that you can successfully negotiate a close to the transaction. It involves three specific components:

1. *Acknowledge feelings.* If the customer is not happy about a situation, make statements that corroborate the person's feelings. *This is not the same as agreeing with the customer's complaint.* If appropriate, let the customer know that you understand why he or she is upset—or, at the very least, acknowledge that he or she feels this way. For example:

   - "I can see that this is very important to you."

   - "I realize that this is very frustrating for you."

   - "Obviously, this is not what you were hoping to get."

2. *Focus on the customer's concerns.* Our normal reaction is to defend or restate our policies, which customers do not care about because they are focused only on what matters to them. Address this by making statements that acknowledge the customer's agenda, such as:

   - "I want to find a mutually acceptable solution for this."

   - "I realize that you need this resolved as quickly as possible."

   - "Let's see if we can find another way to make this work."

3. *Offer solutions.* Even when you are delivering bad news, or can't give customers what they want, there is almost always something that you can offer to a customer—such as other goods or services, alternative approaches, referral to other resources, or even simply an offer to be helpful. If you can provide options, however small they may be, you provide a possible face-saving way for the customer to agree to a solution and move on.

Once again, this step works because it is so counterintuitive to normal experience. Recently, I was involved in a rear-end collision while waiting at a stoplight. When I called the insurance company of the truck that hit me, a harried claims adjuster sighed, "Sir, you have to understand that I'm overloaded with claims, and every one of these people wants their car fixed soon. You're going to have to wait until I can get to this." So here I am sitting here in a collision shop with a stiff neck, a pounding headache, and a car that has been squished like an accordion, and I'm supposed to be concerned about someone's paperwork? Needless to say, I wasn't happy with this company.

The great irony is that by using empathy statements like the ones mentioned previously I would have been more than happy to wait the three days that it took for the claim to be processed. Imagine if I had instead been told, "I'm sorry that you were in an accident with our client, and I want to make sure you're back in your car as soon as possible. We are looking at about a three-day lead time, but I will personally make sure that we have things resolved by Thursday afternoon. Is there anything else we can do for you?" I would have gotten off the phone quickly, happily, and with good feelings about the insurance company, and the adjuster would have done *no* extra work compared with the first conversation.

The subject of showing empathy to customers is so important that we devote a substantial part of Chapter 6 to specific techniques for how to communicate with empathy. In the meantime, a key point for this stage is that empathy is a *technique*, not just a *feeling*. By saying things that acknowledge and understand a customer's feelings, you not only help the person feel better but make it much easier to bring a transaction to a conclusion on your terms. It costs nothing; doesn't require changing your policies; and, best of all, becomes a good habit with time and practice.

Now, let's pull all three of these concepts together by looking again at the situation we described earlier—you are behind the counter of a retail store, a customer wants a refund, and you don't accept returns on sale merchandise. Compare how this situation works with and without staging.

Without staging:

Customer: I'd like to return these pants. My wife hates the color.

You: Sorry, we don't take returns on sale merchandise.

In this case, the customer is very likely to react badly, and you will be faced with the dual problem of defending the store's policy and enduring the customer's wrath. Now, let's try it again using staging.

With staging:

Customer: I'd like to return these pants. My wife hates the color.

You: (*Step 1—Introduce*) I certainly understand. I hate it when people don't like what I've bought too. (*Step 2—Explain*) Our store's pricing policy is unfortunately designed around not taking returns on sale merchandise, so that we can keep our prices lower for you on everything else. Is there anything else that we can do for you?

At this point, the customer may still not be happy about the situation—but in all likelihood *the person won't be angry at you*. With your response, you have demonstrated that you care about the customer while still defending the store's policy. And as you continue to use the third step of staging, empathy, you will continue to defuse what could otherwise be an uncomfortable situation.

Customer: That's frustrating. I really don't want these pants.

You: (*Step 3—Empathize*) I don't blame you for being frustrated. I wish we could give you a refund on these.

Customer: Well, it sounds like you're doing the best you can. Thanks anyway.

At this point, the customer will probably leave the counter, pants in hand. But some very important things happened in this transaction because you used staging, instead of just stating your policy:

- You kept a disagreement from turning into a confrontation.

- You sent the customer away peacefully without caving in and violating your store's policy.

- The customer was able to save face by having his feelings understood.

- Although the customer may be frustrated by the situation, he is much less likely to avoid your store in the future.

Above all, you accomplished all of these things by using a technique, which in turn helped you to say the right thing when you needed to. Staging helps you focus on delivering messages in the customer's best interest, simply by following the next steps in the process. In the process, you develop a communications style that is uniquely customer focused, which will serve you well in all of your everyday interactions with other people.

IT'S NEVER JUST THE SITUATION

Staging underscores a point that is perhaps the most fundamental concept of customer relations:

Customer conflicts are not caused by the situation—they are caused by the way the situation is communicated.

And we truly mean any situation. As mentioned earlier, this technique is frequently employed by emergency service personnel when they are communicating with people in a crisis. When police officers, firefighters, or paramedics are delivering difficult news, they are trained to introduce, explain, and empathize with the people they are speaking with, because these skills are central to keeping the crisis from escalating. It is perhaps in these worst-case situations that we learn how the staging technique allows us to deliver any message as charitably and humanely as possible.

Delivering the Worst Kind of News

A difficult real-life example of staging took place when I was part of the management team of a software company, and one of our star employees—a young woman who had tremendous promise and was loved by everyone—was tragically killed in an automobile accident. To make matters worse, this tragedy happened in the middle of our annual conference, with nearly three hundred of our top customers in attendance.

After privately sharing what had happened with me and the other members of the management team, the company's chief officers had the sad duty of interrupting the festive occasion of our conference, gathering together all of our employees and all of our conference attendees in separate meetings, and delivering some of the worst news imaginable. What they said at each of these meetings was a classic example of staging.

- First, they *introduced* what they were about to say. "We are meeting today because of something that happened last night. I have to prepare each of you for some very difficult news."

- Next, they *explained* what happened. "Late last night, there was a tragic automobile accident involving one of our employees. I wish that there was an easier way to say this, but unfortunately this employee was killed in the accident."

- Then, they did something that was perhaps most important of all. They stood silently for a period of time, to allow the people in the gathering to react. People sobbed, turned to each other, hugged, and started to grasp the reality of what had happened. It was, in a sense, the group equivalent of waiting for a customer to respond.

- Finally, they brought a sense of closure to this process by *empathizing* with everyone's reactions—by sharing how they themselves felt, by noting that this was the first time this had ever happened in the company's twenty-five-plus year history, and by discussing what support and counseling resources would be available over the next few hours and days. ■

Most situations that call for staging are far less difficult than this one. However, the important point is that any message—no matter how bad it is, and no matter how poorly it may be received by another person—can be communicated successfully without leading to conflict between you and the recipient.

Perhaps the most important point about staging is that it is not so much an attitude as a skill that you learn and practice—and just like lifting weights, it gets easier the more "reps" that you perform. It represents a process that runs counter to human nature, and when you follow the steps and work the process, good things happen between you and customers that you normally wouldn't expect. In time, you will find that people almost naturally react better to you, argue less, and have a higher opinion of you and your organization—and, even more important, you will find a newfound confidence in being able to deliver any message to any customer.

CHAPTER

GETTING INTO YOUR CUSTOMER'S HEAD

You get behind the wheel of your car and drive through the city streets wishing that all of these slow, obnoxious pedestrians would hurry up and get out of your way. Minutes later, you step out of your car and walk across the street, and suddenly you are annoyed at how these impatient drivers are whizzing by too close to you in their cars. As you keep getting in and out of your car, your perception continues to shift smoothly and automatically—from driver to pedestrian and back again—to fit whatever you are at the moment.

Exactly the same phenomenon occurs between you and the customers you serve. Speak with a group of service employees about what bothers them the most, and they will probably have stories about obnoxious, demanding customers. Then, go speak with a group of customers about what bothers them, and they will invariably share tales of rude, indifferent service employees. Better yet, speak to the same person about his or her experiences with both groups, and you will likely hear that person talk about both things without missing a beat! The pull of human nature is extremely strong, and our basic instincts overwhelmingly drive us to perceive and respond to situations from the viewpoint of our own interests.

More often than not, this perceptional shift colors the way that each of us acts out the roles of a customer transaction. Customers, and the people who serve them, each naturally see the world in terms of how it affects *them*—a phenomenon that often leads both parties to becoming locked in battle to defend their interests. If you look critically at what is said in the heat of a difficult customer problem, you will frequently find two people who are both failing to address the other person's reality in any tangible way, with results that are often similar to pushing on a door marked PULL.

Conversely, speaking from a customer's perspective is a very powerful but underutilized technique that will make a real change in how customers react to you. Getting into a customer's mind-set may seem like simple courtesy, but in reality, it is more a matter of psycholinguistics that you can learn and control. In this chapter, we will look at three simple techniques that will help you to quickly "think like a customer," which in turn will lead to smoother transactions with customers who like and respect you.

THE *JEOPARDY!* TECHNIQUE—PUTTING THINGS IN THE FORM OF A QUESTION

The popular TV game show *Jeopardy!* is famous for insisting that its contestants always word their responses in the form of a question.[1] Ironically, a similar technique can become the key to winning the jackpot with your customers. By making the simple change of learning to respond to people with *questions* rather than with *statements*, where appropriate, you can make a real difference in the way customers feel and respond to you.

Once again, this is a concept that is best explained by example. Let's compare a couple of different conversations and see the big difference the right kinds of questions can make:

Customer: I'm looking for an inexpensive set of golf clubs.

Clerk: Our least expensive clubs are over there, for $200 a set.

Customer: Are they any good?

Clerk: It depends. I think they are pretty good.

Customer: And what about these more expensive ones over here?

Clerk: They are a little lighter and easier to swing than the other set.

Most of us wouldn't raise any red flags about this discussion. The clerk is probably being reasonably polite and does not hesitate to respond to the customer. The information he is giving is accurate. Conversations like this are typical of the kinds of transactions that go on thousands of times every day with customers where you live. However, there is one very important thing missing here—the customer is doing all the driving, and the clerk is doing nothing but responding very specifically to his questions. Now, let's try this same situation again, using the *Jeopardy!* approach:

Customer: I'm looking for an inexpensive set of golf clubs.

Clerk: Great! I have some good sets to show you. Could you tell me a little bit about your golf habits?

Customer: I'm just a weekend duffer. I don't really need a top-of-the-line set.

Clerk: Great. It sounds like you've spent some time on the links, so I'm curious: What are some of the things that you liked—and didn't like—about the clubs you have already used?

Customer: Well, first of all, those rental clubs are heavy. And I never liked the feel of the putter.

Clerk: I'm glad you mentioned both of those things. In general, there is a relationship between cost and weight. Also, because the putter is so important, some people often pair an inexpensive set of clubs with a good putter. Do you have a sense of what kind of price range you are looking for?

Do you notice a difference between these two discussions? In the second case, the clerk not only responds but also follows up with *questions* each time—and the customer, in turn, is responding to these questions and opening up with valuable information that will help the clerk to sell him the best set of golf clubs. But you are also seeing much more than a simple transfer of information going on here. There are some very important—but unspoken—things going on at the same time that these questions are being asked:

- The customer feels that the clerk is taking an interest in him and his needs.

- A level of trust is being built between the clerk and the customer.

- The transaction is much less likely to become adversarial.

- The customer may choose a more expensive set of golf clubs.

- After the transaction is over, the customer will probably feel very good about his purchase.

All of these benefits, and more, can be yours in nearly any customer situation, by simply changing the punctuation of your sentences to end with a question mark.

People often feel that their success with customers revolves around what they say. Salespeople, in particular, often feel that the more eloquent they are, the better impression they will make. But experts in sales universally say that the people who sell the most are the ones who draw out their customers and get *them* talking about what *they* want. Questions are an ideal way to get customers talking, and in turn start building a good relationship with them. It works because you are putting the spotlight on the customer's favorite person—himself.

There is sound psychology behind the process of asking people questions. From its earliest days, psychotherapy has in large part been a process of getting people to open up and talk, to probe their state of mind, and to help them solve their own problems, rather than simply telling them what to do. In much the same way, the right kinds of questions can make you look good by helping customers to solve their own problems.

At the same time, this approach doesn't mean that you should randomly start asking people about anything, such as the weather, politics, or their vacations. The right questions should ideally focus customers toward quickly resolving their issues while at the same time building a bridge of respect, trust, and understanding between you and the customer. You could summarize this approach by using the following four criteria for your customer questions:

1. *Targeted.* An ideal question should follow directly from what a customer *just told you*. For example, if someone comes into your deli and asks where the hot sauce is, you might ask the customer what kind of food he or she plans to use it with. Likewise, a person looking for a baseball cap might be asked if he or she prefers wool or cotton caps. Perhaps the easiest thing

to remember about asking customers questions is to start by listening—because they invariably will give you the clues you need about what to ask them.

2. *Relevant.* Customers approach you with an issue or a problem. Does your question address this agenda? When someone is looking for a jacket, for example, your questions might revolve around how much warmth she is looking for—or what kinds of activities she is planning for it. A good litmus test for questions like these is whether the customer's answers will ultimately help you to serve her better.

3. *Benefit Driven.* Some customer environments practice asking lots of questions, but they are meant to benefit the *person asking* rather than the customer. These questions range from ones used to qualify a sales prospect, such as the ubiquitous "Are you planning to buy a car today?" that you hear from many auto dealers, all the way to the myriad name, rank, and serial number questions that get asked at the doctor's office.

   Questions like these may be important or even necessary, but relative to building a customer relationship, they don't count as the kinds of questions we are discussing here. To get close to customers, find questions aimed toward benefits for *them*—what they want, what they don't want, or what will make their lives better.

4. *Respectful.* No matter how much you are trying to help, be careful that your questions do not invade someone's privacy or get too personal. It is okay to ask customers how they plan to use the minivan that they are looking at, but it is not appropriate to probe about their marital status or children. Likewise, outside of legitimate circumstances such as taking a credit or an insurance application, detailed questions about personal finances are similarly off-limits. Moreover, beyond the bounds of privacy lie the bounds of propriety—for example, if someone is looking at a party dress in your store, it is not a good idea to ask her if she has a date! Always keep your interest in the customer pleasant, businesslike, and professional.

You could sum up all these guidelines into a single key point: *Ask questions that will help and benefit the customer.* It is a skill that you can develop in stages, that gets better with practice. And when

WHEN IS A QUESTION NOT A QUESTION?

"You know, I hate it when I ask someone, 'How are you?' and the person actually starts telling me how he is!"

This comment from a friend of mine sums up a common dilemma in asking people questions: the fact that some of these questions have become so implanted in our vernacular speech that we no longer *think* of them as questions. Therefore, these phrases do not have the desired effect in getting a customer to open up or feel cared about.

The only effective way to pose a question that has become a catchphrase is to *change its wording*. For example, if you really want to know how a person is feeling, you might instead ask, "How are things going today?" Or, if you observe a particular situation with a customer, you might address it directly by asking, "How are you and your little darlings doing this afternoon?"

Some other examples of customer questions that have become nonquestions over time include "Can I help you?" and "Do you have any questions?" and "Will that be all?" The sentiments behind these questions are appropriate and have their proper place at times—but they don't count as questions designed to get a customer to open up.

you reach a point where this approach becomes natural, you will see a tangible difference in your dealings with people. More people will be cooperative, and fewer people will be confrontational. Transactions will go more quickly and smoothly. And perhaps most important, you will discover a newfound confidence when a customer first approaches you, knowing that you intuitively know what to say and do to put him at ease, and help him feel good about you.

Finally, there is one more important benefit to asking a lot of questions around customers—it makes *you* look very intelligent. In a very real sense, we could have titled this part of the chapter "How to Get Yourself Promoted," because people who can draw their customers out invariably appear smarter and more competent than those who do not. Asking questions is not only a sign of interest but also of expertise, and knowing how to do it well can become an important part of your own professional image.

I personally learned this lesson early in my career, as a strategy for supporting unfamiliar computer equipment. Our company's product ran on two different kinds of computers: One type was fairly common and the other had just a handful of users. When people would call with problems on this latter system, I was often stumped and would go directly to our company's engineers, who would generally respond with more questions—"What was he doing?" "Did she close the files?" "Did he reboot his system?" I would then go back to the customers with these questions to try to troubleshoot the problem.

Over time, I wrote down these questions and used them to help future callers narrow down what was happening with their problems. Once I started doing this, a curious thing happened over time: Customers soon started asking for me specifically by name, because of my so-called expertise on this very complex computer system—even though *I had never once sat down in front of it and used it*. Over time, growing positive comments from customers led directly to my being given increasing levels of responsibility, which in turn started me on a path that led me to eventually becoming director of customer support for the entire division. Not a bad return from asking people a few extra questions on the phone!

Bringing this concept full circle to your own customer relationships, the art of asking good questions is a microcosm of how we interact with people in general. It is a structured technique that, in turn, changes the feelings and emotions on both sides of the transaction. And the comparison to the TV show *Jeopardy!* is an apt one—just like this game show uses a formula to define how its contestants can win, this technique is a formula that you can use to win with customers, as well as with people in all areas of your life. Make this part of your normal style of interacting with others, and you will discover how much it benefits both you *and* your customers.

WHEN THE CUSTOMER IS ALWAYS WRONG—USING THE "I" TECHNIQUE

Now, let's move on to a much more delicate situation: What do you say when a customer has done something wrong, or is about to do something that is a really bad idea, and you need to let the person know about it? Most of us who work with the public eventually run into customer situations like the following:

- The customer's computer crashed, and he or she lost work because a backup copy was never made.

- The customer did something that voided the warranty on his or her merchandise.

- The customer is trying to use a complex piece of machinery without the proper training.

Many people feel that they are in no-win situations with transactions like these. When they tell customers what they should have done, or shouldn't do, they frequently offend these customers. But the alternative is to absolve them of responsibility, often in violation of their company's procedures, or let them go ahead and make a mistake. None of these scenarios are win-win situations for either you or your customers.

One effective technique for communicating in these situations is what we call the *"I" technique*. We give it this name because it involves describing the customer's behavior from *your own* frame of reference, with *you* as the focus of attention, rather than the customer—and then focusing on how to solve the problem. It is a counter-intuitive but effective way of telling a customer what he or she did wrong, or is about to do wrong, without hurting the person's feelings. There are two steps to this process:

Step 1. Talk about yourself. Find a way to phrase your comments so that you are talking about yourself, and not the customer. For example, if a customer does something wrong, say, "I get frustrated when I've done that." Or when a customer doesn't know what he or she is doing, say, "I know from experience that it takes time to learn how to use this." The important principle is to avoid mentioning the customer's own poor behavior wherever and whenever possible.

Some people may think to themselves, "How do I talk about myself when, in point of fact, a customer is doing something uniquely stupid that I would never do?" The answer is that you can always draw on your experience as an *observer*, if not as a participant. This means that you can almost always make an "I" statement of the form, "I know that a lot of people have trouble with this," which still avoids putting blame on the customer. Either way, the key principle is to make sure that your first sentence always has *I* and not *you* in it.

Step 2. Talk about solutions. The previous step lays the groundwork for making recommendations to resolve the issue—and these recommendations should be phrased in terms of *what will help the customer* rather than *what the customer should do*. For example, "You will have to pay to fix this" should instead be phrased as "Here are what options we have," while "You need to learn how to use this" could become "I'd like to discuss some possible training options for you."

This step is important, because the act of proposing a solution further shifts the focus from blaming the customer to helping the person. More important, by not putting the customer on the defensive as you discuss the problem, he or she is much more likely to be receptive to these solutions. Taken together, both steps result in substantially easier transactions, as customers focus on solutions rather than on defending themselves.

Let's take the examples we just mentioned and look at how you put the "I" technique to work with them:

EXAMPLE 1:

The customer's computer crashed, and he or she lost work because a backup copy was never made.

Normal response: "You should have made a backup copy of your work."

"I" technique: "I get really frustrated when I forget to make a copy of my data and my system crashes. If these data are extremely important, I do have some third-party resources that might be able to help you with data recovery."

EXAMPLE 2:

The customer did something that voided the warranty on his or her merchandise.

Normal response: "You did something wrong that has voided your warranty."

"I" technique: "I like to tinker with things sometimes, too. Even though this modification means that we can't cover this under warranty, you do have some other options at this point."

EXAMPLE 3:

The customer is trying to use a complex piece of machinery without the proper training.

Normal response: "You should have learned how to use this first."

"I" technique: "I know how hard it is to use these without the proper training. I'm going to make some recommendations on training resources for you, so that you have a good experience with this."

In the 1970s, social learning researcher Albert Bandura proposed that much of our behavior is influenced by *modeling*—that is, we learn what to do—or not do—by watching or hearing about how other people perform a behavior. His theories ranged from how children learn behaviors they see on the playground to how we are influenced by television programs or celebrity endorsements. According to modeling theorists, we are programmed as a species to be strongly influenced by the behavior of others, because we cannot possibly learn every adaptive behavior ourselves.[2]

When you use the "I" technique to discuss a behavior with a customer, you are effectively modeling the customer's own behavior so that he or she can see it from the perspective of an outside observer. The customer is watching you describe yourself doing a behavior, with no criticism directed at anyone but yourself, so that he or she can learn from it without feeling defensive. And then when you move to the next step of the process and offer solutions, the customer is much more likely to listen to these solutions and leave the transaction satisfied.

The "I" technique is effective precisely because it is so rarely used. The pull of human nature is so strong that nearly every transaction like this is normally handled, at some level, by blaming the customer. As a result, it is very refreshing for customers to hear responses that don't put them on the defensive, and people generally respond very well to them.

Should "I" Leave My Husband?

A national advice columnist once put his own version of the "I" technique to work, with hilarious results. In his Salon.com advice column "Mr. Blue," noted author and radio personality Garrison Keillor once received a letter from a woman who was considering whether to leave her loving but sexually tame husband to, as she put it, "live out my Harlequinesque fantasies," while worrying that she might become a lonely spinster after leaving her husband and friends behind. She closed her letter with "What to do?"

Compared with most advice columnists, Keillor took a very imaginative tack. He said that the two of them were in the same boat, because at age 58, he was wondering if he should chuck his successful life as a writer to become a pop singer. He went on to say that his wife enjoyed his singing around the house, and that perhaps he should go out and buy singer clothes, but worried that he would be a flop and endure public criticism for it. He then closed his reply with "What to do?"[3] ∎

While Garrison Keillor's answer was more than a little tongue-in-cheek, it also does a good job of demonstrating the impact of the "I" technique. Keillor, in all likelihood, felt that this woman was considering doing something stupid. But instead of telling her she would be stupid, which might elicit a defensive response, he instead presented a mental image of a portly, bespectacled, fifty-eight-year-old wanna-be pop singer giving up a stellar writing career, and let her fill in the blanks.

In real-life customer transactions, of course, you would not want to employ the humor and gentle sarcasm that was effective for this advice column. For example, if you were a psychotherapist and this woman were your client, you might instead use the "I" technique more charitably and say something like, "I understand what it is like to be torn between two sets of desires. Let's look at this." Either way, the impact of turning attention onto you and away from the customer represents a powerful way of modeling behaviors that will benefit him or her.

Naturally, this technique does not apply in cases where you are trying to stop inappropriate or unacceptable customer behavior. When someone is abusive, sexually aggressive, racist, or otherwise beyond the bounds of acceptable behavior, these situations call for unequivocal action, rather than delicate communications. But for the much more common situation where you are trying to prevent self-inflicted customer problems, the "I" technique represents a powerful and diplomatic method to help customers take responsibility for their own behavior, in a way that benefits everyone.

ROLE REVERSAL: SPEAKING LIKE A CUSTOMER

One additional technique that can make a major difference when you are communicating with customers—particularly when the news is unwelcome—is to anticipate their likely reactions, and then speak from their frame of reference *before* they respond. This simple but counterintuitive method will often defuse a bad customer reaction from happening in the first place, by making it clear that you understand and acknowledge how it will affect the person.

For example, one day I was sitting in my dentist's chair, expecting to get a simple filling for a cracked tooth. He looked at the X-rays, then turned to me and first did a good job of staging. "I see what's going on here. If you'll look here, you'll see where the tooth structure has become weak, and is letting decay grow further." But then he took a very unusual way to describe what I needed. Patting me on the shoulder, he said, "You're going to need a crown. You didn't want to hear that. You're thinking that crowns are expensive and no fun. And you're right. But here is how it's going to benefit you."

He made his point—well enough that I am now the proud owner of a new dental crown. How often do you hear someone say, "You didn't want to hear that" or "You've got concerns about this, and you're right"? As we discussed previously, because of our innate perception shift, we tend not to word situations from the customer's point of view. However, by making a few simple changes in how you word things, you can make a dramatic difference in how a customer will respond to you.

Let's look at some examples of how this process works:

EXAMPLE 1:

A customer has just missed the last flight of the day.

Speaking normally: "We'll have to book you on another flight tomorrow."

Speaking like a customer: "It's no fun being stuck in a strange town overnight. Let's see what we can do to make you comfortable tonight, and get you on your way again in another twelve hours."

EXAMPLE 2:

You have to charge someone a late fee because he or she returned a video a day late.

Speaking normally: "Unfortunately, that is our policy."

Speaking like a customer: "Late fees are really annoying. Even when they are necessary, you hate to pay them."

EXAMPLE 3:

It is Saturday night, and someone has just come to your clinic to get a tetanus shot after accidentally slicing his hand instead of his bagel. It will be a forty-five-minute wait until he can be seen.

Speaking normally: "Please have a seat until the doctor can see you."

Speaking like a customer: "I'll bet you had better plans for a Saturday night than sitting in our waiting room."

In each of these cases, we presume that you have already told the person the bad news—using the techniques discussed earlier in this book, hopefully—and now you are preempting any negative response by saying exactly what *he or she* was going to say, and doing it *first*. When done well, a customer should be silently saying to himself or herself, "Gosh, that's my line!" But more important, you are showing customers at a very personal level that you are thinking the same way that they are. This "commonality of thought" helps customers view you as someone like themselves, and this in turn helps your transactions with them go much more smoothly.

Early in the twentieth century, philosopher Martin Buber defined human relationships as having one of two forms: "I-Thou" relationships, where we and others have a shared reality involving each other's thoughts and feelings, and "I-It" relationships, where we view those around us as static objects.[4] Most customer relationships are frankly of the "I-It" form, where the focus remains on our own policies, procedures, and duties. By making proactive statements that share the reality of our customer's experience, we accomplish more than providing better service—we create a different relationship that ultimately benefits us even more than the customer.

THE ULTIMATE GOAL: THINK LIKE A CUSTOMER

One thing that all three of these techniques have in common is the ability to help us think and respond like customers themselves do—and, moreover, they are all structured techniques, rather than just feelings or attitudes. They do not require a transformation of your personality to put them into use. Instead, you learn and practice different ways to communicate the same messages, which create measurably different outcomes than what normally happens in a customer transaction.

Perhaps more important, these techniques fundamentally change the dynamics of how we interact with customers. Many people look at "thinking like a customer" as a matter of altruism, where we push our concerns into the background and focus on someone else. The problem with this view is that, far too often, altruism lasts about as long as the short walk between your last motivational seminar and your next real-world customer situation. This is because, in the absence of specific approaches and techniques, the pull of human nature is usually far too strong to resist while we are in the trenches with real customers.

Here, by comparison, we are proposing an approach that is more like athletic training than attitude adjustment. It involves a process with specific steps, and working these steps day in and day out delivers results that far exceed simply setting out to be "nice." When you become good at these skills, customer interactions become much more predictable, more successful, and more fun—which, in turn, affects the success and pleasure you derive from your own career working with people.

In my own experience as a real-world customer support manager, watching these techniques take shape among the many and varied personalities in live call centers and training workshops is nothing short of amazing. You really can learn to get into a customer's mind-set and think like he or she does, and the end product of this process is a set of interpersonal and leadership skills that will stick with you for the rest of your life.

6

RESPECT AND EMPATHY: MORE THAN A FEELING

I f you ask an average person how to give someone a good customer experience, he or she might say, "Develop a good attitude." But what creates a good attitude? Is it having a positive, sunny disposition toward every customer? Going out of your way to help people? Always having a smile on your face?

These are all good things to do. But for many people, believe it or not, they also represent a trap. Because when we feel that good service basically means being nice to people, we set out with the best of intentions to put a good face forward to customers—and then discover that these good intentions don't make it any easier when we have to say no to people, set boundaries, or are faced with someone's unhappiness. These intentions are even less effective when we run into the buzz saw of customers who behave poorly, demand more than they are reasonably entitled to, are rude to us, or confront us. As a result, many of us resign ourselves to a grudging truce—we may be good at being nice to *nice* people, but our human nature takes over in those tougher situations that are common to customer service.

That is where this chapter comes in. Respect and empathy are, in fact, the cornerstones of a peak customer experience. However, they are not feelings—they are *skills.* In the following sections, we will look at some simple techniques for developing respect and empathy as a learned communications skill. These skills don't even require you to necessarily *feel* warm and fuzzy toward a customer—they simply take the guesswork out of what to *say*, in ways that will demonstrate this sense of respect and empathy while maintaining your boundaries about what you can reasonably do for the customer.

These techniques are easy to learn and use, because they involve simple rules that are based on what customers themselves are saying or feeling. But above all, they work remarkably well. By the time that they become second nature, both you and your customer will perceive a marked difference in your level of warmth and understanding toward people, and this in turn will further build the sense of confidence and professionalism that you feel in working with the public.

LOOKING AT RESPECT

The term *respect* has its roots in the Latin term for "looking back," and even today, its definition involves responding in relation to something—such as another person's needs or wants. It fundamentally involves acknowledging what is important to people, and sharing this sense of importance. In a customer situation, respect means understanding the agenda that a customer presents to you, and then responding specifically to this agenda.

Respect is another one of those virtues that sound obvious in theory but are often lacking in practice. Think back to the last bad experience that you had as a customer. What happened? In all likelihood, you came to someone with a set of expectations, and then he or she did not show an appropriate level of *respect* for those expectations:

- You expected your car repair to be ready on time, and instead it was late—with no explanation or apology.

- The computer you ordered was dead on arrival, and the service technician you called seemed much more interested in the company's rules and procedures than in your inconvenience.

- You said you were in a rush, and they were in no hurry to respond.

- You pointed out an overcharge on your hotel bill, and the desk clerk sullenly and silently rang up a new receipt.

- You noticed a stain on your dress when you picked up your dry cleaning, and the clerk shrugged as you pointed it out to him.

The common denominator among all of these situations is a simple lack of respect. You are upset not because you did not get what you wanted—in fact, in many of these cases, you ultimately got what you asked for, whether it was having your computer fixed or your bill corrected—but because they didn't *care* about what this situation *meant* to you. And the word that probably comes to mind as you think about these scenarios is that you felt *disrespected*.

Now, let's shift gears for a moment and step on the other side of the counter. Why would nice people like us *not* show respect to customers? Because we naturally tend to pay more attention to how a situation impacts *us*. When you work with customers, it can become all too easy to focus on the mechanics of what you do for them and see them as an endless, faceless stream of auto repairs, lunch orders, or dental procedures. But in reality, these practical issues are usually "gift wrapped" with each customer's feelings about them, including:

- *Their level of urgency.* ("My daughter is getting married tomorrow—can you fix this?")

- *The degree of expertise required.* ("You didn't fix my brakes properly last time—can you put your best mechanic on this?")

- *How critical the problem is to them.* ("If I can't get on this flight, I'm going to miss an important speaking engagement.")

- *Their personal frustration.* ("This is the fourth time I've been back.")

These feelings are often more important than the practicalities of what you are doing. They vary with each customer's situation: One person may be making a routine request with modest expectations, whereas another may feel he or she has an extremely urgent problem requiring immediate action. Either way, respect is fundamentally a matter of acknowledging both the customer's problem *and* the customer's agenda.

Demonstrating Respect: Using "Phrase Substitution"

When you are face-to-face with a customer, the transaction normally goes something like this:

1. A customer asks you something.

2. You make a decision about the person's request.

3. You share your decision with the customer.

The hard part is step 2, where you usually have to decide between one of two outcomes. You can do what the customer asked, or you can't. You know the answer, or you don't. You have the authority to fix the customer's problem, or you don't. The *easy* part is step 3—and that is where a simple yet powerful technique that we call *phrase substitution* comes in.

Phrase substitution takes the process of showing respect to customers and puts it on autopilot. It involves taking the kinds of things you would normally say to people, and coming up with *planned, rehearsed* phrases to replace them—phrases that say exactly the same thing, but in a way that is:

-   Enthusiastic

-   Responsive

-   Acknowledges the customer's agenda

Phrase substitution works so well because it involves reengineering the *exact same message* that you would say otherwise, by using new words that create a win-win situation for both you and the customer. Let's look at a quick example of how it works in practice:

Before:

Customer: Could you help me?

You: OK.

Customer: I need to find a jar of pickled beets.

You: They're in aisle 14.

After:

Customer: Could you help me?

You: Absolutely! What can I do for you?

Customer: I need to find a jar of pickled beets.

You: I know exactly where they are. Go two rows down from here, and make a left on aisle 14.

Now, let's take stock of what has just happened, as a result of using simply a little bit of phrase substitution:

- You have done no extra work.

- You have made yourself seem much more competent.

- You have proactively offered to help, rather than just passively responding.

- Above all, you have painlessly shown respect to the customer's request.

In other words, you have a much happier customer—and a much better reputation at work—all for the cost of just changing a few words. Let's break down the mechanics of creating these phrases into its three component parts:

1. *Enthusiasm.* We show enthusiasm through a number of cues, including our facial expression; tone of voice; and, above all, what we say. By changing our words to be enthusiastic ones, we follow the classic behavioral psychology of acting "as if," which in turn can affect feelings and behavior. Table 6-1 outlines some examples of rephrasing what you say to show more enthusiasm.

Table 6-1. Showing enthusiasm.

Before phrase substitution	After phrase substitution
I can.	I sure can!
I can't.	I wish I could!
Yes.	Absolutely!
We're out of stock.	Our customers can't get enough of this!
You are correct.	That's exactly what I wanted to hear!

2. *Responsiveness.* Enthusiasm is important, but it isn't enough by itself if you do not respond in kind to what customers are saying to you. Here again, the right phrases can convey your interest in the person in front of you, such as the examples in Table 6-2.

3. *Acknowledgment of the Customer's Agenda.* Finally, the things we tell customers need to shift gears toward their interests—and away from our natural tendency to focus on our own constraints or procedures, as shown in Table 6-3.

Table 6-2. Being responsive.

Before phrase substitution	After phrase substitution
I don't know. I'd have to ask someone.	I can find out!
That would work.	I'd recommend this one for you.
That won't work.	In my experience, there's another alternative that would be better for you.
It'll be at least another hour.	We're going to finish this as soon as we possibly can. I'm estimating an hour.
That isn't my department.	I know where you can get an answer to that question.

Table 6-3. Acknowledging the customer's agenda.

Before phrase substitution	After phrase substitution
Next person in line, please.	Welcome! What can I do for you?
You'll have to come back.	I don't want you to have to wait.
I'm sorry.	This shouldn't have happened to you.
That won't work.	Here's what you can do. . . .
It costs this much.	Here is our most affordable model.

The trick with all of these examples is that you must plan and rehearse these phrases ahead of time, much like an actor or actress rehearses lines before appearing on stage. The time to develop a new way of speaking isn't when a situation is heading toward you at 80 miles an hour—it's when you have time to think, reflect, and choose a new way of speaking that fits your unique personality. Then, with practice, you will find these new patterns creeping into your normal speech. It's a small amount of "off-camera" effort that yields a substantial return when you are in front of actual customers.

As you can see from the previous examples, the same concept works equally well when you have to say no to people—again, by using known, prepared phrases that show enthusiasm for the customer and his or her agenda. Let's try another situation:

Before:

Customer: Can I have a box seat for today's game?

You: We're sold out.

After:

Customer: Can I have a box seat for today's game?

You: I wish you could! We have a great crowd at the ballpark today, and every seat is sold out.

Again, by using some simple phrases—that you have planned and rehearsed in advance—you have accomplished two important things. First, you've shown the customer that you wanted him or her to attend the ball game ("I wish you could"). Second, you have shared what a good product your team has on the field ("We have a great crowd at the ballpark today").

This technique even works well when you don't *feel* a great deal of respect toward a particular customer. Imagine that someone is very upset, to the point where he is flailing his arms and shaking his head. You certainly don't *feel* enthusiastic about dealing with him at this moment. But by responding to his issues with statements like, "Absolutely" or "We certainly can," you are creating an environment of respect that has nothing to do with how you are feeling at the moment—no matter how you feel inside. Even when you disagree with a customer, you can—and should—still use phrase substitution, and it will still have the desired effect of showing respect for what a customer is saying.

Beyond your basic communications skills, demonstrating respect is perhaps the most important skill in a customer transaction—respect for the customer's time, feelings, and his or her reasons for seeking your assistance. There are times where showing this respect must involve action, such as going above and beyond the call of duty in a critical situation or personally ensuring that a situation has been resolved. But perhaps the most important measure of respect lies in what you say to customers, and phrase substitution represents a simple, practical way to make this sense of respect part of your natural routine with customers.

Done well, the phrase substitution technique will usually create less work—and shorter transactions—than more typical responses will. And as an added bonus, learning to speak this way will change the way others look at you at work, because you are adopting the language of leadership in what you naturally say. It costs nothing, requires no changes to your service policies, and is easy to learn—but putting it into practice will deliver considerable benefits to both you and your customers.

UNDERSTANDING EMPATHY

In an earlier chapter, we touched on the importance of empathizing with a customer's feelings as you deliver information to him or her. Here, we will examine some specific ways to show empathy in all of your communications with a customer.

Empathy is similar to respect, but not quite the same. Whereas respect is about acknowledging and responding to what people want, empathy is more about understanding their *feelings*—in fact, the word springs from the Greek terms for "passion" and "feelings." Empathy implies that you personally share what the other person is feeling.

These feelings are often more important than they appear on the surface. For example, when someone contacts a call center with a computer problem, there may be much more going on than the computer problem itself:

■   The person may be seeking reassurance as he or she uses a computer for the first time.

- The person may be trying to get something to work to avoid looking bad in front of his or her manager.

- The person may have an important deadline looming.

- The person may be trying to convince a spouse that he or she didn't make a mistake in buying this computer.

In each of these cases, the person's feelings are probably more important than the problem itself. If you can successfully reassure these feelings, you and the customer are much more likely to work cooperatively toward a solution. Conversely, have you ever had a situation where the problem itself was resolved satisfactorily, but you received no empathy? If so, you realize that even when you technically "do your job," ignoring or being insensitive to a customer's feelings can make a bad impression on the customer—and, more important, can prolong a difficult transaction.

These feelings are all part of being a customer, and indeed of being human. No matter how proud we are on the outside, we universally want both our problem solved *and* our feelings validated. We all want to be accepted and understood, fear appearing inept in front of other people, and feel upset when people don't take us seriously. This means that what you say to a customer—regarding both the problem and the feelings behind the problem—has an important, if unspoken, impact on the customer's self-image.

Empathy is the act of addressing other people's feelings in a way that helps them feel good about themselves—and feel good about you. With customers, empathy is more than a state of mind: It is an organized approach to saying things that reduce customer defensiveness to produce shorter and easier transactions. As with respect, it is a skill that need not depend on how "nice" the customer is, and it gets easier with practice.

Demonstrating Empathy: The "Playback" Approach

Showing empathy to customers is a structured communications skill and not just a feeling. It involves providing customers with a playback of what they just said worded in such a way that you demonstrate acceptance of their feelings. Here are four specific techniques that you can use to do this—any or all of which may come into play depending on the situation:

"THIS IDIOT WANTS TO BUY ANOTHER CAR"

You wouldn't know it to look at me, but I have a bum shoulder, most likely a remnant of my childhood exploits as a defensive tackle on the local football team. Once in a while, I have to wear my arm in a sling when I overexert myself. A few years ago, this physical situation led me to a very interesting customer situation.

One day, soon after moving to a new city to take on a management position, I decided to treat myself to a new car. I read the reviews, took several test drives, and purchased a sporty little black sedan. It was a great car, but soon enough, I discovered a slight problem—that shoulder. Every two weeks or so, I drove several hundred miles with my wife to visit her family, and over that much of a distance, the car's manual steering made my arm throb and ache.

After several weeks of putting up with this discomfort, it was clear that I really needed to get another car. So, have you ever tried to trade in a car that you have only owned for three months? If you haven't, allow me to share some of the things that I was greeted with:

- "You know, you just bought this car three months ago." (No! Really?)

- "Trading in a car this soon is going to cost you a lot of money."

- "This is a very unusual situation."

- "We'll have to see what we can do in a case like this."

In short, as I went from dealership to dealership, I became convinced that these salespeople were not actually trying to sell me a car—instead they were, in reality, engaged in a contest to see which of them could make me feel more stupid! But finally I went to one more dealership, whose salesperson instead said things like:

- "I totally understand situations like this, Rich."

- "Things like this happen all the time."

- "We can get you fixed up again in a much more comfortable car. It's no big deal—your payments will go up a little bit, but we'll work it all out in the transaction."

- "A car is an important purchase, and you need to do what's right for you."

Guess where I bought my next car?

---

1. *Acknowledge feelings and frustrations.* Even when you do not agree with a customer, you can still show you understand how important the situation is to him or her. By using the customer's own statements, you personalize your response in a way that builds trust and good feelings.

    Example: "I realize that you really wanted to have these prints back by Monday."

2. *Share common experiences.* Telling stories of your own past experiences not only shows empathy but also helps to frame the transaction as a discussion between equals. As an added

bonus, sharing these experiences also lets you show your own competence and expertise in handling the customer's problems.

Example: "I've had similar problems with this model, and I know exactly what to do."

3. *Use the customer's own feeling statements.* This technique shows respect for a customer's agenda by incorporating his or her own feelings within your response, using the form of "Because you ____, I ____." For example, you might say, "Because you are in a rush, I am going to show you the fastest way to do this." By chaining the customer's own words with your response, this powerful technique creates acceptance and understanding of the customer, which is often as important as the response itself.

Example: "Because you were unhappy with this dish, I'd like to suggest some alternatives."

4. *Reassure concerns and self-deprecating statements.* When a customer says, "I'm really stupid," you are not being asked to agree with him or her! In cases like these, silence is viewed by the customer as tacit agreement. Actively reassure people who criticize themselves.

Example: "Don't worry; you are doing great. A lot of very intelligent people are using computers for the first time, like you are."

The common denominator among all these responses is that they play back at least a little bit of what the customer just told you in a way that acknowledges the feelings behind the problem. When you agree with a customer's feelings, share your own experience, use her feeling statements, or address her concerns about herself, you explicitly recognize and accept her feelings, which in turn lowers the emotional barriers between you and the customer. Table 6-4 shows some examples of the difference this approach can make.

The responses in Table 6-4 aren't just a matter of being "nicer"—they are specific techniques that cause customers to feel empathy, and react accordingly. With practice, these four approaches can serve as ways to create an environment that lowers customers' defenses, increases their cooperation with you, and builds a productive relationship between equals. And when sales enters the equation, these skills

Table 6-4. Using playback.

Without playback	With playback
You'll have to wait in line.	Don't you hate it when everyone shows up at the same time?
OK, I can do that.	That's a piece of cake—I've done hundreds of these.
This is the best I can do.	I realize you want X, so we're going to come as close as possible by doing Y.
I see.	That's very understandable. Everyone gets frustrated with that.

are even more critical. When you have a financial stake in a customer's buying decisions, developing a genuine sense of empathy can be the most important way to improve your own bottom line.

As with other communications skills, playback is *not* the same as agreeing with someone. You can disagree with people and still demonstrate acceptance that they feel the way they do—and, above all, acknowledge that these feelings are important to them. Ironically, by doing this first, it will be much *easier* to subsequently disagree with people. Compare the following two scenarios:

EXAMPLE 1:
Customer: I'm missing my family reunion, and I demand a seat on the next flight!

You: I'm sorry, sir, the flight is full.

EXAMPLE 2:
Customer: I'm missing my family reunion, and I demand a seat on the next flight!

You: Wow, I don't blame you for being upset about that! Because you need to get there ASAP, I'd like to see how soon we can get you out of here. Even though the next flight is full, here are some options. . . .

In the second case, the customer is no closer to getting a seat on the next flight than he was in the first case. However, by addressing his feelings—and, more important, addressing them first—you create

a zone of trust and comfort from which you can both negotiate a mutually acceptable solution. Perhaps the greatest secret of showing empathy with customers is that it is even more important when you cannot
say yes to them—when you are most tempted to turn inward and defend yourself. This is precisely why empathetic responses are particularly useful in difficult customer situations.

Above all, the playback technique addresses feelings that are spoken: A customer shares a concern about something, and you acknowledge and reassure him or her. The next level of empathy—the
advanced course, if you will—comes in when you can *anticipate* what
a customer must be feeling, and then respond to these *anticipated*
feelings with empathy statements.

Naturally, you always need to be a little careful about presuming
what a customer is or is not feeling, so that you don't second-guess the
person. However, there are times when the emotions involved are so
obvious that the right words can make a great deal of difference. Let's
say that you are the desk clerk at a hotel where an extremely long line
of people are waiting to check in. An obviously tired and stressed
young woman slouches toward your counter with several young children and a pile of luggage in tow. It's more than okay to say something,
and the difference between "Next, please" and "I'm sorry that you had
to wait so long. I've got a nice room just down the hall waiting for all
of you" is incredible.

Police officers, who make a career of defusing confrontations, are
masters of this technique. After someone gets arrested, what do you
think that police officers say to the handcuffed suspect during that
long ride in the patrol car? Personally, I've never had the pleasure, but
a good friend of mine who is a former police officer once told me that
is when savvy cops turn on the empathy. For example, she personally
would say things like, "I can tell you're probably a good person. You
got caught doing something stupid, like most of us do at some point.
But if you learn from it, things are going to be OK." As she puts it, "In
a situation like this, the officer has all the power, but treating someone
with civility is the best thing—not only for the arrested person but for
the safety of everyone who subsequently handles him or her."

Although most customer situations aren't so critical that they involve handcuffs, the principles remain the same: Listen when customers express their feelings, or use your best judgment to imagine what
they are feeling, and then say things designed specifically to respond to
these feelings in order to foster warmth, understanding, and smoother
transactions. With time and practice, these empathy responses can

become as natural to you as the defensive replies most people use, and this sense of empathy will in turn have a major impact on your interpersonal skills with customers.

MOVING FROM PERSONAL FEELINGS TO PROFESSIONAL SKILLS

Many people who serve the public don't realize that most customers really want three things from us. The first is the obvious thing that they are asking for, which springs from doing your job—be it a hamburger, a doctor's appointment, a ticket on the ski lift, or whatever else. The second is to have their needs treated with respect. The third is empathy for what they are feeling. Most customers will never ask you for these latter two things, but ignoring them can often cause ill will and difficult customer transactions. Conversely, when you become good at sensing and responding to all three of these needs, you will sense a real change from customers.

Respect and empathy are among the most important things you can share with a customer in any situation. But how you demonstrate both of them has much less to do with feelings and much more to do with practicing specific communications skills than you might think. If you are seeing a pattern to many of the techniques we have covered to this point, it is this: Think like a customer, and learn and practice the phrases that speak to that customer's mind-set.

This brings home a deeper point that excellent customer service is less a matter of personality and more a matter of specific communications skills. The so-called nice people who don't know what to say in the right situation will still leave customers unhappy, whereas average people who apply the right transaction skills professionally—and sincerely—will do a great job. Respect and empathy are two great examples of how small changes in these communications skills can truly make anyone a star in front of customers.

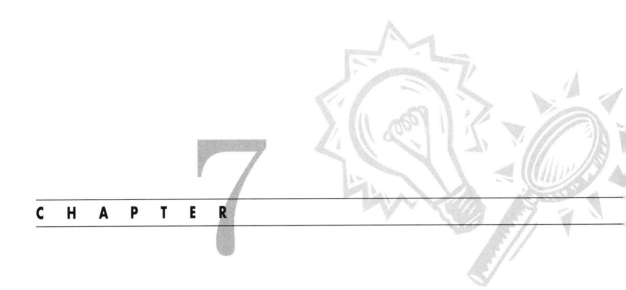

CHAPTER 7

HOW TO (ALMOST) NEVER SAY NO

"We're in the business of saying no."

How many workplaces would have a slogan like this? Probably not many. However, we know from experience that the word *no* is one of the most common words uttered to customers. And as people who serve the public, we also know that when we say no to a customer during a transaction, our problems are often just beginning.

This chapter presents a unique solution to the problem of saying no to people: Stop saying it! As incredible as it might sound, there is usually no need to *ever* utter a nay-saying phrase, whether it is the garden variety no, or its close relatives such as, "Sorry, we can't do that" or "I'd like to help you, but we can't." Our goal here is to cut statements like this from your vocabulary—permanently.

Once in a great while, I have the talent to read minds, and I believe that I can read yours right now. "What? How can I *never* say no to customers? What if they demand things that I can't provide? What if they are asking for something totally outrageous? What if they want me to fix a problem that is *their fault*?" But rest assured, you really can avoid telling someone no, in just about any situation that you can imagine, including these and many more. What's more, you and your customer will both feel much better doing it that way! Read on, and you will learn exactly how to do it.

Here, we will discuss a specific technique that you can use to keep from saying no, while still respecting the boundaries of doing your job. It may take a little extra practice to feel natural, because we are strongly programmed to set limits, enforce rules, and defend ourselves. But once you master it, you will do much more than take the word *no* out of your vocabulary—you will take a big step in preventing conflicts from starting and escalating. This, in turn, will give you the ammunition you need to keep most customer transactions from ever becoming difficult ones. Master it, and you will discover that many of your most stressful customer situations are suddenly "no" problem.

HOW TO STOP SAYING NO: DOING THE CAN-CAN

If you are a native speaker of English, you may not be aware that in much of the world, there are strong cultural taboos against using the word *no*. At a business meeting in Tokyo or New Delhi, it is considered insulting to contradict someone publicly by saying no. In these parts of the world, disagreements are instead framed with polite conversation about the benefits of doing things differently, whether they are formal contract negotiations or a debate on where to go for dinner. And in many countries, such as China, their native languages don't even have a word that translates to "no"![1]

These cultures have a head start on a positive, constructive way of communicating with people that helps bring people to agreement, without crossing boundaries on either side. But for those of us who don't share such a cultural background, we present a simple rule that helps us achieve the same outcome in our own customer interactions. We call this technique the *Can-Can*.

In the nineteenth century, the cancan was a popular dance revue made famous by the Moulin Rouge in Paris.[2] Here, the term refers to an extremely powerful technique designed to prevent people from becoming angry when you cannot do what they want. Here is how it works:

Always respond with what you *can* acknowledge and what you *can* do.

This technique works, and works well, because it shifts your focus—and that of your customer—from the glass being half empty to being half full. It focuses on solutions rather than problems, and on the future rather than the past. And underlying it is the simple but powerful idea that in any situation, there is always something you *can* do for a customer.

This technique is simple, but not intuitive. Why? Because people generally don't ask for service when they are having a fine day and want to tell us what nice people we are. They want service because their tire is flat, their order didn't get delivered, or they are hungry and want to get fed. So, what is our basic, innate, human response when someone confronts us with a problem? It is to defend ourselves, of course. We have an inherited tendency to see the world through our eyes, and not the eyes of our customers.

This leads us into situations like one that I personally encountered a while back: I had ordered something online, looked at the receipt a few minutes later, and noticed that I had mistyped my credit card number. Immediately, I picked up the telephone and called their so-called customer service number to straighten out the mistake. The conversation that followed went something like this:

Me: I just ordered something online from your store and typed in the wrong credit card number. Can you help me correct this?

Store: We can't do anything about that here. Those orders get handled in our warehouse.

Me: Could I call the warehouse?

Store: We don't give out the number to the warehouse.

Me: So how do I fix this?

Store: I'd have to try sending a fax to the warehouse.

Me: (long pause) Well . . . could you do that?

Store: Uh, I guess so. Gimme your name.

You can probably guess the rest of the story from here. The person who answered the call did nothing, and eventually the warehouse—whose number apparently remains a state secret—contacted me a day later, complaining that my credit card number was incorrect. I had a few choice words in reply and have never ordered from the company since.

So, what happened here, beyond the obvious bad attitude? A communications style that remained totally in the frame of reference of the person receiving the call, where every single thing that he uttered revolved around what he "can't" do. Aside from clearly being impolite, this person failed because he remained stuck focusing on his own rules and procedures, no matter how technically correct he was.

By comparison, the Can-Can is a simple technique where you take statements about what you *can't* do and replace them with statements about what you *can* acknowledge and *can* do. For example, Table 7-1 examines how the Can-Can might have changed the outcome of the previous situation. Note that we are not changing their procedures— we are still presuming that the person taking the call needs to let the warehouse handle the problem. However, by responding with what he *can* acknowledge and *can* do, the feelings surrounding the situation now become totally different.

Now, let's take a look at a situation where years ago, as a call center manager, I had an interesting opportunity to put the Can-Can to work in real life. One afternoon, I was doing some routine monitoring of one of our agents' phone calls. He was speaking with a very angry person who (a) had never obtained any training on how to use our company's software product, (b) had done something he shouldn't have, and (c) had completely messed up all of his company's financial information. In his mind this was all our fault, and he was angrily demanding that we fly someone immediately to his office in Chicago to "fix everything."

This particular agent was calm, patient, and unflappable as this

Table 7-1. Using the Can-Can.

Can't	Can-Can
We can't do anything about that here.	That sounds really frustrating. Don't worry, this will get taken care of shortly.
We don't give out the number to the warehouse.	There is no need to worry about this. The folks at our warehouse will contact you as soon as they try to process your order.
I'd have to try sending a fax to the warehouse.	To make sure they see this as soon as possible, I could send them a fax.

customer continued to carry on, and thinking that he had matters well in hand, I signed off the call and went back to work. A few minutes later, he showed up at my office door, and I greeted him with, "Hi, Steve! I was just listening to your last call, and you were doing a great job with that man." His response was, "He's still on the line. He wants to speak with you, because you're the boss. And he is still demanding that we fly someone to Chicago tomorrow."

My reaction? "Excellent! Have a seat. Let's get him on the speaker-phone, and we'll use this as a coaching opportunity!" (Did I tell you that my staff always thought I was a little strange?) Then we got the customer back on the phone, and here are some of the things that I said to him:

Me: Hi, Michael! I was just speaking with our technician Steve, and I understand that you are having some problems with our software. What can we do to help you?

Michael: My orders are all wrong! Your software messed everything up permanently! You need to send someone here to straighten this out!

Me: I can tell that you're very frustrated about this. And I have some good news for you—we can, in fact, send someone out to help you! The only thing is that on-site visits like these cost several thousand dollars, and our trainers are usually booked three to five weeks in advance. So, I'm wondering is there anything else we can do, right here on the phone, to help straighten out this situation?

Michael: I don't want to pay to have someone come out!

Me: I completely understand that! That's why I'd like to see what else we can do to help you right now for free.

The key here was that everything I said in this discussion was focused on what I CAN acknowledge ("I can tell that you're very frustrated"), followed immediately by what I CAN do (such as sending someone out for a cost or helping him on the phone). In fact, if you reread the previous dialogue, you'll see that the word *can* is used more frequently than any other word except the all-important *you*. Throughout the rest of this conversation, my approach was the same:

- I never told him that we "couldn't" do anything.

- I never told him that he should have been trained first.

- I steadfastly refused to say anything that wasn't designed to be helpful to *him*.

The results? After a few more seconds of this exchange, things had calmed down considerably, and we were now both talking rationally about what his problem was—and soon, what *we* could do to help *him* make the best use of this software, within our boundaries of providing technical support and paid training. He eventually agreed to fix the problem himself with our guidance, and we set up a visit from a salesperson in his area to arrange for him to get training. More important, we parted at the end of the phone call as friends—and, in the process, I got to coach one of our top team members on how to never, ever say no.

In much the same way, learning to word things to a customer's benefit in any situation—particularly when he or she pushes you to do things that you cannot responsibly do—is often the quickest way *out* of that situation. It works precisely because it goes against our normal self-protective nature and moves us from confrontation to solution. Let's take a look at the specifics of how to put this principle to work in real life, and soon you too will never say never.

THE CAN-CAN IN DETAIL

Have you ever observed the mother of a young toddler in the supermarket as she goes past the candy racks at the checkout counter? The child's behavior is instinctive—he or she wants some candy, *now*. Listen closely the next time that you see this scenario, and there is a good chance that the mother will respond with something that *benefits the child*—for example, "You can have dessert when we get home," or "After we're done here, let's go to the park—would you enjoy that?"

There is an important reason that mothers do this: It works. And more to the point, they have probably learned the hard way that the more obvious, direct answer—"No, you can't have any candy. Please be quiet."—often leads to an escalating tug-of-war with a screaming kid. So, they naturally and instinctively learn to resolve conflict by seeking what benefits both them *and* their child.

This leads us to a key difference between how mothers handle their children and how most of us handle our customers: We don't have to take our customers home with us and raise them for the next twenty years! As a result, it becomes much easier to respond with statements that focus on our limits, such as, "No, I'm sorry, we can't do that." In our fantasies, the customer will then respond by saying, "Silly me—you're right!" and walk away—but in reality, he or she instead often behaves much as the toddler would by arguing with us. This is why you need a new way of disagreeing with people—one that makes both you and the customer feel better.

This is where the Can-Can comes in. It is a simple but important tool for preventing confrontations when you cannot give customers what they are asking for. As with many of the techniques that we have described to this point, it works because of a powerful concept in human psychology—that people have a strong, innate ability to categorize what they hear and experience, which triggers our natural friend-versus-foe instinct. This means that when we say the right things to customers—or, more accurately, when we say things the right way to customers—they are much more likely to cooperate with us because it is very hard to fight with an ally. Conversely, when we say things that challenge customers or ignore their interests—*even when these things are correct*—we often kindle the hot buttons of frustration or disrespect that can spark a confrontation. This is why it is critical that we learn and practice ways to stay in the customer's own frame of reference.

The Can-Can provides an easy, structural method for speaking in the customer's interest, in a way that eventually becomes our natural response. Let's break down the mechanics of how it works in a little more detail.

Step 1: What You CAN Acknowledge

In Chapter 3, we looked at the key components of what you first say to a customer: acknowledging his or her needs and feelings around an underlying principle that *feelings are never wrong*. This opening statement becomes even more critical when a customer wants something that you cannot provide. By opening with something you *can* acknowledge, you send a clear message to a customer that you understand and respect his or her agenda, even when you cannot directly provide what the person is asking for.

These acknowledgments can range from the situation itself to the customer's feelings. Either way, they have a common purpose: to share agreement and acknowledgment of at least one thing that is in the customer's self-interest—which, in turn, changes the customer's stance from "me versus you" to one of "you and me versus the problem." Table 7-2 shows some examples of common acknowledgments.

Each of these opening acknowledgments has a common purpose: to speak to the customer's own interest in a way that builds trust and empathy. More important, they create that all-important first impression, which guides how a customer reacts from then on. No matter what you acknowledge or how you choose to word it, speaking from a customer's perspective puts the thought first and foremost in the person's mind that *your first priority is to help him or her*.

Step 2: What You CAN Do

Here's where the rubber meets the road. The customer wants something. And, because we are such nice people, if we could possibly give it to him or her, we would. But we can't. So now, after we acknowledge the customer, we reach that critical fork in the road of how we should respond to the request.

Most people would take the obvious fork in the road and say no.

Table 7-2. Examples of acknowledgment.

Type of acknowledgment	What it involves	Example
Common ground	Share your knowledge, expertise, or understanding about a situation.	"That situation has happened to me, too."
The "I" technique	Model appropriate behavior by putting it in the first person.	"I get frustrated when something goes wrong, and the right answer was in the manual all along."
The silver lining	Point out the benefits of a situation.	"Even though this is broken, there is actually a much better product out now."
The customer's feelings	Acknowledge that the situation is frustrating to the customer.	"That sounds like no fun at all."

Whether it is a blunt refusal or a polite, diplomatic explanation of what our limits are, we still overwhelmingly respond to the customer's need by talking about ourselves. What we can't do. Why we won't do it. What we expected the customer to do first. What the policy manual says. In short, everything *but* the one thing that will actually resolve the situation: namely, *what you can do for the customer*.

Now, I'd like you to stop and think back to your last argument with someone at home. What finally resolved the problem? For most people, I bet that after breathlessly trying to convince the other person how wrong he or she was, one of you finally acknowledged that the other person had a point about *something*—perhaps even a very small thing. And chances are that once there was even a tiny acknowledgment of the other person's interests, the floodgates opened for serious negotiations to solve the problem.

The same thing happens with you and your customers: We trigger the natural friend-versus-foe reflex by *finding a way to take their side*. This means resisting the natural temptation to say no, and instead looking for ways—even very small ways—to say yes.

Let's take a look in Table 7-3 at some examples of finding something that you *can* do, and see what a difference it makes.

Most people would agree that the *can* responses on the right sound a lot better to customers than the *can't* responses on the left. They are certainly more helpful, and much more likely to elicit a reasonable response from the customer. More important, the act of *trying* to work with a customer, in and of itself, will change the dynamics of the discussion in a positive way.

So why don't more of us talk about what we *can* do in real life?

Table 7-3. Examples of what you *can* do.

Can't do	Can do
I'm not the right person to fix this problem.	I'm going to put you in touch with the right person to fix this problem.
It's the end of my shift.	My partner Sally is going to help you with this problem.
I can't give you a refund.	I can give you a 20 percent discount.
We can't possibly do that.	Let's look at some other options.

Aside from an almost irresistible urge to protect our interests, customer problems often come at us like a runaway train and don't leave us a lot of time to think logically. Which leads us to perhaps the greatest secret of all in using the Can-Can effectively: *Prepare and rehearse your most common "can-do" responses ahead of time.* Do you work at an auto repair shop? Know what to say when a repair takes too long. Answer the phones at an insurance agency? Know how to handle at-fault accidents, claim problems, and rate increases. And if you work in retail, you should completely nail what to say about your store's refund policy—for example, even when someone absolutely cannot return something, you can still suggest donating it for a tax deduction or gift wrapping it for someone else (using the "I" technique, of course). Whatever your unique job situation is, there are common transactions for which you can practice what you *can* do.

An equally important point is that any situation—and that literally means *any* situation—can still be worded to a customer's benefit:

- When someone owes you taxes, you can help him or her work out a payment plan.

- When a person is at fault in an accident, you can help him or her make things whole.

- When a customer wants a discontinued product, you can learn about his or her needs.

- When there is bad news of any kind, you can help people look at their options.

Let's take, for example, my neighbor who is a loss prevention specialist for a large retailer—in other words, he apprehends shoplifters. He is unarmed, his customers are often bigger and faster than he is, and they *really* don't want to be there. So how does he do a good job? By using his own version of the Can-Can: When he confronts shoplifters, one of the first things he tells them is that it would be in *their* best interest to come back to the store with him—because they might be able to settle the matter directly with the store and avoid criminal charges. In short, he keeps them from running away by offering them a better deal than calling the police.

Whatever the reality of your job is, a new and much more positive way to handle your unique customer problems by focusing on what you *can* do is waiting to be discovered. When you seek out and practice this seemingly unnatural way of communicating with your own customers, you will start getting results immediately—and once it becomes second nature, you will find that it helps transform even your most difficult customer encounters into a win-win situation for everyone.

Step 3: What to Say Instead of No

In an ideal world, a customer asks for X, and you acknowledge the person politely and say that you can do Y instead. Then the person thanks you and walks away satisfied. But in the real world, simply telling a customer that you can do something else can seem like a futile effort at diversion—much like what comedy troupe Monty Python portrayed in their "Cheese Shop" skit, where a proprietor tries hard to keep up appearances with a customer when, in fact, he has no cheese at all.[3]

When someone wants something badly enough and you can't provide it, how do you respond directly to this fact without focusing on what you *can't* do? By using two magic phrases that refocus the customer back on what is possible: "I wish" and "Even though."

Both of these phrases work powerfully well because, while they honestly convey your limits, they do so *as an ally of the customer*—and, more important, they begin sentences that allow you to shift the focus of the conversation back to what you *can* do. The key lies in using them as follows:

E X A M P L E   1 :

I wish I could do X—but I can do Y.

or

Even though I can't do X, I'd be happy to do Y.

E X A M P L E   2 :

I wish that the store were open later, but I'd be glad to help you now.

Even though we cannot give you a refund, I'd like to see if we can arrange a store credit.

I wish we could get you on the nonstop flight, but since a ticket for that flight would cost several hundred dollars more, I'm going to try to get you on a connecting flight that arrives within an hour of it.

Even though the company had to cancel your insurance after the accident, I've lined up some alternative coverage for you.

In each of these cases, you are still letting the customer know that he or she cannot get what he or she wants. But using the naturally empathetic introductions "I wish" or "Even though"—and, more important, chaining them to what you *can* do—you are much more likely to end up with a thank you to each of these statements instead of a fight. Even when customers want something badly and continue to argue for it, they will still know that they are dealing with someone who is on their side—and, in all likelihood, will negotiate a solution in good faith, as a partner rather than an adversary.

Remember that you must follow up these phrases *immediately* with what you *can* do—otherwise, you may make things worse instead of better. This is because all too often, these phrases are unthinkingly used to defend ourselves—for example, "I wish we could help you, but we can't." "Even though you want this, we still have to follow our policy." In fact, statements like these are so widespread that people have a term for them: "Yeah, but." As a rule of thumb, as long as the rest of the sentence is designed to help the customer, "I wish" and "Even though" will get you through almost any situation where you have to diplomatically negotiate alternatives.

Putting the Can-Can Together

The Can-Can keeps difficult situations from escalating by using a one-two punch of powerful psychology—first by acknowledging the customer, to build a relationship based on mutual respect, and then by speaking to his or her interests by focusing on what you *can* do. In Table 7-4, let's take some typical customer situations and see how the Can-Can technique can change how customers react to you.

In each of these cases, the message is the same—only the wording changes and, more important, the focus behind it. You move from your perspective ("You have to pay for this damage") to the customer's ("Everything is OK"), without changing the basics of the situation. Actually, you are doing nothing more sophisticated than speaking to a customer the same way that you would address a close friend or relative in the same situation—and in return, you create an environment where the customer will usually respond the same way that a friend would. This, in a nutshell, is where the beauty of the Can-Can lies: It is

Table 7-4. The Can-Can in practice.

Situation	Human nature	The Can-Can
A customer wants to purchase something that is out of stock.	"I'm sorry, sir, we're out of stock."	**Can acknowledge:** "I wish that we had this in stock, so that you could have had this today." **Can do:** "I can help you order this."
A customer's son breaks a piece of merchandise.	"Ma'am, I'm sorry, but your son broke this item, and you have to pay for it."	**Can acknowledge:** "We had a small mishap when your son was playing with our merchandise. The important thing is that he is OK, and no one was hurt. Even though we do have to charge you for the merchandise, we certainly understand situations like this." **Can do:** "I can take care of this at the register up front for you."
A customer wants a refund for a product that he has damaged, and you cannot give him one.	"Sorry, ma'am, I can't give you a refund on damaged merchandise."	**Can acknowledge:** "I hate it when things like this break." **Can do:** "Even though we can't refund damaged merchandise, I can give you our best price on a more durable model."
A party of five has just shown up at your restaurant for dinner, and you won't be open for another fifteen minutes.	"Sorry, we're not open yet."	**Can acknowledge:** "Thanks for coming!" **Can do:** "I can seat you in just a few more minutes."

a structured technique for what to say, which, in turn, has the effect of taking your service quality to a much more intimate and personal level.

"Love Means Never Having to Say You're Sorry"

Do you notice one common denominator among the human nature responses in Table 7-4? They almost always begin with "I'm sorry"—which is truly ironic, because they convey no regret whatsoever. And unlike the line shown here from the movie *Love Story*,[4] "I'm sorry" is a nearly universal phrase that serves the functional purpose of excusing ourselves before we deliver bad news.

This is a good example of a service catchphrase that has long since lost its original meaning yet has become a nearly addictive part of our vocabulary. Try an experiment the next time that you have to deliver bad news to a customer—make it a point *not* to start your sentence with "I'm sorry." In all likelihood, it will feel awkward and strange at first, sort of like answering the doorbell in your pajamas. But as you replace this catchphrase with Can-Can statements like the ones offered previously, the difference in a customer's reaction will be remarkable!

There are times when true regret is very appropriate, and in such cases the right apology would be *specific* and *personal*—for example, "I am very sorry that we spilled salad dressing on you, and we want to make the situation right." But in general, the unvarnished phase "I'm sorry" should be stricken forever from your vocabulary. ■

BEYOND THE CAN-CAN

You may have noticed that the title of this chapter is "How to (Almost) Never Say No." Where does the *almost* come in? There are a few situations where this technique has its limits. By understanding them ahead of time, you can make the best use of this technique—and, more important, know where it may not be appropriate. Here are some of the most common exceptions to using the Can-Can:

■ *The Moral High Ground.* On the whole, customers respond well when we are trying to speak to their interests, but they aren't stupid. When you are in a situation where your answer—or your organization's answer—is indefensible, no amount of customer skills can make it otherwise. For example, when someone lands in the hospital following an accident, and his spouse rushes in wanting to see him, no response other than "yes" will be acceptable—nor should it be. Some other examples of where the moral high ground comes into play include:

■ When customers are not getting services to which they are legitimately entitled

■ When following your policies would be unjust or insensitive

■ When the stakes are high and the response is inadequate—for example, when people need help in an emergency

Even in these difficult cases, it still makes sense to keep the customer's interests front and center in what you say, particularly compared with the defensive and insincere responses that people often get in these situations. But above all, keep in mind that any communications technique is only as good as the service behind it.

■ *Crossing Boundaries.* When customers want something that they can't get, use the Can-Can. When there is a misunderstanding between your organization and a customer, use the Can-Can. But when a customer is stealing an armload of toilet paper from your rest room, it may be time to use another communications technique called "call the police." When people openly break rules, harass people, or go beyond the boundaries of civilized behavior, they are the ones choosing to step outside the realm of diplomacy.

■ *The Never Satisfied.* Most people get upset because they are, well, legitimately upset. But a few people intentionally *choose* to be upset, because it is their normal negotiating strategy—because, sadly, they have a personality that believes hostility will get them what they want (often, at a cost of alienating everyone with whom they interact). With people like these, nothing that you propose in good faith will be acceptable, and they will grind away at you until they get what they want.

How can you tell the difference between the unsatisfied and the never will be satisfied? Normally, the giveaway is a complete unwillingness to negotiate or acknowledge you, combined with an unreasonable request. The people who say, "Don't you know who I am?" and demand a free upgrade at your hotel, or wave a so-called defective product with a small scratch in front of you and demand a steep discount, are fundamentally different people from the normal disgruntled customer.

When your legitimate efforts to resolve things don't meet with cooperation or success, these situations become a matter of setting appropriate boundaries while still acknowledging the customer's feelings. Of course, if there is anything that you can legitimately do to satisfy these customers, by all means do so. But if you cannot, in all good faith, give in to their demands, the solution is deceptively simple: *Keep politely repeating the Can-Can* until they give up. In other words:

1. Ask them what they want.

2. Acknowledge their concerns.

3. Set boundaries in terms of what you can do. (I wish I could . . . but I can . . .)

4. Go back to step 1, and repeat until the situation is resolved or escalated to someone else.

In my own personal experience with tough customers, two or three repetitions are normally all it takes before they realize that their game plan will not work and move on. This technique of repetition borrows from an approach known as *fogging*, a key component of assertiveness training that springs from the granddaddy of all self-help books, psychologist Dr. Manuel Smith's *When I Say No, I Feel Guilty*—so named because when you patiently repeat your intentions, the other person's provocations become as ineffective as hurling things into a fog bank.[5] When done politely and with class, it is extraordinarily effective with your most unreasonable customers.

At the same time, realize that these situations are normally an exception and not the rule. In the vast majority of cases, we need to give each and every customer the benefit of the doubt, and use the Can-Can to treat his or her concerns with respect and dignity. More important, by making a habit of speaking in a customer's best interest, we become more keenly aware of the exceptions and treat them as the special cases that they are.

THE CAN-CAN WAY OF LIFE

The amazing thing about how the Can-Can works is that it doesn't change the situation—just the way you describe the situation. Your customers are still having their cars towed away, paying for things they damaged, and keeping their nonrefundable merchandise. You are just changing the frame of reference, in a way that both saves face for the customer and paves the way to a solution. More important, by staying within the customer's frame of reference, you avoid the hot buttons that often cause confrontations to begin or escalate in the first place.

In the process, learning and practicing the Can-Can will create a subtle but important change in the way that you see customer situations. It changes your fundamental stance from one of defensiveness to one of open-ended possibilities. This, in turn, helps develop a mindset that helps you become a genuine friend and partner with your customers, in a way that changes the entire customer relationship. Above all, the Can-Can is a clear, easy-to-learn technique for preventing confrontations with customers, particularly when customers want things that they cannot get. It takes the essence of the Golden Rule—do unto others as you would have them do unto you—and turns it into simple guidelines for what you say:

- Don't say no—find small ways to say yes.

- Word things in the customer's best interest.

- Take a genuine interest in the customer's problems.

When you put the Can-Can to work in your own life with customers, you do much more than simply negotiate solutions with them—you reach out to these customers as people and build personal connections that benefit both you and your organization. This technique, combined with the other skills in this book, helps you to effortlessly manage potentially difficult or contentious situations with any customer. By incorporating the Can-Can into your normal style, you will never, ever look at the word *no* quite the same way again.

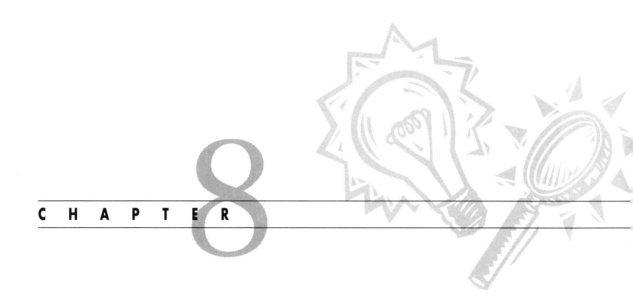

8

HOW TO BECOME A HUMAN BOMB SQUAD

Okay, let's see a show of hands—how many of you have never, ever been an angry customer yourself? Bad customer experiences are universal to all of us, and no matter how polite or accommodating we are, there is a point past which we are going to become frustrated and show it. And for those of us who work with the public, most of us are all too familiar with the experience of customers getting upset with us.

At the same time, all too often, people equate the words *customer service* with "dealing with angry people." They presume that anger is a fact of life in a profession that, by its nature, involves dealing with people who have problems. They resign themselves to being at the mercy of the situations that they and their customers find themselves in. And they are wrong.

First and foremost, the vast majority of angry customer situations should never happen in the first place. In Chapter 7, we focused on how to keep situations from getting out of hand—by speaking in a way that always makes you the customer's advocate and avoiding the hot buttons that can set people off. In my own experience, having literally overseen tens of thousands of customer transactions, truly angry encounters are extremely rare when you have the right skills—and they should be. So above all, the best way to handle upset customers is to keep them from ever getting that way.

At the same time, anyone who works with customers long enough will eventually find themselves face-to-face with someone's anger—because it is part of being human. Given this fact of life, managing confrontation remains an important part of your tool kit for managing customer transactions. More important, knowing how to handle these situations professionally will substantially boost your confidence level in working with the public, which will in turn make *all* of your customer interactions go better. It is a little like being in law enforcement or the military: You hope to never have to use your weapons, but it is good to know that they are there when you need them.

This chapter focuses on a simple, three-step process for cooling things down and negotiating a clearheaded solution when customers turn up the heat. The goal is to reduce the hostility level of a customer, step by step, and quickly move to a neutral zone where you can negotiate alternatives rationally and solve the problem. By putting this technique into practice, you can quickly become a human bomb squad capable of defusing hostile customers in almost any situation.

UNDERSTANDING WHY WE GET ANGRY

According to psychologists, anger is a natural human response to a threat, and an adaptive survival trait. We become angry when we feel challenged, hurt, or at risk, by preparing physiologically to fight or defend ourselves. Our adrenaline levels increase, our muscles tense, our pulse rate and breathing levels increase, and our emotions reach a boiling point. This fight-or-flight response is a universal trait among people, and even across species—for example, when you approach a helpless baby animal, the mother animal will often confront and threaten you, even when it puts her own life at risk. It is one of our most powerful and intimate emotions.[1]

This means that when a customer is upset because she has been waiting too long, she is essentially using the same skills that her ancestors did to outrun or fight a hungry predator, but translated to the modern-day situations that surround her own life. If you work with customers long enough, you can identify certain common situations that are at the root of most customer confrontations, and you can use this knowledge to understand and manage these situations better. Some of the most typical reasons for customer anger include:

■ *A Real or Perceived Injustice.* We carry around in our minds an image of how life should be, and when reality does not match these expectations, we feel upset. Noted psychiatrist and *Feeling Good* author Dr. David Burns refers to this as the "should-y" approach to life, because we focus on how things "should" be, and notes that this is frequently the root cause of much of our unhappiness.[2]

The obvious customer example of this is a product or service failure—for example, when someone's new minivan breaks down repeatedly on a family vacation, the person may understandably be at a boiling point when he or she returns to the auto dealership. However, there are more subtle expectations in a customer transaction as well, such as how people are treated—for example, if a sales clerk gives a customer exactly what he or she asks for, but won't acknowledge the person or make eye contact, this may also provoke a hostile response.

■ *Failure to "Execute" Properly.* An even more obvious source of anger is when commitments are made to customers but not kept. When the customer expected a return call last week, for example, and your company didn't follow through until a week later, misunderstandings can cause frayed tempers. Similarly, when an executive gets on a plane in Seattle and expects to arrive for a meeting in San Francisco in a couple hours, but is now into her fourth hour on board as you circle the airport, the gap between your timetable and reality can cause bad feelings to erupt.

■ *Poor Treatment by Others.* Getting a customer angry doesn't even require *you* to do anything wrong! A customer's past experience with other people can spill over into his or her interactions with you, even before you do or say anything. When customers are used to dealing with rude, indifferent sales clerks at other auto repair shops, they may come into your shop with all guns blazing, no matter how hard everyone tries. Similarly, the run-in that they had with your boss last week might lead them to have a chip on their shoulder when they deal with you.

■ *The Customer's Own Personality.* Some people simply have a shorter fuse than other people. By nature of their temperament, they are easily provoked and aggravated in public transactions. Still others unfortunately incorporate anger as a normal part of their negotiating strategy, because they have grown to feel that it often gets them what they want.

The common denominator across each of these situations is that in every case the customer feels that something should—or should not—have happened. In other words, there is a gap between the customer's expectations and reality. It is within this gap that most confrontations with customers begin. Typically, when a situation gets out of hand, it goes through a set of predictable stages:

1. The customer confronts us with this gap, and his or her feelings about it.

2. We feel defensive and respond to this confrontation by defending ourselves.

3. The customer keeps trying to close the gap, we keep on defending ourselves, and both parties keep talking past each other.

From there, the situation keeps spiraling downward until one party eventually gives up, or the situation is escalated to someone higher up in the chain of command. More often than not, both parties leave the transaction exhausted and upset, and neither person goes away satisfied—no matter what the outcome is.

There is a better way—and its first step lies in understanding these root causes of customer anger. By knowing the most common reasons why customers get upset—and, more important, knowing how they often lead customers to react—you take the first step in seeing the situation from a customer's perspective. From there, you can use structured communications skills that can effectively defuse the conflict, and allow both sides to negotiate a win-win solution as partners.

DEFUSING A CRISIS: THE TRIPLE-A APPROACH

No matter what the cause, anger universally feels inappropriate and uncomfortable when we are on the receiving end of it—particularly from a relative stranger such as a customer. When someone yells at you, hurls biting sarcasm at you, or confronts you with his or her physical presence, it is natural to feel intimidated. It is unquestionably one of the most difficult experiences of working with the public.

This discomfort makes it hard for most of us to handle anger effectively. Left to our own instincts, a customer's anger often leads us to either react with hostility ourselves, or withdraw emotionally—both of which are self-protective responses that usually make the situation worse rather than better. But the good news is that angry customer situations *can* be understood and managed by using a step-by-step process that addresses the customer's feelings, gathers information, and negotiates a solution. We can call this process the Triple-A approach, named after its three key steps:

1. *Acknowledgment*—acknowledge feelings and give the problem importance.

2. *Assessment*—gather facts and assess the situation.

3. *Alternatives*—sell alternatives and set boundaries.

These steps play several important roles in defusing a customer crisis:

- They give the angry person attention and empathy.

- They create a neutral zone where a customer can openly express his or her feelings.

- They create time and space for strong emotions to subside.

- They turn a confrontation into an information-gathering process.

- They provide the setting for a face-saving resolution.

The goal of the Triple-A approach is to reduce a customer's hostility level *in stages*. These steps are not magic words that suddenly turn off a person's anger—because anger, unfortunately, does not turn on or off like a light switch. Instead, this approach is a process that, when followed in order, will progressively turn down the heat until you and the customer both reach a point where you can calmly and rationally negotiate a solution. Let's look at each of these steps in detail.

Step 1: Acknowledgment

The first and most important step in defusing any customer crisis is acknowledging the customer and his or her issue. In Chapter 3, we discussed the importance of acknowledging customer feelings in the opening seconds of a transaction. When someone is upset, this takes on even more critical importance, and a good first acknowledgment is the single most important aspect of defusing a difficult customer situation. When you acknowledge the customer first, you are giving his or her problem a sense of importance, and starting to build a level of trust that lets you mediate a solution much more effectively.

The fundamental principle behind using acknowledgment in a customer crisis is one that we have also discussed before: *Feelings are never wrong.* In other words, you can't always agree with the customer's viewpoint, but you can *always* acknowledge his or her feelings. You can always agree that what a customer is feeling is important *to him or her* and use that shared understanding to start communicating productively about the problem.

Although this principle may sound great in theory, be aware that it is challenging and takes practice to become natural. There are three key components of a good first acknowledgment for an angry customer, and all of them work against our nature:

1. *It requires talking about the customer and not yourself.* In real life, when someone confronts you, your self-protective instinct slams into high gear and you quickly focus on what *you* won't do and why *you* won't do it. This strategy makes perfect sense if you are trying to scare off someone who is threatening you, but in the workplace, it makes for a poor customer retention strategy. Conversely, when you lead by talking about customer's favorite subject—themselves—it starts to make a positive change in a difficult situation.

2. *It requires discussing their feelings.* When someone is upset, another innate response is often to withdraw. This is why people often respond to angry customers in a colorless monotone that tiptoes around their feelings—which, in turn, makes them even angrier! Conversely, meeting these feelings head-on ("Boy, you must be really frustrated about this!") gives these feelings a face-saving legitimacy that short-circuits their need to defend their anger.

3. *It requires acknowledging the situation as* the customer *sees it.* Many angry customer situations are fundamentally

adversarial in nature. For example, your customer thinks that your product is shoddy or wants to get home after the last train just left the platform. In cases like these, your first instinct is to focus on who is right, which means that you defend your product, or remind the customer about the train schedule. But to lower the heat, you must instead lead by acknowledging these very real customer feelings, *even when you do not agree with them*.

On top of all of these things is the fact that angry customers are, well, angry. When someone loudly insists that you fix something *now*, wants you to personally contact the president of your Fortune 500 company, or demands that you give back three times his or her money, your first instinct is to defend yourself—at which point you usually get yourself into more trouble! An angry person is trying to get your attention and will instinctively escalate the situation if he or she is not getting it. Learning to give the customer this attention, on his or her terms, is a counterintuitive but important first step toward managing the person's anger.

Here are a couple of examples of how to acknowledge people when they are upset:

EXAMPLE 1:
A customer comes in complaining that a product is defective—and in reality, this person broke it by misusing it.

- You *can't* agree that the product is defective.

- You *can*—and should—agree that it is frustrating to have a product break down.

What you shouldn't say: "But, sir, you broke this by misuse."

What you should say: "I agree, it's really frustrating when parts like this break down. It's a shame that our warranty doesn't cover accidents like this. Let's see what we can do to help you out here."

EXAMPLE 2:
A customer claims that another sales associate told him or her one price, and the sign lists a higher price.

- You *can't* agree with the customer yet—you still need to investigate what happened.

■ You *can* tell the person that you will do what you can to clear things up.

What you shouldn't say: "Sir, the sign lists a higher price."

What you should say: "I certainly can't blame you for not wanting to pay more money. Let me speak with my manager and see if we can get this straightened out."

Will a good acknowledgment stop an angry person from being angry? The answer is sometimes—but not always. The goal of a good acknowledgment is not necessarily to completely dissolve a person's anger. Rather, the goal is to identify yourself quickly as a friend versus a foe while lowering the anger level so that you can start to negotiate a solution with the customer. It represents a first, but very important, step within a broader process of defusing a difficult situation.

Step 2: Assessment

Have you ever spoken with police officers after an automobile accident or a break-in? If you have, you probably remember one key thing from the exchange: *They ask lots of questions.*

Assessment—or, in plain English, the art of asking good questions—is perhaps the key difference between handling angry customer transactions and normal ones. Assessment has an obvious purpose, which is to gather facts and information about the situation, but there are also some subtle but important reasons that you need to do it when someone is angry:

■ It gives the angry customer time to calm down.

■ It demonstrates interest in the customer's problem.

■ It helps you learn things about the situation that may help to negotiate a solution.

Assessment questions work best when you preface your questions with a calming, helpful statement, such as:

■ "I'd like to see what we can do to help you. First, let me just get a little information about this issue."

Then, ask emotionally neutral, factual questions that help you assess the situation:

WHEN SILENCE REALLY IS GOLDEN

One other "question" that deserves special mention in tough situations is the judicious use of silence—specifically, a planned pregnant pause that leads the customer to help you resolve his or her concerns. While an unvarnished lack of response is clearly not a good idea, consider introducing a short silence with a phrase such as, "Let me think about what we might do here" or "I'm thinking about what options we have." Because it is human nature to fill in periods of silence, a properly placed break can often lead an angry customer to break the silence—and a possible stalemate—by proposing a solution to the issue. For example:

> *Customer:* Look, I'm tired of talking about this. This problem ruined my vacation, and I want a complete refund.

> *You:* I can see how frustrated you are about this. Let me think through some options for a moment. . . [pause].

> *Customer:* Look, I'll tell you what—if you could just upgrade me to a better room, at least I'd feel better.

> *You:* Great! I think that would certainly be appropriate. I'll set that up right now.

In most cases, calm and patient questions will help set the stage to resolve an angry customer's issue—but when things get very tense, sometimes saying nothing can be the best response of all.

- "Can you tell me what was happening when the problem occurred?"

- "Is this the first time you have used this product?"

- "What kinds of things have you tried already?"

As customers respond, listen patiently, make eye contact when appropriate, and acknowledge the person's responses in a nonjudgmental manner. At a minimum, use short response statements such as "I see" or "OK"—and where appropriate, find ways to paraphrase the person's answers, in a way that shows that you understand his or her feelings. For example:

> *You:* I can tell that you are pretty upset about this. Can you tell me what happened?

> *Customer:* I certainly can! I was driving along in your rental car on the freeway, and a tire blew out! I spun around and then had to limp across three lanes of oncoming traffic to get over the shoulder.

> *You:* Wow—that certainly is scary! I'm glad you weren't hurt. So you were on a freeway—how fast would you say the car was going when the tire burst?

> *Customer:* Almost 75 miles an hour. That was really a jolt when it happened.

> *You:* Absolutely. Were all your passengers OK?

Customer: Thank goodness, we're all fine. We rented this car so we could move to Oklahoma, and it's packed to the gills with stuff, too.

You: I'm sorry that this happened—moving is a stressful time even when car problems don't happen. Did you have any damage to your luggage?

Several important things are going on in this exchange. First, by asking questions and paraphrasing the customer, you are demonstrating interest in the situation. Second, you are giving the customer the time and space to decompress from a very emotional experience. Third, you are gathering valuable data about both the condition of your car and the circumstances of the incident. On one hand, you clearly need to check the condition of this car's tires and make sure that future customers are safe driving it. On the other hand, you have also learned that it was overloaded and the driver was speeding, which is potentially useful information if the customer were to eventually litigate against your company. In either case, you are gathering valuable data while you helped the customer calm down and negotiate a solution.

Above all, asking good assessment questions helps put you in a mind-set of being curious rather than furious. Beyond the obvious transfer of information between you and the customer, these questions create a zone of neutrality that prepares both of you for the final step of resolving the issue. When done well, it helps customers feel better about both you and the situation and sets the stage for them to eventually leave the transaction satisfied.

Step 3: Alternatives

Remember the Can-Can technique described in Chapter 7, where you focus on what you *can* do for a customer? Once you have acknowledged an angry customer and gathered information about the person's situation, you return once again to the art of focusing on what you *can* accomplish to resolve a situation—by providing alternatives to the angry customer, and negotiating a resolution to the issue.

Once again, the key principle to remember at this stage is that there are *always* alternatives. Satisfying the customer's wishes is the best solution—and you should always do your best to make this happen. But if you cannot accommodate what the customer wants, you now have two choices: You can tell the customer no or present the customer with alternatives. Amazingly, human nature often leads most people to make the first choice—but the second choice almost always leads to a much better outcome, for several reasons:

- You are showing the customer that you are still trying to help him or her.

- You may find another way to satisfy the customer's needs.

- You provide the customer a means of saving face.

Here are a couple of examples of how giving alternatives works better than contesting the customer:

EXAMPLE 1:

A customer accidentally leaves his digital music player in the pocket of one of his jeans when he does the laundry, ruining it.

Not good: "I'm sorry, sir, we can't take responsibility for that."

Better: "Even though we can't cover this under warranty, I have a couple of ideas. We could switch you to a less-expensive model or perhaps upgrade to a new player with better features. Which direction would make more sense for you?"

EXAMPLE 2:

A customer complains that her favorite dish is no longer on the menu. (And even if you wanted to ask the kitchen to make it, the ingredients aren't even in stock.)

Not good: Ma'am, I'm afraid you'll have to order something else.

Better: I can suggest a couple dishes that other customers have been ordering in place of this one.

In both of these cases, you have no control over the customer's desired outcome: You cannot replace the cellular phone, and you cannot prepare the missing dish on the menu. But by focusing on alternatives, you change the dynamics of the situation to one of being the customer's advocate, even as you set boundaries. This does not mean that customers will not negotiate or even continue to argue with you—remember, after all, that they came into this situation because of a gap between their expectations and reality. But providing alternatives *does* mean that you will reach a solution much sooner, and with fewer hard feelings, than if you do not.

Taken together, this three-step process will make a real difference in what happens when a customer comes to the table in anger. Skilled professionals look at angry customers in much the same way that airline pilots look at turbulence—as situations that are never comfortable, but manageable with the right skills. By looking at these situations as a process, and following the right steps in this process, you can truly bring the vast majority of them to a successful conclusion.

PUTTING THE TRIPLE-A TECHNIQUE TO WORK

Now, let's pull all three steps of the Triple-A technique together and look at how you might use them in a typical real-world situation.

Imagine that you work in a small, upscale toy store in a downtown shopping district. One afternoon, a woman storms into the store, marches up to the counter, and starts to confront you. First, let's take a look at how discussions like this *normally* go:

You: Can I help you?

Customer: Yes—you stupid idiots wouldn't give my son his money back on this broken toy, on his birthday! He just came home in tears. I am *outraged* about this. How *dare* you tell my son that he can't get his money back on this rotten, defective product!

You: Whoa, calm down, ma'am. This is a small store, and we don't give refunds for any products.

Sound familiar? This is how many, if not most, people react in the face of a torrent of hostility—they set boundaries and defend themselves. Following human nature is understandable at a time like this, because these situations are intensely uncomfortable. But let's predict the results: Do you think that (a) she will calm down, and (b) she will suddenly respect your store's policy and leave quietly? I don't think so! So let's try this again, but using the Triple-A approach.

Step 1: Acknowledgment

You: Can I help you?

Customer: Yes—you stupid idiots wouldn't give my son his money back on this broken toy, on his birthday! He just came home in tears. I am *outraged* about this. How *dare* you tell my son that he can't get his money back on this rotten, defective product!

You: I can tell by your tone of voice how upset you are, and I'm sorry this happened.

Customer: You'd better be sorry! You people ruined his big day!

You: I know that my kids would be very upset if their birthday presents got broken too. Let's see what we can do about this.

Customer: All right.

At this point, is the customer happy? No. Has she stopped being angry? Probably not yet. But by acknowledging her feelings—every time she speaks up—you are lowering the hostility level to a point where both of you can have a meaningful discussion. Notice that, at this point, you are not yet speaking about who is at fault in the situation or what you will do about it—you are simply acknowledging the customer's feelings, at a level where everyone can share common ground. Once you reach this point, you can then move on to the next phase and start assessing the situation.

Step 2: Assessment

You: Did you bring the toy back with you?

Customer: Yes, I have it right here. [Places it on the counter.]

You: I see . . . you bought your son one of our Whistle Stop Railroad sets. I can see why he really wanted this—it's a really nice set. Tell me what happened with it.

Customer: Bobby was putting it together, and the main track platform snapped in half. Take a look. . . .

You: I see . . . you're absolutely right. And I presume that made it impossible for him to finish assembling it?

Customer: Exactly. The track sections won't stay together with the platform broken like this.

By asking questions—and, more important, by *not judging the answers* at this point—things have now progressed from a diatribe to a dialogue. Now, we can move to the most crucial part of the discussion, which is negotiating alternatives and bringing the issue to a close.

Like many real-life situations, there may in fact be no clear right or wrong answer here. Your small toy store has a no-refund policy, and it is not entirely clear at this point whether you are dealing with a defective product, a child who played too roughly with it, or both. On top of this, you have a very upset mother defending a son who has lost an expensive present on his birthday. Finally, depending on your position at this store, there may be constraints on what you personally can offer the customer. Depending on the specific factors of the situation, your options might include:

- Helping her arrange for the toy to be repaired

- Offering a discount on a replacement or another toy

- Making a onetime exception to your policy for the sake of customer goodwill and refunding the price of the product

- Contacting the store's manager to further negotiate a resolution

Personally, I am a big fan of giving customers the best experience that you possibly can—but, more important, I also want you to be able to handle difficult situations even when your options are limited. So, for this example, let's take a middle ground and presume that you are authorized to offer the customer a discount but not a refund. As long as you keep your focus on what you *can* do for the customer and continue to acknowledge her feelings, your chances of success are still very good. Let's start this negotiation by asking the customer what *she* wants, and follow along from there:

Step 3: Alternatives

You: Tell me, what would make your son happiest at this point?

Customer: Bobby has wanted a train set for months. When he came back to the store, he just wanted his money back so he could go buy another model at a department store. That's why he was so crushed when your people were so rude to him this morning.

You: I'm really sorry if he wasn't treated well, and I can see why you are upset. And I still want your son to have a happy birthday.

Customer: So what can we do about this?

You: If I could give your son his money back, I certainly would, and I'm sorry if my coworkers were too blunt with him this morning about our store's refund policy. Here's one thought I have: I could, in a situation like this, sell you a replacement product at our cost, which is about 40 percent off. What I'm thinking is, if we sold you a more basic model of the Whistle Stop Train set at cost, he could have a working track *and* all of the components he bought earlier. Would that make sense for the two of you?

Customer: How much would that be?

You: I could give you this $99 starter kit for $59.95—and send it home with you today, in time for the rest of Bobby's birthday.

Customer: OK, let's do that. I really appreciate all of your help.

Often, a well-intentioned offer in the customer's interest will allow the person to save face, get some of what he or she wants, and close the transaction successfully. But what if your offer still isn't good enough—and you can't do more? Here as well, keeping the focus on the customer's interests will almost always keep lowering the tension and move you toward a solution. For example:

You: I could give you this $99 starter kit for $59.95—and send it home with you today, in time for the rest of Bobby's birthday.

Customer: No way! We've already spent $200 on this set, and I can't afford to spend another $60.

You: I totally understand. Let's look at the options we have from here. First of all, I could call the manufacturer for you and look into getting a replacement part from them. Usually they don't cover breakage, but I could see what I could arrange. Another alternative might be getting this repaired, and I know a good repair location right here in town.

Customer: Bobby really wanted his money back so he could have a train set today.

You: I certainly understand that, and my offer for a discount still stands if you want something for Bobby today. What would your preference be?

Customer: OK—actually, I would appreciate it if you could see what you can do with the manufacturer. Could you call them today?

You: Absolutely! Hopefully, we can still make you a hero for Bobby's birthday. Let's make the call right now. . . .

The key principle here is to continually offer options and empathy, rather than set limits—and each time a customer refuses these options, keep responding with possibilities that benefit *him or her*. Even if you ultimately reach a point where you must say, "I wish that we could do what you would like, but we're still happy to do X," you will normally close the transaction on a much more positive and professional note than where it started—and, in most cases, you will quickly converge to a face-saving solution on both sides. In this particular case, several important things have happened by using this approach:

- You successfully turned an angry confrontation into a rational discussion.

- You honored your management's "no-refund" policy.

- You helped the customer explore other ways of solving the issue.

- You have probably turned an angry customer into a *future* customer.

- Perhaps, most important, you did your best to preserve a happy birthday for the customer's son.

You accomplish all these things by standing human nature on its ear through the use of a step-by-step process that relentlessly keeps the focus on the customer's agenda, even when your options are limited. In real life, I have watched angry situations like this dissolve into professional encounters, over and over again—and with practice, you will see the same things happen with your own angry customers. The Triple-A technique really works, by attacking a very difficult and emotional situation with specific steps that you can control—which, in the process, creates a better outcome for everyone involved.

ANGRY AND ABUSIVE ARE TWO DIFFERENT THINGS

The relationship between you and a customer is fundamentally an unequal one. They can behave more or less as they please, and as a paid

THE MANAGER PARADOX

As a call center manager, I had an ironclad rule that any difficult or abusive customer issue could be transferred to me, for any reason—no questions asked. It rarely happened, thanks in large part to great team members who knew how to handle customers very well, but I noticed something interesting when it did happen: These same customers were rarely abusive to me when I got on the line with them!

This phenomenon is extremely common, and there are perhaps a variety of reasons for it, ranging from customers having more respect for a supervisor to their wanting to make themselves appear more reasonable than the employee with whom they spoke. In either event, probably 90 percent of the time, a distress call from someone on my team usually led to a calm and rational exchange between me and the same customer.

This same class consciousness seems to apply universally to almost any workplace. For example, I have heard stories of patients being abusive to nurses and then being polite to the doctor, or unruly passengers who hassle flight attendants and then calm down when the captain comes out to speak with them. There is even a term for it: "kissing up and kicking down." So, as unfair and frustrating as it might seem when you are on the frontlines, remember that calming down an out-of-control customer may be as close as a call to your supervisor.

professional, it is your job to take care of them—even when they are rude, angry, or unpleasant. But you are also a human being, and there are limits to what kind of behavior you can—or should—tolerate from customers. Here are some examples of conduct that crosses the line:

- Screaming and yelling

- Repeated use of obscene language

- Racist, sexist, or other inappropriate remarks

- Any implied threat of physical intimidation or violence

At a deeper level, you should trust your own good judgment about when a situation is getting out of hand—when your gut tells you that it is time to back away from a situation, the best and safest course on both sides is generally to listen to it. Here are some steps to take when customer behavior crosses the line from angry to abusive:

- *Be prepared.* Perhaps the most important tool for handling an abusive customer situation is something that you do before the customer ever shows up— namely, knowing the options at your workplace for handling abusive situations, and discussing them in advance with your manager. This can range from a policy to get a supervisor involved, all the way to panic buttons in high-security environments such as banks or airport terminals. Knowing what your options are ahead of time not only protects you but also gives you the confidence to try to defuse situations, knowing that there is backup available when you need it.

■ *Set limits.* When customers are simply angry, your response should be all about them—by acknowledging, assessing, and providing alternatives. However, when the person starts crossing personal boundaries, the situation is about you as well, and it is perfectly acceptable to set a limit on the customer's behavior in these cases.

Perhaps the most effective way to set limits is to *give the customer a choice of whether the transaction will continue,* tied in with an offer to continue helping him or her. For example:

■ "I would like to help you, but you will have to stop using that language with me."

■ "I want to assist you, but I am personally offended by your comment about my race."

Depending on the situation, and your own personality, a sense of humor may even serve as a face-saving way out of an offensive encounter—for example, I once overheard a customer service agent respond to a customer's tirade by saying, "My husband doesn't get away with talking to me like this, so neither should you." But when a personal boundary has been crossed, the decision to lighten the mood is yours and yours alone: If it feels right, and will help defuse the tension, by all means go ahead.

Either way, when boundaries are calmly stated, it then becomes the customer's choice whether you can continue to provide assistance or not. In many cases, a customer will apologize and the situation can get back on track. However, if the person continues to be abusive, he or she is the one who chose to end the transaction. Where appropriate, this is often the point at which a manager must be called—but in either case, within the limits of your own workplace's policy, you have laid the groundwork to walk away, hang up the phone, or call security.

■ *Get to a safe place.* The vast majority of customer transactions are safe—even very angry ones—but in a small minority of cases, often involving emotionally unstable people, a customer transaction can erupt into violence. Always trust your own feelings when a situation feels unsafe, and use any reasonable means necessary to excuse yourself and/or call for backup, to protect yourself and others.

Above all, remember that many abusive customer situations are so-called crimes of passion where customers are frustrated by how they are being treated, so the greater a customer's hostility level, the more critical it is to speak to his or her interests and use your communications skills to defuse the situation. By using a consistent approach of respecting the customer *and* respecting yourself, you can successfully manage the vast majority of difficult customer situations while setting appropriate boundaries on customer behavior.

THE PARADOX OF ANGRY CUSTOMERS

In closing, we need to remember that angry customers are not an alien species—they are a fraternity of which we are all a part. This common shared experience helps us to understand what procedural skills will defuse encounters with angry customers, and why human nature fails us so badly when they occur. And as uncomfortable as these situations may be, learning to master them can add a tremendous level of confidence to your everyday work with customers.

Because customer anger is a common shared experience, there is a deeper issue to handling these situations properly that many people find ironic: Your angriest customers often become your *best* customers, and your strongest supporters, if you learn to take good care of them. And paradoxically, people who are the most skilled at defusing conflict tend to experience much less of it in the first place. These skills not only build your own self-esteem but also inoculate you against the minefield that most people face when they serve the public.

Difficult customer situations are never fun for people on either side of the transaction. Nevertheless, there is a tremendous satisfaction that comes from being able to minister to the needs of every person with whom you deal, even when his or her emotions get the upper hand. So, in a sense, you should view skills for crisis customer situations in much the same way as first aid or CPR training—as something that you hopefully use very rarely, if ever, but that nonetheless greatly enriches your own personal growth in working with your fellow human beings.

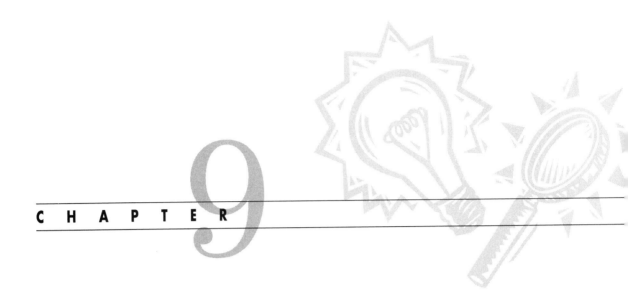

MANAGING SPECIFIC CUSTOMER PERSONALITIES

You tell a customer how important his problem is to you, and he thanks you warmly for taking such good care of him. Then you tell your next customer the same thing, and she grimaces at you. What happened?

What happened was a simple case of two people with two different personalities. The first person probably values having his feelings acknowledged, whereas the second one prefers to shoot straight and get right down to business. There was nothing wrong with what you said, but it was filtered by how each person sees the world. Understanding these differences, and knowing how to speak to them in a customer transaction, can quickly boost your interpersonal skills to the top of the pack.

By definition, working with the public involves dealing with the full spectrum of human personalities, and different people respond best to different approaches. The good news is that, with a little guidance, you can quickly tell what kind of personality you are dealing with so that you can react accordingly. These techniques ride on top of your own good communications skills, to personalize the service experience in ways that both help customers feel better and make your work with them much easier.

In this chapter, we will explore how to quickly "read" customers in the opening seconds of a transaction, and then relate to them with responses that are tailored just for them. This doesn't mean changing who *you* are: Within your own unique personality, you simply interact with customers in a way that respects who *they* are. In the process, you can learn a great deal about what motivates other people—and about yourself.

YOUR PERSONALITY

Personality defines who you are: your strengths and weaknesses, your likes and dislikes, your motivations and turnoffs. According to psychologists, you developed the vast majority of your personality by age 6—and will keep it for the rest of your life!

How do we describe personality? Your personality is composed of the basic beliefs that guide your behavior. Our personalities are made up of aspects such as:

- How we see the world around us

- How we interpret events

- How we react to situations

- How we solve problems

- Our relationships and interactions with other people

There is a vast core of feelings that nearly all humans share in common—for example, most of us prefer nice people to rude people, and respond better to a handshake than a shove. However, beyond these common feelings, our personality determines on which traits we place our own personal emphasis. One person may crave praise and approval, another one may value high standards, and still another may seek freedom and flexibility. All these traits are equally valid, and there are no "right" or "wrong" personalities.

One even more important aspect of personality is that it strongly affects what kind of people we like—and do not like. When you are a perfectionist, you may see others as sloppy and incompetent, while they, in turn, may think that you are rigid and uptight. When you look critically at what kinds of people you naturally gravitate toward—and, more important, who drives you nuts—personality-type differences are often at the root of each of them. This is why personality-type workshops are often a big part of leadership training. When people understand that others are motivated by different things, and learn to respect and accommodate these differences, they start developing the skills needed to work with diverse groups of people.

As a customer service professional, exactly the same thing is true. Chances are very good that the customers you work best with have certain personality types that are compatible with your own, and the ones you have the hardest time with fall into specific personality types as well. This means that when you start to understand your own personality, and those of other people, an amazing thing happens: The people who were once frustrating are suddenly just *different*. When you understand and respect these differences—and, more important, learn how to communicate with these different personalities in their language—it opens up a whole new world for you.

CUSTOMER PERSONALITIES: FOUR KEY TYPES

People have attempted to describe the human personality since the dawn of time. Early civilizations used the foundations of astrology to ascribe our personalities to the positions of the stars at birth, while later generations used facial features or even the shape of our heads to intuit what we were really like inside. As the field of psychology grew throughout the twentieth century, numerous measures of personality grew as well; one well-known test in use today, the Minnesota Multiphasic Personality Inventory (MMPI), even weighs in at a stupendous five-hundred-plus questions![1]

Since you probably do not have time to ask five hundred questions of most customers, we will focus on four key customer types that most of us can easily recognize and react to, based around a popular personality scale known as the Myers-Briggs Type Indicator (MBTI). These four types summarize the most dominant kinds of personality differences in a way that helps us to understand other people much better.

Based originally on the personality archetypes of psychologist Carl Jung, the MBTI was originally developed by a mother-daughter team of psychologists in the 1940s, and it identified sixteen personality types. By the 1970s, psychologist David Keirsey had combined these types into four clusters with high-minded titles such as the Artisan, the Guardian, the Rationalist, and the Idealist.[2] To put them in more familiar jargon as customer types, let's call them the *Free Spirit*, the *Solid Citizen*, the *Thinker*, and the *Feeler*. You could describe them as follows:

- *Free Spirits* are independent and strong willed.

- *Solid Citizens* are serious, practical, and responsible.

- *Thinkers* are perfectionists who like to solve problems.

- *Feelers* focus on the human side of most issues.

These personality types are neither good nor bad, and there is no one "right" personality. They also do not speak to how good or likeable someone is—you could have a very nice Solid Citizen and a mean, petty Feeler—or vice versa. They simply describe what motivates people, and how they are more likely to react to certain situations. More important, the descriptions of these four types provide you with valuable clues that help you identify what kind of person you are dealing with so that you can respond appropriately—which, in turn, helps create a smoother and more successful customer transaction. Let's take a look at each of these personality types in detail.

The Free Spirit

Rules? What rules? Free Spirits, as the name implies, like to follow their own lead. They are found in all walks of life, from the tie-dyed individualist to the rugged outdoorsman. And they are more common than you might think, making up an estimated 35 to 40 percent of the population.

People in this group tend to favor action. They are willing to make quick decisions and go on impulse. The saying of "Don't just stand there, do something!" was tailor-made for them. They do not like being tied down and are more comfortable with change than most other people—and, conversely, dislike routine more than most. This also means that it is easy for them to change their minds—so no sale is ever final with a Free Spirit!

Here is how to tell when you are dealing with a Free Spirit as a customer:

They like to act quickly. A typical Free Spirit is more of an impulse buyer than most people, and more likely to want immediate gratification when he seeks service.

They tend to be open-minded about alternatives. When most people miss the bus, they sigh and wait for the next one. A Free Spirit would be more likely to say, "Hey, who wants to split a cab?"

They hate *being told what to do*. How many times have customer service people said to you, "You'll have to do X"? This would be a poor choice of words with a Free Spirit. As far as they are concerned, they don't *have* to do anything.

They like to do things their way. Do you like people to meekly nod their heads in rapt attention when you tell them what to do? Don't expect that here. A Free Spirit may respect your expertise, but that won't stop him or her from wanting to take a different path.

So how should you handle a Free Spirit customer? Here are some tips:

Acknowledge their initiative. Free Spirits want to do things their way—which means that they aren't always the best people at following directions or coloring inside the lines. This means that a mind-set of "That's a unique idea" will serve you much better with a Free Spirit than "That's not what I suggested."

Give them options. Free Spirits like choice and hate constraints, so phrase things in terms of options, not pat answers. For example, instead of saying, "I think you should purchase this model television," consider saying, "Here are the pros and cons of these television models. What do you think?"

Ask them what they want. Are you going nuts trying to figure out what a customer wants? There is often a simple solution: Ask! Feel free to point the Free Spirit in a general direction, and then sit back and go with the flow.

The Solid Citizen

Solid Citizens work hard, shoot straight, and give you a good day's work for a good day's pay. People like these form the dependable backbone of our society. And they have lots of company—at roughly 40 to 45 percent of the population, they are the most common of the four main personality types.

People in this group feel a healthy sense of duty and participate actively in society at many levels. You will find them doing responsible jobs, coaching Little League, and setting up neighborhood barbecues. They would generally rather give help than receive it and take pride in a job well done. And at a personal level, they are more serious and down-to-earth than many of their more flamboyant brethren.

If you assume that a customer is a Solid Citizen, you will be right almost half of the time; however, here are some traits to look for, to improve your odds:

They want to get right down to business. Solid Citizens prefer to get to the bottom of things, with as little chitchat as possible. They have little patience for people beating around the bush and talking about extraneous details.

They aren't overly emotional. Stick to facts and not feelings with a Solid Citizen. Although a certain amount of empathy is appropriate with everyone—for example, apologizing for an inconvenience—Solid Citizens would much rather that you fix the problem than gush about the consequences.

They keep commitments and expect the same. Keeping your word is important with every customer, but particularly so with a Solid Citizen. They want you to say what you mean, mean what you say, and deliver what you promise.

They want results. Solid Citizens are focused on the outcome, not the process. The good news in this is that your personal style is less under the microscope than with other personalities, but the flip side is that if you don't deliver, no amount of "nice" will help.

This means that when you have a Solid Citizen as a customer, you should approach him or her as follows:

Be serious. Specifics are good with a Solid Citizen, and wisecracks aren't. Stay on topic, stick to the practicalities, and keep everything on the straight and level.

Be professional. The term *professional* has several meanings, and all of them apply with Solid Citizens: Present yourself as a skilled representative of your company, don't veer into personal territory on your side or theirs, proactively address their issues, and deliver on your commitments.

Get to the point. Respect the time of a Solid Citizen, and save most of your war stories and personal anecdotes for more talkative customers—unless you are providing details that sincerely benefit him or her. Keep on task, and the Solid Citizen will work with you to bring a pleasant and productive transaction to a close.

The Thinker

Thinkers are master problem solvers, and stereotypes of this personality range from scientists and inventors to the mechanic who can nurse a few extra horsepower from a race car. Knowledgeable, rational, and perfectionistic, Thinkers are fueled by a sense of competence. They are also relatively uncommon, making up only 5 to 7 percent of the population. However, they are strongly represented in groups such as engineers, computer experts, financial analysts, and other knowledge workers.

People in this group are natural experimenters and seek to understand the inner workings of the world around them. They take pride in being able to figure things out and in being self-sufficient. They enjoy a good challenge, take pride in contributing their knowledge to the world, and can sometimes tend to be a little hard on themselves in pursuit of the perfect answer.

Here are some of the things to look for when you have a Thinker as a customer:

They tend to be very knowledgeable. These customers are the classic know-it-alls. They like to show their own expertise and don't want to be lumped in the same category as more ignorant customers.

They care about competence. Thinkers usually do their homework before seeking help in a service transaction—so above all, they want to feel that you are as competent as they are, and that you aren't wasting their time.

They want you to think their problem all the way through. A quick way to get on a Thinker's bad side is to say, "Oh, I don't know" or "That should be good enough." They want you to take the time to solve their issues and want you to be sure it's the right answer.

They will question your responses. A Thinker's favorite question is "Why?"—whether it applies to her own curiosity about how things work or she is challenging you to make sure you know what you are doing.

Here are some of the most effective ways to take good care of a customer who is a Thinker:

Share your knowledge, and acknowledge theirs. Drop hints about what you know about a situation while making it clear that you respect what they have already tried. Above all, avoid what I call the "airline pilot problem," where a pilot announces over the intercom that this is his or her first flight. Show your expertise or transfer the problem to someone who has the proper knowledge.

Stick to the facts. You can't just talk Thinkers into something—you need to *prove* it to them. Stay focused on *why* something is a good solution, and listen carefully to any feedback that they offer in return.

Be prepared to defend your advice. Thinkers often need to develop trust in you and your recommendations, so keep your facts and expertise at hand when needed. Here again, don't be afraid to honestly say, "I don't know," or to get other experts involved when the situation calls for it.

The Feeler

Feelers represent the human side of customer service. Cheerful and articulate or deep and thoughtful, every relationship in their lives is an important one—even customer relationships. Feelers are often found in professions that teach, entertain, or coach us and constitute between 8 and 10 percent of the population.

People in this group are, by definition, very feeling oriented and place a great deal of value on the interpersonal aspects of what they do. Feelers are born communicators, with many business leaders, speakers, and writers (including this one!) among their ranks. They tend to be among your more personable and congenial customers, but the flip side of this is that they have very high expectations for how you treat them.

Here are some of the things that Feelers often have in common as customers:

They want you to care. Nothing irritates Feelers more than being treated like just a number. Even if you give them everything they ask for, you will create a poor impression on them if you are cold or indifferent.

They want to be taken seriously. Feelers want their needs acknowledged—and won't hesitate to let you know about it when they aren't! They expect you to respect them as people, and pay attention to how a situation affects them.

They care about your feelings, and their own. When you treat Feelers well, you will find that they care about you as people more than most customers—but, conversely, they expect you to be sensitive to how they feel, more so than most customers.

Style and substance both matter. Resolving problems is important for every customer. But, ironically, a Feeler will often remember being treated well *without* a solution more kindly than being treated apathetically *with* a solution.

Here are some tips for handling customers who are Feelers:

Show your concern. Respond directly to their situation, and be proactive about how you plan to help them—both to acknowledge them and to express your personal interest. With Feelers, it's all about how much you care.

Respond to their feelings. If a Feeler mentions that a situation affects his or her son's softball game, the word *softball* needs to be somewhere in your response. Never ignore cues that Feelers give you about how something affects their life. With Feelers, you are ministering to two situations: the problem itself and its impact on them.

Give the problem importance. Everything matters to Feelers, and responding in a way that gives their issues your undivided attention and interest is one of the fastest ways to their heart.

Together, these four personality types describe the vast majority of people whom you encounter. Of course, no one is completely a stereotype. Many people combine traits from any or all of these types, and our own unique personalities ride on top of these core traits. But once you know the basics, you will find it much easier to smoke out what your customer's preferences are in the first few seconds of the transaction, and respond accordingly—which, in turn, will make a real difference in how these people interact with *you*.

HOW TO SAY THE SAME THING IN FOUR DIFFERENT LANGUAGES

So, now that you understand the basics of customer personality types, how does this affect the way that you communicate with customers? Think of it a bit like a chocolate cake—your basic communications skills form this cake's primary ingredients, and your understanding of personality is like the icing that goes on top. Knowing how to tweak your basic response style to suit your customer's personality is one of those master skills that will help you communicate well with an even broader range of customers and situations.

In a sense, you could view these personalities as different languages, where you say the same thing in different ways, depending on the customer. Let's take a look at three different phrases, and how you might express them for each personality type. First, let's start with a simple instruction statement, as shown in Table 9-1.

Table 9-1. How to say "Let's try this."

Personality type	Response
Free Spirit	That's a good thought. Here is why I would try it this way.
Solid Citizen	Let's try this.
Thinker	In my experience, I've found that this approach works best.
Feeler	I understand your concerns and want to make it right. Here is what I'd like to try with you.

Now, let's move to something you would, of course, never say directly to a customer—that they are about to do something stupid. Although you would certainly word this diplomatically for any customer, different forms of this statement are still more effective for specific personality types, as shown in Table 9-2.

Table 9-2. How to say "That would be a really stupid thing to do."

Personality type	Response
Free Thinker	I can see why you did it that way, but I've got an even better idea.
Solid Citizen	I don't think that's the best way.
Thinker	Here are some of the things I see about doing things that way.
Feeler	That was a really good try. I've got another idea—what do you think?

And, finally, even the way you compliment people can make a difference to different personalities. Let's take a look at how you tell someone that they did a nice job in Table 9-3.

Table 9-3. How to say "Nice job."

Personality type	Response
Free Thinker	That's a very creative approach.
Solid Citizen	Nice job.
Thinker	You did a great job of figuring that out.
Feeler	I can tell you really care about what you're doing.

Left to our own human nature, we tend to gravitate toward the style of response that best fits our *own* personality. This means that Solid Citizens often play things completely straight, Thinkers start troubleshooting immediately, Feelers gush about how the other person must feel, and so forth—and then they each wonder why, for example, 20 percent of their customers do not respond well to their practicality, their knowledge, or their great depth of concern. By comparison, knowing how to speak the language of the customer in front of you can make a real difference and help you hit a home run nearly every time you step up to the plate. It is yet another case where a few small adjustments, based on known principles of behavioral psychology, can make a world of difference.

PERSONALITY AND YOU

Understanding customer personalities isn't just a good way to learn about other people. It also teaches you a lot about yourself—and your relationships with other people of every personality type. This knowledge can then become a powerful tool in broadening your human relations skills with everyone you meet, both inside and outside of your customer transactions.

Another important reason to understand personality is to make yourself aware of subtle biases that you may have toward customers, based on their own personalities. If you look critically at customers whom you have more trouble getting along with, don't be surprised if personality differences are at the root of many of them. For example:

- A Thinker may view a Feeler as wishy-washy, touchy-feely, and indecisive.

- A Feeler may view a Thinker as cold, heartless, and hide bound by rules.

- A Free Spirit may think that a Solid Citizen is unresponsive and dull.

- A Solid Citizen may think that a Free Spirit is pushy and abrasive—and so on.

Remember that traits are neither good nor bad—and when you understand the factors behind everyone's unique personality, it makes it much easier to see other people as just being different from you, as opposed to being good or bad. This understanding is often a breakthrough that helps open your mind to good relationships with a much wider range of people. Once you learn about the impact of personality type on how people communicate and respond to each other, you will suddenly start to see others in a whole new light.

While learning personality skills is clearly a good thing for your customers, the benefits to you are even greater. First of all, this helps your career because leadership is, by definition, the ability to deal with and motivate many different personalities, and communicating effectively with any person is a natural leadership trait. Second, this understanding makes work a nicer place to be, by creating happier customers, smoother working relationships, and fewer conflicts and misunderstandings. But most of all, understanding personality helps you to know yourself better and to play to your unique strengths as you work with others. It is one of the most tangible gifts from the field of psychology to human understanding, and with surprisingly little effort, one that can make a substantial difference in your own customer service work.

WRAPPING THINGS UP

All good things must come to an end, including customer transactions. Most of us naturally want to help as many people as possible, and our productivity with customers is increasingly gaining the attention of higher-ups in the workplace as well. At the same time, it is easy to feel helpless when customers do not seem to share the same sense of urgency that we have. The good news is that bringing transactions smoothly and quickly to a close, in a way that still sends customers away happy, is easier than many people think.

Time-consuming customer transactions may seem like random events, but there is a pattern to most of them. If you look critically at what happens when things take a longer time than the situation itself warrants, you are often dealing with one of a few known, predictable types of customers. These include:

- *The Talkaholic.* Someone who cannot stop talking and lacks the normal sense of closure that most of us have when a transaction is coming to an end

- *The Strong, Silent Type.* Someone who does not communicate well, and leaves you feeling stuck as you try to pry needed information from him or her

- *The Nonlinear Thinker.* Someone—often highly intelligent—who doesn't predictably follow directions or listen to what you say

- *The Needy Novice.* Someone who is brand new to something, and wants you to spend inappropriate amounts of time teaching new things from scratch

There are known, practical techniques that you can follow to manage each of these customer types in order to bring the transaction to a productive close. In this chapter, we will examine each of these situations, as well as a general approach that you can use to bring most normal customer transactions in for a smooth landing, with good feelings on all sides.

THE TALKAHOLIC

It is a busy morning in the shoe department of the major retailer where you work. Shortly after 10 A.M., a cheerful woman walks over and asks to try on a pair of pumps. As you help her slip them on, she tells you about what was wrong with the last pair she bought . . . and how important the right heel height is . . . and what people said the last time she wore a blue pair with a teal dress . . . and isn't it terrible what's happened to service in the stores these days? Before you know it, twenty minutes have gone by and she has tried on only three pairs of shoes; many other people have come and gone waiting for help; and since you draw a commission on sales, this is becoming a very expensive conversation with no end in sight.

Chronic talkers are generally very nice people who have the potential to take up a great deal of your time. While you are trying to help them with their business, they are regaling you with stories—not only about your products and services but about their children, their vacation, their bad back, or whatever else is on their mind. And more often than not, it is a one-way conversation that never seems to end. Some things that these people have in common include:

- They like to interact with people and be the center of attention.

- They frequently go off topic from the business at hand.

- They often lack a sense of how or when to bring a conversation to a close.

You have two challenges in dealing with an overly chatty customer. One is to stay on topic and somehow close the transaction in a timely fashion. The other equally important challenge is to make this customer feel good—and listened to—in a situation where he or she seems to be all but daring you to cut him or her off. Believe it or not, these two goals do not need to be mutually exclusive when you use the right technique.

Handling the Talkaholic: Using the Acknowledging Close

When we are faced with talkative people, we often mistakenly feel that we have only two options: to suffer in silence as they go on and on and on or to butt in and ask them to get back on topic—quite possibly hurting their feelings or even losing their business. But there is, in fact, a third path. A simple, delightful technique will put you back in control of these conversations while making the customer still feel great—and once you learn it, you will be amazed at how effectively it works. We call this technique the *acknowledging close*, and it involves the following three steps:[1]

1. *Break in and enthusiastically acknowledge the last thing the person says*. People often wonder if you should interrupt a talkative person. The answer is yes, you should. You cannot presume that he or she will simply run out of steam and voluntarily give you an opening to speak. But the way that you do it is all important. If you *enthusiastically acknowledge* the last thing that the customer says, you will find that you can successfully break in without making the other person feel like he or she has been cut off. Here is an example of how it works:

   Garrulous Gary: I just took this car on vacation last week. You should have seen the places we went! We went to Oklahoma, Texas, and even New Mexico. And boy, talk about scenery—New Mexico is like being in another world, with all those beautiful desert mesas. And we had a good time every night. We even got to see Garth Brooks in Albuquerque—

You: No kidding! You got to see Garth Brooks? I've wanted to see him for *years*.

Can you see why this would be more effective than just changing the subject and asking about his carburetor repair? It works so well because most talkative people don't simply crave speaking—they crave *attention*. And when you sincerely lavish this attention on the other person, you open the door to take the conversation in any direction that you want it to go.

2. *Follow up with a binary question.* The word *binary* is a common term from computers and mathematics, which describes a result that can only be one (yes) or zero (no). In this context, a binary question is one that requires a yes/no or short-statement answer—not one that your chatty customer can answer with a long soliloquy—and, more important, is significant to the customer. Some good examples of binary questions include:

   ■ "Do you prefer an automatic transmission?

   ■ "What color suit are you looking for?"

   ■ "When do you need to pick this up?"

   Normally, you should use a transitional statement such as "By the way" or "One more thing" to bridge smoothly between your acknowledgment of these customers and these questions—in much the same way that you would move on to a new topic in a conversation with a good friend. Combined with a good acknowledgment, binary questions form a powerful one-two punch because immediately after showering the customer with attention, you start asking things *that are in his or her interest.* Together, they create an atmosphere that is all about the customer, while giving you the tools you need to keep the transaction moving forward.

3. *Continue using binary questions to take control of the conversation.* This is far and away the most critical part of the process. When you enthusiastically acknowledge someone, and then pop a binary question, something magical happens: You get the floor back! And if you get it back once, you can get it back again . . . and again . . . as long as you politely and firmly *keep asking binary questions.*

This means that as soon as the other person answers—boom! Jump in with another binary question before he or she has a chance to say anything else. And, perhaps more important, keep enthusiastically acknowledging and encouraging these short answers. Here is a short example of how the process works:

Chatty Charlene: So I was in Chicago last week, and, wow, you should see the size of those thick-crust pizzas! I thought I was going to be full for a week, and—

You: You know, Charlene, from everything I've heard, it sounds like I could easily eat my way through Chicago! Now, I just have a few more questions about your tax form. Do you have any dependents?

Chatty Charlene: Yes, I have two.

You: Great! How old are they?

Chatty Charlene: Eight and eleven. They're adorable—

You: Excellent! That's going to save you some money! Now, did you have any interest income?

As you can see, this approach takes interrupting other people and raises it to a fine art—by focusing on the other person throughout and speaking to his or her interests. Here are a couple of important postscripts for making it work well with your own customers:

- *Start slow.* For best results, don't use this technique the minute that people start speaking. Give them the time and space to start talking—just as you would with any customer—and acknowledge them normally, to give the relationship a good start. Then jump in as needed, when things start to go off topic or run too long.

- *Know when to break in.* Once, when I taught this technique for a large, global call center operation, people informed me that their rules forbade them to interrupt a customer. My response was: "Do your customers ever breathe?" If so, great! Because when they pause to take their next deep breath, there you are, with an enthusiastic acknowledgment and a binary question. With time and practice, most of us can learn the rhythm of another person's speaking habits and find those small breaks where we can politely and gracefully intervene.

This technique is extraordinarily effective in real life. It makes people feel good even as you get things back on track, because you are giving them lots of positive attention—and you can use it over and over again as needed, whenever a discussion strays too far off topic. Done politely and with class, the acknowledging close technique invariably creates good feelings between you and your customers, as you discreetly work your way back into the driver's seat of the conversation.

THE STRONG, SILENT TYPE

Imagine that you are on the telephone explaining to someone how to use his or her digital video recorder for the first time. You give the person some very detailed technical instructions, and the response is a long, silent pause, followed (maybe) by a simple "OK." Several more long pauses and OKs later, you finally discover that they are far off on the wrong track. And then you start all over again from square one—to which they reply, "OK."

Quiet, withdrawn customers may seem, at first glance, to be the polar opposite of Talkaholics. In fact, they both share a great deal in common. They both lose focus on the transaction because of their personalities. They both have trouble reaching a point of closure when they need help. Most important, both of these customer types can take up a great deal of your time, unless you handle them properly. Some things common to timid customers include:

- They are often intimidated by your products or services.

- They may be embarrassed to ask for help.

- They frequently find it difficult to communicate clearly and proactively.

The reasons for this may range from personal style all the way to full-blown social anxiety disorder, but either way, your mission is the same: to create a zone of comfort that helps them come out of their shell, so that you can gain sufficient information to solve their problems. Handled with care and sensitivity, the right approach can help these transactions go much more quickly and easily.

Handling the Strong, Silent Type: Using Feathering

This technique gets its name from gently brushing against an issue, rather than hitting it head-on. It is very effective for drawing out a shy or reticent person, so that you can more quickly get the information that you need to close the transaction. Here is how it works:

1. *Listen carefully and intently.* Unlike talkative people—who must be interrupted to keep the conversation on track—shy people need time and space to express themselves. A transaction with them will, ironically, be *more* productive if you take care not to interrupt them.

2. *Respond with a roughly equal mix of questions, feedback, and reassurance.* When someone is unresponsive, it is best to assume that he or she is uncomfortable. Ironically, some service people respond to quiet customers by doing exactly the thing that many of them fear: turning the spotlight on them even brighter. ("Hello? Are you still there?") Instead, gently ask nonthreatening questions, give positive feedback to each and every answer, and reassure the customer that things are going well, as in the following example:

   You: Tell me what you are seeing on your screen now, Tim.

   Timid Tim: Um . . . a login screen?

   You: Perfect—that's exactly what I was hoping you would see. Now, could you try your user name and password and see if it accepts them?

   Timid Tim: OK.

   You: Excellent. Did it log you in?

   Timid Tim: Yeah.

   You: Good. Now we're getting somewhere. I think you're going to be OK.

3. *Go slowly and avoid information overload.* With talkative customers, you deal with them by being articulate, enthusiastic, and (politely) aggressive enough to jump in on the discussion. With a timid customer, by comparison, easy does it. The less you say, and the more gently you say it, the more likely it is that the customer will process what you are saying and stay within his or her own personal comfort zone.

Do you remember what it was like the last time someone was too loud, spoke too fast, and interrupted you too much? That is perhaps a little what it is like for a shy person when you respond with the perky, articulate style that many people think of as being customer service. Slow down; give these customers time and space; and, paradoxically, you will often find that they open up and start communicating more freely.

4. *Check understanding frequently.* At regular intervals, make sure that the other person understands you as things proceed. This is extremely important, because shy people will frequently be embarrassed to question information that they do not understand. As they respond, use positive statements like "Exactly," "That's absolutely correct," or whatever best fits the situation, to actively verify their responses.

In my experience, shy customers are often polite, cooperative, and appreciate your sincere respect more than most people. And, surprisingly, many of them actually become very articulate and focused as the transaction proceeds, once they feel safe and comfortable in dealing with you. By using the *feathering* technique, you accomplish two important goals: You help people feel much better about doing business with you and your organization and, in the process, you send them away happy much more quickly.

THE NONLINEAR THINKER

My late father was the smartest person I ever knew. He had a Ph.D. in engineering, wrote several books that were knee-deep in mathematical equations, and eventually became the president of a major university. So when he started to use a computer later in life, and would occasionally call his son the software expert for assistance, I was in for a big surprise—it often took ages to explain even the simplest things to him. Why? Because he was *too* smart for his own good. I would tell him to do X; wait breathlessly for the results; and, eventually, he would blithely explain that he was trying to do Y instead, because he thought it might work better. And so our phone calls would drag on and on, as he kept trying different things rather than simply following my directions.

My dad has plenty of company. He is among a class of customers that I refer to as nonlinear thinkers, because they do not process information in a straight line like most of us. Whether they have a short attention span, a superhigh intellect, or simply a strong desire to figure things out for themselves, they often require more patience and diplomacy than most customers. They are particularly the bane of people who work in call centers, who silently wish that they could just reach through the telephone line and *show* them exactly what to do. However, they can easily consume lots of your time in any work setting. Some things they tend to have in common include the following:

- They tend to march to their own drummers.

- They go off on tangents and frequently veer off topic.

- They will not predictably follow your directions.

Like the two previous types of customers we have discussed, nonlinear thinkers have the potential to take up a great deal of your time—and they are particularly challenging when you *know* the solution but feel stuck moving them toward it. With these customers, your challenge is to rein in their tangents and move forward while making them feel good about the process. Here as well, a specific technique can often quickly get things back on track.

Handling the Nonlinear Thinker: Using the Acknowledging Return

We intentionally call this technique the *acknowledging return*, because it shares a great deal in common with the acknowledging close technique for talkative people. In both cases, you acknowledge the customer and then take steps to bring the transaction back on track. Here is how the process works when a customer's focus is scattered.

1. *Acknowledge their tangents.* Many people become frustrated when a customer goes off target and does not do what they ask. Predictably, when people show this frustration, it leads to hard feelings or even an overt lack of cooperation. Instead, move *with* your customer, and acknowledge the direction in which he or she is going for the express purpose of then bringing him or her back on task. Let's compare the difference:

   Not so good:

   You: OK, now I'd like you to press the TUNING MENU button on the receiver.

Sally Scattered: (presses the MAIN MENU button) I thought there were some tuning features over here.

You: That isn't what I asked you to do!

Better:

You: OK, now I'd like you to press the TUNING MENU button on the receiver.

Sally Scattered: (presses the MAIN MENU button) I thought there were some tuning features over here.

You: I can see why you're doing that. You'd think that a MAIN MENU button would have everything under it! But believe it or not, they actually have a separate TUNING MENU button on this model.

2. *Explain your position.* Now comes the important part: Give a clear explanation of why you want the customer to do what you want. Many nonlinear thinkers implicitly assume that they know better than other people, or they have issues with trusting others. To break through this trust barrier, show your knowledge of the situation to build the other person's confidence in you. For example:

You: Before we troubleshoot your engine problem, I'd like you to check the idling RPM on your tachometer.

Owen Drummer: Really? Are you sure?

You: Absolutely! I race these cars on the weekends and know them like the back of my hand.

3. *Return them back on track.* Once you've acknowledged the customer, and explained what you would like him or her to do, take the lead back and proactively move the person to the next steps in the process.

4. *Repeat as needed.* Wouldn't it be nice if you could just acknowledge the customer *once*, and explain yourself *once*, and then have him or her be blissfully compliant afterward? Sorry, but you're in the business of customer service, not total personality transformation! Be prepared to repeat the acknowledge/explain/return cycle each time that the customer goes off on a tangent, but do it politely and cooperatively.

Nonlinear thinkers form an important segment of your customer base. If it wasn't for them, we wouldn't have people like Thomas Edison, Albert Einstein, or the person who has been fiddling around with something in your store for the past twenty minutes. By getting into their mind-set, and matching their nature with your expertise, you can turn most of your encounters with these fascinating and intelligent customers into productive ones.

THE NEEDY NOVICE

Congratulations—you made a big sale yesterday. You sold a top-of-the-line digital music-mixing console to an amateur musician who recently came into some money. But today, he's back in the store again. It turns out that he doesn't know a fader from a fruitcake, the manual is like Greek to him, and he wants *you* to show him how to use this expensive new toy. You gamely try to cover some of the basics with him, but things aren't going well at all, and this is shaping up to be a very long day. What to do now?

People who require more help than you can legitimately provide within a service transaction often fall into one of three categories:

1. *The Skills Challenged*—People who are out of their depth using your product or service.

2. *Service as Unpaid Consulting*—People who seek an inappropriate amount of resources.

3. *The Service Paradox*—When you give people really good service, their needs and demands may increase.

Every business has customers who need more resources than you can legitimately provide. Handling this issue properly requires care, sensitivity, and often a team approach with other people in your organization. At the same time, the right approach can resolve the vast majority of these situations while still preserving good feelings on all sides.

Handling the Needy Novice: Setting Positive Boundaries

When I managed software customer support centers, my team and I often dealt with novice customers who needed more time than we could reasonably provide—for example, when an employer would throw a manual at someone who knew little about computers and order him or her to "figure out" our complex product. In training the rest of the team, I explained my approach with these customers as follows: "We are in the business of making people happy. If you feel that spending an extra few minutes with a customer will make that person happy, do it. If you feel that spending an extra hour will make that person happy, do it. But if you know in your heart that no reasonable amount of time will make the person happy, then direct the customer to those resources that will make him or her *really* happy."

When we are confronted with customers who need way too much help, most of us see it as an issue of setting boundaries. Instead, I truly see it as an issue of *making people happy*—and when you change your perspective to that of your customer's interests, you will ironically handle the transaction much *faster* than if you see it as a simple tug-of-war. Here's how you make it happen:

1. *Refer them to more appropriate resources or training.* Your job isn't to say no, but to help customers get to the resources they need—which aren't you. This means that your main focus is—no surprise, if you have read this far in the book—what you *can* do for them. Know your options, and focus on leading customers to those options that are best for them.

2. *Sell the benefits of these resources to them.* What is the first thing that most people want to say when someone asks for too much? Usually, it is some variant of "You are asking for too much." Instead, understand what *benefits* the customer when you set reasonable limits, and lead with these benefits. Compare the following two examples:

Not so good:

Norbert Newbie: My boss told me that this thing here on my desk is a PC! How do I use it?

You: I'm sorry, but we can't train people how to use a computer from scratch on the phone.

Better:

Norbert Newbie: My boss told me that this thing here on my desk is a PC! How do I use it?

You: I'll be glad to help you. If you are new to using a personal computer, you have several good options. I respect your time, and you would get very frustrated if I tried to teach you by pushing one word at a time to you through the telephone. Instead, I normally recommend some live face-to-face assistance, where someone can actually show you how to use your system. Where are you located?

In the first case, there are several problems going on: You are probably hurting Norbert's feelings; you are making your organization seem callous and indifferent; and perhaps, most important, Norbert is probably going to fight you and take up more of your time. (Or he might try to negotiate, and say, "Can't you just help me with X?") With the second approach, leading with benefits makes it much easier to close the transaction, even when you must ultimately set boundaries on how far you can help.

3. *Protect the customer's dignity.* Let's be honest. Novice customers who ask lots of questions can be very frustrating. And if you are very good at something, it can be far too easy to see these customers as slow and dimwitted. Unfortunately, too many customer service professionals telegraph this impression to the customer, with statements such as, "You should have been trained on this" or "Most people already know how to do that." This is both hurtful to customers' feelings and totally unnecessary—and, more important, risks losing them as paying customers.

Instead, use the fundamental principles of respect and empathy to make customers feel better, no matter what the situation is. Use emotionally neutral phrases that focus on the situation ("Lawn mowers are hard to assemble") and not the person ("You can't assemble this"). More important, seek legitimate things to acknowledge—for example, how lots of people struggle with these products at first, or what a good job the customer did trying to figure things out on his own.

When you use the *positive boundaries* approach, bear in mind that you are still setting appropriate limits with customers; however, you are just doing it in a way that speaks to the customer's own interest and, therefore, makes it much easier for him or her to buy in and do what's best for both parties. It creates win-win situations on each side, simply by changing the mechanics of what you say. By shifting your focus toward that of the customer, you ironically set limits much more quickly while preserving good relationships with the vast majority of your novice customers.

THE VERBAL RECEIPT

Once you get past specific customer types, there is one more reason that customers take too much of your time—and in all likelihood, this one is your fault!

Have you ever had dinner guests who stayed too long, and didn't leave until late into the evening? Perhaps they were impolite and weren't thinking of you. But if you look back critically at the situation, the reason was probably because you didn't drop an explicit enough hint that the evening was over. When customers dawdle without a legitimate reason, there is often a similar cause, because you haven't given them the hint.

Think back to the last time that you, as a customer, hung around asking a lot of questions. Why did you do that? Probably because either (a) you lacked trust in the person serving you, or (b) important information was still being withheld from you—or both. Far too many transactions go something like this:

You: Hi. I'm dropping off my car for a tune-up.

Service person: OK.

You: So, when do you expect it to be finished?

Service person: Depends on how backed up we get.

You: What's your best estimate?

Service person: Oh, I don't know—sometime late this afternoon.

You: Should I call this afternoon?

Service person: You could.

Even though you are dealing with an auto service clerk, it feels more like you are dealing with a dentist—because it's like pulling teeth to get the information you need. Multiply this type of response across all of this person's customers, and the odds are that he frequently has people backed up while customers interrogate him. This, in a nutshell, is the cause of many long transactions and disagreements.

The solution to this is to give people a *verbal receipt* that provides a proactive summary of action items from the transaction and verifies the customer's acceptance of these action items. This verbal receipt helps to set customer expectations at the end of the transaction, and it sets the stage to close the transaction smoothly. Here are its key steps:

1. *Establish ownership.* Take charge of the transaction until it is closed or has been actively handed off to the person at the next level of follow-up.

    Example: "I can take care of this problem for you."

2. *Be proactive in initiating follow-up.* Be the first to suggest what you know needs to be done in a customer situation.

    Example: "From what you have told me, I would like to send you an upgrade."

3. *Communicate action items clearly to the customer.* End the transaction with a clear summary of the next steps, and the customer's agreement.

    Example: "I will deliver this upgrade via e-mail at the close of this call, and once you receive it, I would like you to download the file attached to it and follow the instructions. Would that be OK for you?"

By giving every customer a verbal receipt, you accomplish several objectives, including the following:

■ You build trust with the customer that you know what you are doing.

■ You give the customer an opportunity to close the transaction gracefully.

■ You clear up any potential misunderstandings before the customer leaves.

■ You prevent needless follow-ups. For example, as many as two-thirds of calls to computer help desks are simply to check the status of existing problems, according to figures from the Service and Support Professionals Association (SSPA).[2]

■ You create an aura of competence and professionalism whose impact goes far beyond the individual customer and into your career as a whole.

Perhaps, most important, you give the transaction a natural point to close, where both parties can walk away satisfied. It is the customer equivalent of telling your dinner guests that it's late, and you'd like to call it a night. Done well, it is perhaps one of the most powerful tools for closing a transaction on your terms.

You may have noticed a common thread among all these techniques for handling time-consuming transactions, which is that they each involve responding in kind to the person in front of you. When someone craves attention by talking too much, you show him or her attention. When someone is shy, you go slowly and gently. When someone is scattered, you acknowledge his or her tangents. When someone is new to something, you show him or her how to get effective assistance. And for everyone, you provide a proactive summary of what *they* want. In each of these cases, you are looking at the world through your customer's eyes, and in each case benefiting your own productivity in the process.

There are, of course, situations where time with customers should be spent liberally. We all have a sense of when to rise to the occasion for difficult customer problems or critical situations, and, at a deeper level, when to value quality over quantity. When you combine this with an understanding of why people take up your time—and, more important, techniques to manage these situations—you will find yourself in charge of the time you spend with customers, rather than the other way around.

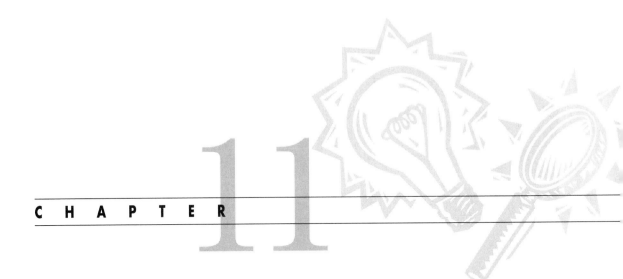

11

THE TOUGH CASES

I n the pleasant and somewhat artificially constrained world of customer service training, it can seem all too easy to provide pat answers to hypothetical situations. But then, when you return to the real world, life has a way of confronting you with tough, challenging problems that aren't in the script—problems where the stakes are high, and saying the wrong thing could lead to serious consequences.

Most of us know what to say when a customer needs assistance or wants a refund. But what if you are facing the shutdown of a customer's entire plant? Or something has gone terribly wrong—and it's your fault? Or how about a customer who wants to be, shall we say, more than a customer? It is at points such as these that perfecting your own communications skills can truly be life changing.

This is why I personally am a big fan of exploring and role-playing worst-case scenarios. As a trainer, I always ask people to share their toughest customer problems, and it is a special delight for me when they come up with situations that involve strong emotions and serious repercussions—because they provide an important learning moment for all of us. They teach us how the right skills can help us make the best of *any* situation involving other people.

This chapter is designed to be such a learning moment. It presents several difficult situations that, although fictional, serve as a composite of the kinds of tough, real-world issues that people actually face in working with customers. They all underscore how your communications skills can be even more powerful than the situation itself, and can bring even the toughest problems to a successful resolution.

CASE 1: OOPS!

As the valet parking manager at one of your city's most posh hotels, driving exotic luxury cars is all in a night's work—and one of the nice perks of the job. Tonight, a well-dressed couple is dropping off a shiny new Jaguar, and you politely take the keys, slip behind the wheel, and speed down the ramp into the hotel's parking garage. As you make the turn into the first level of the lot, a bird suddenly darts in front of your windshield. As you instinctively swerve to miss it, you are suddenly thrown back in your seat with a sickening crunch as the car slams headfirst into the rear fender of another customer's BMW.

Dazed but physically unhurt, you climb out of the car to survey the damage—the front of the Jaguar now looks like an exploding cigar, and the BMW's rear fender and wheel well are totally demolished. You now need to speak to both customers and let them know what happened to their cars. ∎

When my late father chaired the civil engineering department of a major university, his office prominently featured a poster of a group of nineteenth-century engineers, in top hats and coats, gathered around a collapsed bridge where an oncoming railroad train had hurtled into the ravine below. The caption? A popular expletive that need not be repeated here. But his point was an important one—we are human, and are all at risk of making mistakes, some of which could be very big ones.

Cases where you are at fault present a unique challenge with customers. Our natural instincts to defend ourselves really kick into high gear when we have done something that puts us at risk, and society encourages this trait in many ways. Insurance companies typically instruct us not to admit fault when we are involved in an accident. In crisis situations, many companies often forbid anyone but corporate spokespeople from making comments. And even the humblest small businesses often fear the financial or legal consequences of admitting to a mistake.

All of these psychological and social pressures lead us to one place: the urge to vigorously defend ourselves when we do something wrong, which is precisely the wrong thing to do in a situation like this. Instead, let's break this down from a customer's perspective. Here, the customers are dealing with:

- Hearing some very unexpected bad news

- A situation that causes them considerable inconvenience

- In all likelihood, a sense of being wronged and wanting recompense

In short, you have all of the same elements of what happens when a customer gets angry about anything—regardless of fault. This means that shifting gears, from self-defense to a process for delivering bad news and defusing anger, represents your best hope for managing the situation. Here are some of the steps you should take:

Step 1: Use Staging to Deliver the Bad News

This is a situation that is tailor-made for staging. Your first priority with the customer is to blunt the impact of a very difficult message, by delivering it in stages—so your first priority *before* you contact the customer is to prepare a good introduction and a good explanation. For example:

Step 1. Introduce. "We had a situation involving your vehicle this evening."

Step 2. Explain. "I'm going to try to break down what happened. As your vehicle was being driven into our parking garage, we had an incident where a bird flew at your windshield. In reacting to this, there was a collision between your vehicle and another one."

Step 3. Empathize. "I am terribly sorry this happened, and we are going to do everything possible to make this situation right."

You then need to prepare for the customers' reaction to the situation. If you are sincere, you may be pleasantly surprised to find that they react professionally and cooperate with you. On the other hand, if they respond emotionally or get upset, remember that your best hope of defusing the situation lies in continuing to empathize with whatever they say, no matter what. For example:

Customer: This car cost $75,000, and now it's ruined!

You: You're right. It's a beautiful car, and I feel terrible that it was involved in an accident.

Customer: I'll have you fired for this!

You: If this happened to my car, I'd be pretty upset too.

Customer: Some night out this turned out to be!

You: You're right. I feel especially bad that this had to ruin a good time for both of you.

More important, you should chain each of these responses to statements that reaffirm that you will do whatever is possible to make the situation right—because, particularly in this case, the customers are much more concerned with the fate of their cars than how apologetic you are. At the same time, reiterating how sorry you are, as often as needed, is still a critical component of this stage of the discussion.

Here as well, the fundamental respect and empathy principle of paraphrasing a customer's own words in your reply will produce a much better outcome than generic responses such as "I'm sorry." Instinctively, we want to withdraw in the face of anger, but if you behave counterintuitively and *move toward the pain,* by responding head-on to a customer's hostile statements with empathy, things will get to a rational point much sooner.

Step 2: Stay in the Customer's Frame of Reference

Once the initial shock of the message has passed, it is equally important to stay focused on the needs of the affected parties. At this point, it is extremely tempting to defend or excuse yourself—particularly if the customers involved are upset—but, paradoxically, keeping your focus on them is the only true way out of the situation.

The most effective thing that you can do at this stage is to focus on the next steps that benefit the customers, such as trading insurance and contact information, contacting the authorities to file an accident report, and arranging for transportation home. Aside from dealing with necessary practicalities, these assessment questions play an important role in defusing the strong feelings that may remain at this point.

Good things to say at this stage of the transaction include:

- "I'd like to trade insurance information with you, so that we can get a claim moving forward."

- "Do you have any valuables that you would like to remove from the vehicle?"

- "What can we do to help you get back home after this is over? Can we arrange a rental car to come pick you up?"

All of these statements offer to assist the customers—and better yet, most are in the form of a question, which gives *them* a chance to discuss how they feel. By staying locked in on what you can do to benefit them, you stand your best chance of keeping the situation on an even keel.

Step 3: Acknowledge the Reality of the Situation

Conversely, most statements about you or your business would be a bad idea at this point:

- "This wasn't my fault."

- "It was an accident."

- "Normally this never happens."

At a moment like this, probably the last thing that these customers care about is you or your business. On the other hand, they now care a great deal about something that really *did* happen to them. So, as tempting as it is, save any self-protective statements for your interview with the insurance company; right now, you need to acknowledge how this situation affects each of your customers and keep your focus on their needs.

Finally, in any accident, there is the big question of admitting fault—particularly when a customer is pressuring you to do so. As a matter of personal ethics, I am normally a big fan of admitting errors and making things right, with customers and everyone else. But what if you are constrained—say, for example, by your employer's policies—from admitting fault? Focus on what you *can* do, such as assuring the customer that you will cooperate fully with the authorities, and will do everything that you can to make sure the situation is made right for them. When you position yourself as an ally of customers, even in a situation like this, the odds are very high that things will still end on a cooperative and professional note.

CASE 2: THE STAKES ARE HIGH

You are the shipping supervisor at a manufacturing facility, and the phone is already ringing as you come into your office Monday morning at 7:30 A.M. On the other end of the line is Darlene, the purchaser for one of your major customers. There is a clear sense of urgency in her voice as she tells you that a shipment of gears from your company, which was supposed to arrive by the weekend, never showed up.

As she talks, you frantically search your desk and pull up the order—which, according to your records, should have shipped last week. She goes on to tell you that without this shipment they will run out of inventory by noon today, and will have to shut down an entire engine plant and send three hundred employees home. ∎

This delightful example came from a student in one of my recent workshops, who was a project manager for a major manufacturing company. Although taking great pains to point out that this situation had never happened (and, of course, *wouldn't* happen) at her company, she felt that this was a great example of a critical real-world problem from her profession. Here are some of the steps you can use when the stakes are high:

Step 1: Show Respect for the Agenda

What is the first thing that crosses your mind when a situation like this erupts? No contest: probably "Oh, my God, I hope this isn't *my* fault!" But when the stakes are high, trying to establish fault or be self-protective is absolutely the worst thing that you can say—particularly when a plant may be going on shutdown in a few hours. Instead, the first and most critical thing that you can do here is to use the phrase substitution technique to create phrases *based around what they just told you*, which address and respect their agenda, such as:

- "We are going to do everything we can to make sure those gears get to your plant."

- "Given that your production is at risk, I want to make sure that our senior management is involved. I'm going to get our company president in teleconference with us momentarily."

- "We both want to find out how this happened, of course, but my first concern is making sure that you can keep running today."

Step 2: Demonstrate Competence

We discussed earlier how certain personality types value your competence above all else. This is a *situation* where showing your competence is equally paramount. Verbally demonstrate that you are on top of the situation and transparently discuss the steps in the process as you are speaking with the other person:

- "I am starting to trace what has happened to these gears as we speak."

- "I just spoke with our shipping team, and I'm going to break down what we've discovered so far."

- "So far, we have identified that the product is still in transit with the delivery carrier."

Step 3: Explore Alternatives

Many difficult transactions revolve around negotiating alternatives—and this is especially the case when the stakes are extremely high. If there is not a quick, closed-form solution to a problem like this—such as finding out that the missing shipment will arrive that morning—you must ultimately focus on options:

- "What is the minimum number of gears that you have to have for today's production?"

- "We can charter an air shipment to have a replacement order arrive this afternoon. Would that be in time to keep your plant open?"

> ■ "Is there anything else we can do while the parts are in transit?"

Here again, much like the auto accident situation mentioned earlier, self-defense should be off the agenda—at least in *this* discussion. If you can document that your products left the plant, and it feels appropriate to slip that into the discussion, fine—as long as you keep your focus on the fact that the *customer* doesn't have these products yet. And at a deeper level, it is important to keep the tone of the conversation calm and factual. In a situation like this, results are going to be more important than feelings. By using the same competence and professionalism that you would show in a less-critical situation, but with the appropriate level of urgency, the chances are very good that you and the other party will work cooperatively to resolve this issue to the best extent possible.

CASE 3: MR. ANGRY

You are a gate agent for Good Time Airlines. Mr. Angry is a customer of yours who is not having a good time. Here are some of the things that have gone wrong for him:

- Because of an equipment malfunction, his flight was diverted to your airport yesterday evening, and he has been stuck there since then.

- He was ticketed to go home to Columbia, South Carolina. His bags, however, were sent to Colombia, South America.

- He is 6 feet 10 inches tall, and the airline lost his first-class upgrade and stuffed him like a sardine in coach between two screaming children.

- You have just given away the last seat home tonight to the person in line in front of him, and the next available flight out is tomorrow.

And, on top of it all, he is, as his nickname implies, a pretty angry kind of guy. Your mission is to calm him down, and send him away from the counter with a ticket for tomorrow's flight. ■

This is a problem that, in a sense, has as much to do with mathematics as it does with customer service. Why? Because it reflects a situation that can happen with any business that serves enough customers. Let's say that, on average, 5 percent of your customers will have one thing go wrong with your company. Take it a step further, and perhaps 1.5 percent will have two things go wrong. And 0.5 percent will have three things go wrong. Keep pushing the numbers, and with enough people, you are bound to have someone who wins what I call "the poor bastard award," where *everything* goes wrong. Here, we will look at what to do with the people who win this award in your business.

Earlier in this book, we devoted an entire chapter to how to manage a situation where someone is angry. Here, we will take things a step further and look at what you do when someone is *really* angry— and somewhat justified in his or her anger. Let's break this down into the three steps of managing a hostile situation:

Step 1: Acknowledgment

When someone is extremely upset, you are—by definition—being put on the defensive. It is one thing for someone to be unhappy about something, and quite another when someone is hurling a stream of insults at you. But if you want to defuse the crisis, this is exactly the time when you need to stay focused and speak from the customer's frame of reference.

In a case like this, where a customer truly is on the short end of the stick, it is critically important to acknowledge the frustration behind the person's concerns—early, often, and repeatedly. More important, these acknowledgments need to be *specific*, *sincere*, and *detailed* to break through the other person's defenses. Some things that you might say in a situation like this include:

- "You've been through a horrible experience."

- "I've rarely seen this many things go wrong, and I will do whatever I can to make things whole for the rest of your trip."

- "I'd be upset if I had the same kinds of experiences."

Personally, I sometimes even use the "poor bastard" analogy with customers themselves and break down the percentages of what happened—and have found that it serves as a powerful acknowledgment of what went wrong, which lets me commiserate with them while providing a very subtle defense of how things usually work.

A sharp observer might wonder if acknowledging that someone's claims have merit might open up an employer to further trouble, such as legal action. Although I respect this viewpoint, I also do not feel that it applies in this case. What has happened has happened, the outcome can be clearly documented, and the customer's feelings are now raging full tilt. In my experience, you have a clear fork in the road here: You can keep mum and greatly *increase* the risk of subsequent action or gain respect by clearly and openly acknowledging the customer's frustrations. In this case, the long way around is the shortest way home.

Step 2: Assessment

Assessment questions are always a good way to both gather data and give a customer time and space to calm down. In a case like this, they also serve to give the customer's problems a needed importance while providing you with an opportunity to show your concern for the person's well-being. Some areas of questions here include:

- *What happened.* "I'd like to know more about what happened when you tried to use your first-class upgrade."

- *Current status.* "Have you received an update on when your baggage will be delivered?"

- *How the customer is doing.* "Do you need any amenities to see you through until tomorrow?"

By focusing on the customer's welfare, and providing a sympathetic ear for his concerns, you can help build a level of trust and confidence that will help you through the next phase of the process—presenting alternatives.

Step 3: Alternatives

When someone feels truly wronged, the most critical part of the discussion clearly revolves around negotiating a satisfactory solution. And when you are dealing with the worst-case scenario where someone is deeply affected *and* very angry, there are two key points to keep in mind:

1. *Become the customer's advocate.* Amazingly, in a situation like this, many well-meaning customer service agents would

emphasize the negative and lead their response with "I'm sorry, but the last flight is sold out, and you'll have to wait until tomorrow." Although this may seem like an honest and self-protective thing to say, in this case you would be waving a red flag in front of a bull—because you aren't addressing *his* concerns or *his* feelings first, in a situation where your airline caused the problem.

The fundamental principle of negotiating alternatives is to always word things to the customer's benefit, and this is never more important than in a situation like this—once again, we call this stage the Can-Can because it focuses on what you *can* acknowledge and *can* do. For example:

- Don't tell the customer that he probably can't fly home tonight; ask him if he would prefer to stand by for the last flight, or would rather have a comfortable hotel room to unwind for the night. Better yet, if possible, explore options such as alternate airports or transportation arrangements.

- Don't tell him that there is nothing more you can do. Ask him what you can do to make him comfortable until you can get him on his way home.

- Don't tell him that his bags will take a long time to come back. Tell him everything that you will do to make sure they are delivered back to his home.

Above all, if this person is anxious to get home that evening, there is no question that until the last flight physically leaves the ground, you must do whatever you can to get this person on board it. If there is even the most microscopic possibility that this person could still get on this flight, you need to hold out as much hope as possible, and do your best to be helpful.

2. *Seek the moral high ground.* In a situation such as this, you also run into the issue of being on the moral high ground, where some kind of recompense is probably called for. Never dismiss a disgruntled customer's claims without doing everything possible—involving higher-ups where needed—to offer a just settlement to the injured party. In my experience, small gestures made early on in the transaction can often prevent much bigger problems later, not to mention helping to defuse the situation at hand.

Worst-case scenarios with customers are never fun for either party—but my own consistent experience is that, with the right approach, they can be managed just like any other situation. Follow the right communications process while keeping your focus on the customer, and the overwhelming odds are that even Mr. Angry will eventually shake your hand and walk away with a ticket in hand for tomorrow's flight.

CASE 4: PAINTING THE TOWN RED

It's Saturday morning at the local home center where you work, and the aisles are bustling with customers. As a floor clerk in the paint department, you are cheerfully dealing with a steady stream of people mixing various shades of colors for their weekend projects.

Suddenly, the calm of the line is interrupted by a loud crash. As you glance in the direction of the noise, you see a wall of paint cans tumbling to the floor. Rivers of paint are splattering over everything from merchandise to passing customers to even the brand-new lawn tractor sitting in the middle of the center aisle. As you rush over, you see a very red-faced woman with a little girl who points to the paint cans, smiles at you angelically, and says, "My mommy didn't mean to knock them over—it was an accident." ∎

In Chapter 3, we spent a great deal of time looking at the opening approach to a typical customer transaction. But what about the case where a customer causes a problem? Your goals are perhaps a little different, because in this case, you are out to both protect the customer and solicit his or her cooperation. But you are still serving the customer—and to resolve the situation with class, your opening approach should still be very similar. Let's look at how you put these skills to work in a delicate customer scenario:

Step 1: People First, Paint Cans Second

First impressions are important, particularly when a customer is embarrassed and uncomfortable. You can never go wrong when the first thing you say focuses on the most important thing, namely everyone's safety and well-being. For example:

- "Are you both OK?"

- "I'm really glad that no one was hurt."

- "Let's get both of you away from the spill."

Situations like this are often a matter of perspective. One day, my wife nicked the bumper of her car, and I was a little frustrated, because it cost us $100 to fix the dent. Months later, she drove around a blind curve and ran full speed into the back of a truck that was parked in the roadway, and totally destroyed the car—and I was positively overjoyed about spending several thousand dollars on a brand-new vehicle! Why? Because she walked away without a scratch, and cars are much, much easier to replace than your spouse. In any situation, always put people first.

Step 2: Keep Things Light

There are times to be firm and serious. This is not one of them. Any customer in a situation like this is going to feel extremely embarrassed and defensive, and any responses that you can make to break the tension will benefit the ultimate outcome as well as the customer's feelings. For example:

- "That is a truly impressive amount of paint!"

- "I always thought this store would look good in red."

- "We were hoping that this morning would be less dull, and we got our wish!"

As always, use humor only to the extent where it feels natural and comfortable for you—and always be sure that you are laughing at the situation and not the customer! But in general, a light touch goes a long way when a customer gets into an embarrassing situation.

Step 3: Keep Things Professional

Once the shock of the incident has worn off, and the initial tension and embarrassment start to fade away, things will ultimately move forward to deal with the practicalities of the situation. At a typical retailer, particularly for a large store, this step will involve people such as your store manager and/or security team. Even when you are trying to investigate situations and establish fault, being cordial and supportive will help bring these situations to a successful resolution.

Does a customer bear responsibility for situations like this? It depends. According to my retail sources, many stores consider situations such as these to be part of the cost of doing business—if not, in fact, their fault for having cans stacked where they could be knocked over. Even in cases where a customer does bear responsibility for property damage, the focus should be on working out a resolution in a way that least impacts the customer. Being helpful and solicitous in situations like these, keeping a "no fault" attitude for as long as possible, and being polite and professional will make a lasting impression on both the customer *and* everyone she shares the incident with.

CASE 5: TOO CLOSE TO YOUR CUSTOMER

Steve is an important client of your firm, and as one of the brightest young women in your office, you've been assigned to his account. You handle all of the financial transactions between his company and yours and keep in touch with him by telephone and e-mail. You do a great job and get rave reviews from both Steve and your managers about the professional relationship you have built with him.

Soon you are at a conference out of town and meet Steve in person for the first time. You greet each other warmly and exchange pleasantries. Then he puts his arm around you, tells you how much he *really* has appreciated all of your help—and, as he draws closer, asks if the two of you could discuss his account further in the privacy of his hotel room. ∎

This is a situation that transcends customer service and communications skills and focuses on your rights as a human being. In the face of overt sexual harassment, a person's value as a customer becomes much less important than your own personal boundaries and safety. You are a paid professional in a situation that has become inappropriately personal, and first and foremost, you have every right to declare the game over and walk away.

At the same time, the right communications skills can still help you to defuse what is often a very delicate and difficult situation. In cases like these, where a customer's behavior is indefensible, your rights and your safety are always the first priority—and when you are confronted with an inappropriate advance, there is frankly no right or wrong way about how you choose to say no. But when you feel that it is easier or safer to give these customers a face-saving way out, you can still use many of the same communications techniques that help defuse other difficult situations.

Step 1: Use the Can-Can to Deflect Inappropriate Requests

Even in an abusive situation, there are still things that you *can* acknowledge and *can* do—namely, you can acknowledge that you can still serve his appropriate needs as a customer, and can do things that do not cross your personal boundaries. For example:

> *You:* I'd like to keep you happy as a client. Even though I can't get personally involved, I can have my colleague Jack meet with you to discuss your issues while you are in town. Would you like me to set up a meeting between the two of you?

Step 2: Provide Alternatives

In cases like these, human nature is to simply tell someone off—and situations like these perhaps merit this more than most. At the same time, a more subtle and face-saving way of achieving the same objective is to provide alternatives that let *him* choose whether the transaction will continue, on *your* terms. For example:

> *You:* I'd like to keep working with you and hope that you will respect my personal boundaries. I never socialize with customers.

> Statements like these—where you start with a benefit to the customer ("I'd like to keep working with you") and a choice that *he* must make ("I hope that you will respect my personal boundaries")—give you power over the transaction while giving the customer a chance to save face.

Step 3: Be Yourself

In less-critical situations, a key component of active listening is using a light touch. Inappropriate sexual behavior is no laughing matter, and you are under no obligation to lighten the mood if it doesn't feel right to do so. But in some cases, some people may turn to their sense of humor to break the tension of a situation like this while still unmistakably getting the point across. For example:

> *You:* My mother always told me never to go anywhere with strangers—let's stay here.

or

> *You:* My husband is always flattered when people want to get to know me better.

Your own judgment plays a key role in whether to break the tension or not. You may feel that a light touch will let the other person save face and preserve the customer relationship—or, conversely, you may feel that it could make it harder for him to take no for an answer. Trust your gut, and do what feels right for you. Above all, be true to your own personality, and don't say anything that feels forced or inappropriate.

These same points apply to any kind of inappropriate customer behavior, including:

- Overt racism, sexism, or other discrimination

- Verbal abuse such as screaming or foul language

- Threatening statements, such as, "I'll have you fired for this"

In each of these cases, the fundamentals remain the same. You can choose to let the customer save face and build safety by using the right communications skills. You can also set conditions where you will still offer to help, but let the customer choose whether the transaction can continue or not. But above all, you have the right to set boundaries and walk away from a situation that has crossed the line of your role as a service professional.

Of course, an even more important issue in a situation like this is to keep yourself safe. At one level, this involves knowing when a situation reaches a point where it is time to call for help or to get out of harm's way. At another level, it means avoiding dangerous situations in advance, such as being alone with clients in secluded locations where you don't have a clear escape plan. Although overt criminal behavior from customers is rare, knowing your options helps you to handle a potentially difficult situation with a clear mind.

Finally, situations like this call for another important form of communication as well—between you and your employer. In any situation where a customer is behaving inappropriately, it is important for your managers and human resource department to be aware of what is going on, for a number of reasons:

- To make others aware of a customer's actions

- To allow your managers to step in and intervene in the situation where appropriate

- To protect other employees who may be victimized by the same customer

- To provide important legal documentation when behavior crosses the line from inappropriate to illegal

Situations such as this clearly go beyond the bounds of a service relationship. The term *service* itself implies being paid to serve other people, but, sadly, some people misinterpret this paid relationship for personal interest. No customer relationship ever takes precedence over your rights to a harassment-free work environment—and where it feels appropriate, the same communications skills that you use with customers in general can serve as a respectful way to set boundaries on customer behavior.

IT'S ALL IN THE FUNDAMENTALS

A popular T-shirt for sale at the Carnegie Hall souvenir shop in New York City reads: "How do you get to Carnegie Hall? Practice, practice, practice!" In much the same sense, the fundamentals of communicating with customers—a science based on known principles of behavioral psychology—can help you to successfully master nearly *any* customer situation that you could possibly encounter, as long as you practice, practice, practice.

The tough cases in this chapter all have one important thing in common: They use the same techniques as more routine customer situations, but adapted to difficult circumstances. There is a clear path between basic customer interactions and the occasions that try any customer's patience. This means that every single customer who crosses your path has the potential to help you to sharpen your skills and to rise to the occasion in those tough situations that make leaders of the best of us.

That great feeling of knowing that you can deal with *anything* is within reach of any person who works with the public. The way that you get there is very similar to how you become a good baseball player or ballerina: Learn the fundamentals, and use them often enough that they become a natural part of your talent. As you send more and more people away satisfied, and handle progressively more challenging situations with ease, you will find a newfound confidence in all your human interactions—and then you, too, will become a natural at handling even the toughest customer problems.

12

PULLING IT ALL TOGETHER

This is one of the most exciting times in history to be serving other people—for two important reasons.

First and foremost, we have learned more in the last few decades about how we interact with each other than we have in the thousands of years that came before. The field of behavioral psychology—barely a century old as of this writing—has created a wealth of knowledge on how we communicate, how different personalities react, how we manage difficult situations, and many more aspects of human behavior. As we stand at the dawn of the twenty-first century, there is a sense that we have only seen the tip of the iceberg.

Second, we now know our customers better than ever. Customer relationships have quickly gone from a soft skill to a science—one that can tell you with remarkable accuracy how many more people will eat at your restaurant if you raise your customer satisfaction levels by 15 percent, or how likely a satisfied customer is to come back. It is now possible to know in excruciating detail how much happier your customers are on a Tuesday versus a Friday, dealing with George versus Sally, and what that means for your sales and profitability. As a result, we no longer guess at the value of good service experiences—we know. And more important, we can now put a price tag on it.

The techniques in this book are a product of these two trends. They represent a shift from the lofty goal of treating people well to the psychology of how to do it. And because they originated in the world of customer contact centers, where everything is measured and fine-tuned, they have a track record of making real, tangible changes in the numerical goals of customer service such as customer satisfaction levels, customer retention and employee turnover, as well as their relationship to overall business success and profitability.

However, there is something even more important than improving bottom lines and performance measures—namely improving your life, both on and off the job. With the help of a little psychology, your own customer service efforts can now move from good intentions to predictable skills, and fundamentally change the way you interact with people. When you become proficient at using these skills, you will gain much more than happy customers, because these skills can also become the fuel that powers your own personal growth and career success.

At a global level, these techniques represent the leading edge of a revolution in customer service. We can already see signs of this revolution in specific organizations that have turned the science of customer contact into market leadership, and specific individuals whose customer skills tower over their peers. From here, as the number of people who learn these methods continues to grow—in much the same way that any new job skill eventually becomes commonplace—we have the potential to create a bold new standard for human relationships in the marketplace.

THE CORE IN COMMON

All the way back in 1936, in his classic book *How to Win Friends and Influence People*, Dale Carnegie laid out several principles for dealing with other people that remain timeless to this day. These include "Be a good listener," "Talk in terms of the other person's interests," and "Never say, 'You're wrong.'"[1] In those days, the fledgling field of psychology was in its early days of examining—scientifically—how and why we behave the way that we do. Today, what we have learned brings the classic advice of Carnegie and others home to where it belongs in the twenty-first century: as a true science of how we interact with each other. The result is nothing less than a revolution in both customer service and human relations.

Between the covers of this book, you have seen a wealth of specific techniques to use in specific customer situations—each of which has its own "recipe" for how to change the way that people react toward you, and to help you build a stronger customer experience. However, these techniques are far from being separate from each other. They form part of a larger philosophy of how to manage your customers, based around three core things that they each have in common:

1. *They involve understanding—and speaking to—the customer's own perspective.* We naturally respond to situations in terms of how they affect our favorite person—ourselves. These techniques all go beyond human nature by saying things that respect what is in a customer's mind while also respecting the boundaries of doing our jobs.

2. *They represent positive responses to difficult situations.* Being upbeat is much more than a state of mind. It is also a technique. There are ways to word things that turn you into an advocate for your customers' interests, which in turn creates a positive, collaborative environment for resolving issues with them as a team.

3. *They rely on precise techniques rather than vague feelings.* Telling employees to simply "think about the customer" usually won't change anything about how they respond to customers. But telling them, for example, to reply with what they *can* acknowledge and *can* do actually gives them something to work with, which they can learn and practice. And when the things that you practice eventually become natural over time, guess what? You suddenly *are* thinking like a customer—and this change is often dramatic and permanent.

Taken together, the skills in this book represent much more than an assortment of specific techniques. They are part of a broader philosophy that treats your customer as an equal and a partner, within the bounds of your job. When they become an integral part of your communications style, you will find that you are naturally empathetic, open, and genuine with your customer while still being true to your own personality—and in the process, will find working with customers to be much easier and more fun.

What this common philosophy means to you is that, in time, these techniques eventually become a mind-set—and this mind-set, in turn, will naturally guide you toward the best things to say and do in any customer situation. Appendix C contains a convenient summary of the skills from each chapter, and if you scan this summary at an overview level and see what these techniques all have in common, you will start developing a frame of mind within which these skills can become second nature to you.

IN CLOSING: THE "A" WORD

Throughout this book, you may have noticed the conspicuous absence of a word that is very common in most customer service books—*attitude.*

This is completely intentional, and there is an important reason for it. Focusing on improving your attitude implies that, left to your own devices, you are normally "bad" and must be trained or reminded to be "good." I do not believe that you are bad. I believe that most of you wake up every morning sincerely wanting to do a good job. My goal in this book is to teach you life skills that help you do a good job.

In a very real sense, you are my customers too, and my job is to give *you* a good customer experience. I want to see you become supremely confident in working with other people. And by focusing on techniques that will make your life easier when you are between the white lines with a customer, I sincerely believe that you will get there. When these techniques become natural to you, the issue of attitude will ultimately take care of itself, and the difference for you and your career—not to mention your customers—will be incredible.

Is having a good attitude important to good customer service? The answer is yes. Are there people who are better suited to it than others? Yes, again. There is something intangible that is common to many of us who work with the public, which can never be measured. It is a desire to nurture other people, and to care about them and their problems. It is what leads us to stand behind a retail counter, take calls in a call center, or work with patients in a hospital. However, this urge is not enough—any more than wanting to play sports alone will make you an excellent baseball player.

This is where skills come in—and one of the great pleasures of my career has been watching seemingly average people become service superstars, over and over again, by simply learning and practicing these skills. And it has been an even greater pleasure to see the impact of these interpersonal and leadership skills on people's lives, as a staggering number of them were eventually promoted into greater levels of responsibility, and many even learned to change the relationships they had with people at home and on the job.

At a broader level, the impact of good customer skills goes far beyond the individual. Statistics show that even small increases in customer retention can nearly double your revenues and profitability, and service quality leaders frequently dominate their markets. At a personal level, having been on the management team of several high-growth companies, I can testify firsthand to the bottom-line impact—on morale, turnover, sales growth, and profitability—when a service team understands the mechanics of good service.

So, in closing, I would like to encourage you to think far beyond attitude, and treat customer service for what it is: a profession. One that has its own unique set of skills, which are every bit as important as those of any other respected field. It is a profession that puts us on the cutting edge of behavioral psychology in how to interact with other people. And above all, one that has limitless potential to improve your professional and personal life, as you in turn help the lives of others. My hope for each of you reading this book is that you will not only learn some new skills but also be truly blessed by the joy that comes from learning to serve other people well.

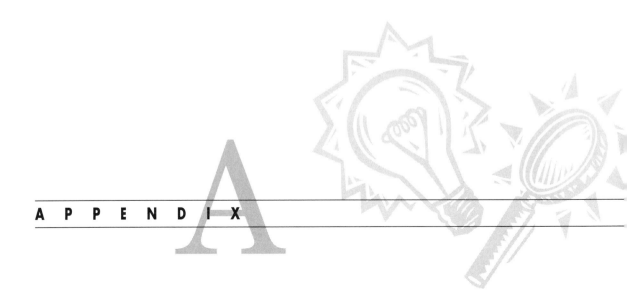

COACHING FOR PEAK CUSTOMER EXPERIENCES

Imagine that you are the head coach of a football team. You decide that you are going to teach the players everything you know about football. So you sit your team down for two straight days of lectures on every aspect of the game but then disappear for the next month while they practice on their own. How well do you think this team will perform on the field? Probably about as well as most frontline teams do when they sit through a session of so-called customer service training and then get turned loose back to their jobs.

One of the great secrets of life is that most behaviors are not trained—they are *coached*. Just like a good football coach is out on the field every day helping players with their mechanics, a good manager or supervisor needs to spend time coaching his or her team on the fundamentals of good communication. And in much the same way that the right customer skills can dramatically change a transaction, the right coaching strategy can make a huge difference in the performance of your team.

This book has focused on improving your own performance with customers. In this appendix, we examine the even more important challenge of improving the customer skills of other people. If your personal customer skills represent a drop of water in a very large river, your coaching skills represent the opportunity to change the course of the entire river, by multiplying the effects of these skills across an entire organization. When you adopt the right philosophy of coaching, and implement a process of long-term personal growth and improvement for every single person on your team, the results spread out far and wide within your workplace.

THE CASE FOR COACHING

Why do we need coaching in the first place? The answer has its roots in the psychology of how we learn.

Once upon a time, learning new skills was seen as a teaching process: Students sat in their seats, listened to a teacher, and had knowledge pushed into their heads one word at a time through their ears. Every student had the same level of instruction, and there was a sink-or-swim mentality where people who learned quickly did well, and people who learned more slowly—or simply learned differently—were often left behind.

Today, learning experts understand that individual coaching can unlock a much higher level of skills in every person, and this in turn has caused a major shift in how we learn—from a teaching model aimed at strong learners to a coaching model aimed at *all* learners. This new approach now affects nearly every level of human learning, from grade school to adult leadership development. Even in regimented environments such as the military, personal coaching and skills development have become the hallmark of elite fighting forces such as the United States Marine Corps and the Green Berets.[1]

Of course, the popular image of a coach remains the men and women who lead athletic teams, because the end product of coaching is better performance, and there are few more public stages for individual and team performance than competitive sports. If you look critically at what happens in athletic coaching, you will find factors that are important in a customer service setting as well, such as:

- Learning to execute the fundamentals
- Instilling hard work and self-discipline
- Providing performance feedback

■ Fine-tuning the mechanics

■ Providing motivation to reach the next level of performance

Above all, coaching is the key ingredient that makes customer skills move from the classroom to the real world. What happens when people are first exposed to structured communications skills such as the ones in this book? In many cases, you will find that success re-quires ongoing practice and reinforcement of these skills, because oth-erwise the pull of human nature is very strong. Supportive coaching will have a major impact on how quickly behavior changes with real customers, because these techniques often only become "real" for many people once they get regular coaching and feedback.

When I trained my own teams on communications skills like these, nearly everyone learned these techniques with great interest and en-thusiasm. Then, when they returned to their desks and got on the tele-phone with customers, you could break them down into the following three groups:

1. People who were already naturals at these skills, but learned some new tips and continued doing an excellent job

2. People who started putting these skills to use and showed gradual improvement

3. People who meant well but succumbed to the pull of human nature in real customer situations

But here is where the magic begins. When you start devoting time and positive attention to the people in groups 2 and 3, things *do* change in the days and weeks that follow. For them, the real training takes place in individual coaching and role-playing sessions, based around their actual customer issues—until one day, you observe these same people in action and notice, "Wow, they are really good at this!" Practice really does make perfect, and to watch it happen across an entire team is nothing short of amazing.

If you are trying to change the service quality of an organization, you must both train people *and* commit to an ongoing process of coaching and feedback. On one hand, this means that you can't just parachute in an instructor for a day and expect substantial changes in service skills. On the other hand, the right kind of coaching can create a transformation that I have personally seen over and over again in my own career: a change from the usual boss and employee roles to a strong, positive team relationship that motivates everyone to new heights of performance. All it takes is a coaching relationship that, in a very real sense, parallels the way that you treat your customers. Let's take a look at how you can put this into practice in your own workplace.

STRENGTH-BASED COACHING

When you see someone who is doing something wrong, the first thing that you should do as a coach is point out the person's flaws and correct his or her behavior, right? Wrong!

Supervisors—particularly newly minted ones—often see their job as one of being an inspector and enforcer, who finds bad things going on and corrects them. This mind-set forms the basis for the all-too-common approach of *deficit-based coaching*. When you use a deficit-based approach, you take an accurate observation of performance that can be improved, and add a layer of moral judgment on top of it. According to the deficit-based view of the world, employees are fundamentally flawed people who need to be pushed to do their jobs correctly. This view quickly becomes a self-fulfilling prophecy.

Deficit-based coaching is simple. It is logical. But it has one flaw: It doesn't work. Think back to your own experience when a boss chewed you out for something. Did you react by saying, "Silly me, she's so right! I'm so glad she pointed that out to me?" In all likelihood, you probably reacted by thinking what a snipe your boss is, how stupid these customers are, what a lousy job you have, and how little appreciation you get for the good things that you do. These are all natural, self-protective reactions that kick into gear when we are criticized. And these reactions often lead us to a subtle but important shift, from wanting to improve our performance to simply not getting caught. From there, it is all too easy to slip into a downward spiral where both sides work in an atmosphere of mistrust and disrespect, with the customers caught in the middle.

This leads us to what I firmly believe is the most effective way to change your team's service skills: Use a *strength-based* coaching approach. Strength-based coaching takes the same approach that you use with customers—namely, forging a win-win relationship—and uses these skills to balance the needs of the organization with your

YOU MESSED UP—GREAT!

Many people thought that I had a strange reaction on those rare occasions when I would hear someone on my team lose his or her cool or say something rude to a customer—"I'm glad I heard that, because it's an opportunity for them to learn some new skills." I would then show up at the person's desk, with a smile on my face, and say, "I can tell that this customer was getting under your skin. Let's do some role-playing and see if I can help you handle these situations more comfortably next time." And the vast majority of the time, these positive sessions were watershed moments where behaviors changed for good.

Did my lack of anger in these situations imply that I was a soft touch who didn't mind customers being treated badly? Not at all! In fact, I was known for having very high standards for how we dealt with our clients—and was very proud of leading a team that ultimately grew to deliver near-perfect customer satisfaction ratings, month in and month out. But by focusing on how we could improve the life skills of people on our team, rather than constantly calling them on the carpet for how they reacted, we had high morale *and* very high service quality.

team's own personal and professional growth. It is based around some fundamental truths about human nature:

- We hate being corrected, but we like being taught new skills.

- We hate looking bad in front of others, but we like being helped when we need it.

- We hate being disrespected, but we like having the potential to grow and improve.

- We hate having our faults catalogued, but we like having our potential recognized.

Strength-based coaching skills, just like customer skills, often go against our human nature as managers—but by the same token, they will significantly change your team's performance when you learn them and use them. There are four key elements to this approach:

1. *There are no mistakes—only lessons.* What happened when you were five years old and you tried finger painting the new sofa? You would probably rather not remember! But in the workplace, what happens when an employee accidentally deletes a customer's data, backs the company truck into someone's car, or says the wrong thing to a customer? With a strength-based coaching approach, you treat the employee with respect and dignity, help him or her learn from what happened, and move on.

With strength-based coaching, the rubber meets the road in those moments where something goes wrong—from everyday errors people make in following procedures to how well they handle themselves in front of customers to those out-and-out disasters that are a fact of life in any real-world business. In a strength-based environment, *everything* is a potential coaching opportunity—and this mind-set, in turn, changes the entire relationship between you and your team.

2. *There are no poor performers—only people who could perform better.* Nearly every new management position I have ever taken came complete with a "guided tour" of who the "good" employees were and who the "bad" employees were. And guess what? By changing the definition of "bad" to "needs more coaching," I frequently watched these same employees grow to become stars—often, purely because no one had taken a positive interest in them before.

   This principle mirrors an important shift in the psychology of how teams learn, from lavishing attention on stronger performers to spending time with weaker ones. For example, in the United States Marine Corps, an ingrained culture of "tending to the bottom quarter" leads to a fighting force who can effectively cover for each other in battle situations. Likewise, in my own experience, time invested with the team members who needed it the most—combined with recognizing their unique strengths—universally had a dramatic impact on the performance of the entire team.

   Are there people who will never perform a job well no matter how much you coach them? Of course. And as a manager, it is your responsibility to make sure that people are in positions that ultimately suit their talents. But when you stop labeling people and start developing them, the results that you get will be incredible.

3. *No criticism.* Really. No criticism. If you are from the old school of management, perhaps the single most productive thing that you can do for your team is to start biting your lip. You can coach all you want, but you cannot criticize people. Because when you create a criticism-free zone in your workplace, an amazing thing will start happening—people will buy in to improving their own performance. People will start coming *to you* and telling you what they messed up, or need to do better. And, more important, they will listen to what you say as a coach, and they will work hard to put it into practice. When you reach that point, it will become a watershed moment for working collaboratively and reaching higher goals as a team.

   Are there ever exceptions to the no criticism rule? Sure.

When someone is stealing office supplies, starting shouting matches with coworkers, or not showing up for work, go ahead and be critical. However, when people are in the uncomfortable position of dealing with the public, and they say or do the wrong thing, criticism will accomplish exactly the opposite of what you are hoping for—because, in most cases, you will compound a simple skills-training problem with the deeper issue of having defensive and disgruntled employees. Conversely, a conscious decision to become a benevolent coaching figure instead of General Patton is often the key to breaking through to better performance.

4. *Get out on the field.* Strength-based coaching doesn't take place through memos and e-mails. It takes place on the floor, at the retail counter, and in people's cubicles. It moves far beyond telling people what to do, into *showing* them through role-playing and positive feedback. When you get to know your team members as people, and get into the rhythm of their workflow instead of just showing up when something goes wrong, learning becomes a continuous process and a natural part of how your team functions.

   This leads to one of the more intangible benefits of strength-based coaching: It's *fun.* When difficult customers would get escalated to me, I'd take great joy in gathering people from my team around the speakerphone and showing them how to handle the customer. When customer situations would implode, it was uplifting to help people turn these situations around in a positive, blame-free atmosphere. Above all, it was delightful to watch people reach their full potential, and accomplish things that they never had before. It's like being a ballplayer who is happiest on the mound instead of in the clubhouse. When you adopt a process of continuous coaching and feedback, you move from being an isolated, feared critic to an integral part of the team.

Sadly, strength-based coaching is not the norm. One day at lunch, I overhead a group of young women discussing their workday at the next table. First, they talked about how Becky got written up for an infraction, and then how Sally was in trouble for something else, and then how Cindy was *really* going to get it once her boss found out about something else. I silently wondered what they did for a living, when it struck me that they seemingly had a full-time profession of punishing each other! Is this office likely to be a hotbed of excellent customer service? You decide.

Strength-based coaching brings several benefits to your organization, including better morale, lower turnover, and higher productivity. It also has benefits for your team members, including personal growth, career development, and a new level of interpersonal and leadership skills. But most important, it is an approach that benefits *you*, in both your growth as a leader and in earning the respect of your team and organization. By putting it in practice, you take a big step toward the ultimate goal of any leader, which is making a real difference in your team's performance.

CUSTOMER SKILLS AS COACHING SKILLS

Quick—think of a group of people who demand your attention, want their needs met, and don't react well to criticism. Your customers, right? Or did your employees come to mind first? Or both?

There is more in common between your customers and your employees than you may realize, such as:

- You serve both groups of people.

- Both groups react emotionally to what you tell them.

- How either group responds depends on how well you communicate with them.

- How well you serve both groups affects your own career.

If you look at it logically, the people you manage are more than your employees; they are your *customers* as well. And the relationships that you build with these internal customers will, in turn, have a tremendous impact on how they treat your external customers.

This means that the same communications skills that you use with customers—and coach your team about—also serve as the linchpin of how you implement strength-based coaching on your own team. Let's take a look at some of the ways that many of the customer skills in this book apply to your own coaching situations.

Active Listening

In Chapter 3, we discussed listening as a very active process, involving showing interest and giving feedback, paraphrasing the other person, gathering information, keeping things light, and using eye contact and body language. The result of this process is a zone of comfort and acceptance, from which people can frankly and productively discuss their issues. Within your team, the same techniques provide a fresh way to approach situations ranging from performance problems to employee concerns.

As an example, let's take a classic situation in a customer contact team—the "I can't get my work done because of all of these customers" problem.

Without active listening:

Manager: I noticed that you still aren't responding to customer e-mails the same day.

Employee: I can't keep up with all these e-mails unless we change my priorities.

Manager: Our standard is same-day response to e-mails, and you told me two weeks ago that you would work harder at meeting it.

Employee: I'm getting too many interruptions.

Manager: We have to get the job done.

In this example, both parties are talking past each other, and neither is listening or responding to what the other person says. In addition, the opening statement from the manager, although technically correct, is confrontational and puts the employee on the defensive. Let's try this again with a more active approach to listening:

With active listening:

Manager: We talked a couple of weeks ago about e-mail response times. How are things going from your end?

Employee: To be totally honest, I can't keep up with all these e-mails unless we change my priorities.

Manager: So you feel that you're still having problems meeting the standard. What do you think is causing the problem?

Employee: I'm getting too many interruptions. In particular, it seems like I'm spending almost half of my time on phone issues coming at me from other agents.

Manager: It sounds like you feel overloaded. What would you recommend that we do?

Employee: I do want to meet our standards—I know that it's important to you. I just don't do well with a lot of random interruptions. I'm wondering, how about if we set up some office hours for me and the other senior agents?

Manager: That's an interesting idea. I'm very concerned about meeting the standard, so perhaps we should consider a schedule for you and the other senior agents to be available to people on the team.

Now, not only are the two parties responding directly to each other but they are now helping to solve each other's concerns, in a more respectful, low-stress atmosphere.

Staging

Staging is a three-step process that helps you deliver difficult messages to people, by breaking them into stages: *introducing* the message, *explaining* the reasons for it, and then *empathizing* with the other person's feelings—whatever these feelings are. It works because it breaks down the emotional content of the message into stages, each of which can be managed with the right communications skills.

Consider the case where an employee is not following procedures. Without staging, it becomes all too easy for human nature to take over, and the employee to get defensive:

Without staging:

You: Steve, I notice that you are not following our assessment script.

Steve: It's not my fault. I can explain. I'm getting some really difficult customers.

Predictably, the employee responds to being confronted by defending himself, rather than speaking to your agenda. Now, let's try this again using staging:

With staging:

You: (Step 1—Introduce) Steve, one of the challenges of an operation like this is that we have to meet our clients' standards, which means that our calls are rated on how well we follow their procedures.

(Step 2—Explain) Since getting low client scores on calls impacts our contractual performance in a very real way, I have to be more careful about everybody following our standard assessment process. I really like the job you do here, so I want to make sure that you get the same good ratings as the rest of us. Do you see any problems that would keep you from following this in the future?

Steve: I hadn't realized how important this was to you. I like this job too, so I'll make it a point to follow the procedures.

You: (Step 3—Empathize) I really appreciate that. I know that you are very conscientious about your work in general, so I'm sure you'll do your best on this too. Thanks!

By using staging with people on your team, you accomplish three important things:

1. You focus on situations rather than personality, by explaining the situation in detail.

2. You give the listener an opportunity to respond professionally instead of emotionally.

3. By empathizing with the response, you are more likely to promote good feelings and cooperation, instead of defensiveness and confrontation.

People mistakenly think that people react only to circumstances. But they really react to the way these circumstances are communicated, and your employees are no different. This is why, particularly as a manager, staging is an important part of your professional tool kit for communicating difficult messages.

The "I" Technique

If you manage a customer contact environment, things are going to go wrong every day—and something is guaranteed to go stupendously

TOO SHRILL? YOU KNOW THE DRILL

Coaching is easy when you are telling nice people that they are doing great things. It gets a little harder when you skate into awkward, personal territory. Whether it is performance problems or interpersonal issues, there is a natural discomfort about telling someone that something isn't good and needs to change.

So, what should you do when you need to tell someone on your team that other people are complaining about, say, how loud and annoying he or she is? You do this by using the same skills that you use with any customer, in any customer situation. Here are some examples:

Staging: "I was talking with some of the team members, and I'm seeing an issue where some people have more sensitivity than others."

"I" technique: "I've noticed, for example, that I sometimes have to speak more softly when other people are trying to concentrate. In the same way, some people seem to be sensitive to the volume of your voice, even several cubicles away. Is this something that you were aware of?"

Can-Can: "Some people have physical issues that they can't help, and I'll always do my best to accommodate that. Do you think that this is something that you can mitigate?"

These are more than communications skills—they are a mind-set. I truly respect the other person whom I want to get along with his or her team members, and I see my role as helping that to happen. But they also serve as an example that almost no topic is too sensitive to address, by using the customer skills that we present in this book.

wrong at least once a week. To keep this reality from turning you into a constant critic, consider using the "I" technique to put your advice in a very nonthreatening light—by speaking in first person. Table A-1 shows some examples of how the "I" technique can change some common team situations.

Using the "I" technique puts things on a collaborative, personal level that lowers defensive barriers, and helps people to really accept and listen to what you are saying. This, in turn, helps lead your coaching efforts away from conflict and toward growth and change. Used appropriately, it is an extremely effective way to get the performance that you want from your team.

The Can-Can

With customers, the Can-Can is a powerful technique to avoid telling customers no. This same approach is equally effective in helping you avoid criticizing or saying no to your employees, by focusing on what you *can* acknowledge and *can* do. Table A-2 shows some examples of using the Can-Can with your team.

In each of these cases, you have a common goal: *Always speak to the other person's interest.* By keeping your focus on what benefits your employees—particularly in a performance or coaching situation— you build the kind of supportive, mutually beneficial relationship where true coaching can take place.

These examples are just the tip of the iceberg. In much the same way, nearly every technique that you use with customers can also be put to productive use with people on

Table A-1. Using the "I" technique as a coach.

Human nature	The "I" technique
You were pretty rude to that last customer.	I can tell that customer was frustrating you.
You dropped the ball with that customer. I want you to pay more attention when someone asks you something, and write it down.	I used to get flustered when customers asked me too many things—but writing things down really helped me a lot. Do you think that the same thing might help you?
When that customer got upset with you, you just stood there like a deer frozen in the headlights and didn't say anything.	I used to get really uncomfortable when customers got angry at me, but eventually I learned how to handle it. Do you want to try a little role-playing and see how you might deal with someone like her next time?

Table A-2. Using the Can–Can as a coach.

Without the Can-Can	With the Can-Can
You messed up.	I can help you do better next time.
You aren't really promotable right now.	We can work together to help you reach your goals here.
You need to do a better job of treating customers well.	I know that you can handle customers even better with some coaching.

your team. In a very real sense, using customer skills in your coaching work lets you "walk the talk" in a very visible way, as you improve these same skills in your own team.

EFFECTIVE COACHING: SOME CLOSING THOUGHTS

One of the great paradoxes about customer service is how something that never touches the customer—namely, your coaching interactions with your team—is probably the single biggest factor in what these customers ultimately experience. In closing, here are some practical recommendations for implementing a coaching process within your own service team:

■ Set realistic expectations for change following individual coaching sessions. Notice and reward small changes in transaction skills.

■ Skills at delivering feedback (staging) and controlling the transaction (acknowledging close, acknowledging return, boundary setting, and so forth) frequently take the most practice and coaching to develop. These skills are generally not human nature for most people, and often take time and patience.

■ Coaching and performance measurement are two separate objectives. When coaching, focus on the development of skills, not grading performance. People tend to be objective about skills, and defensive about performance.

■ Bring your feedback to life using role-playing where possible—skills become real for people when they have the opportunity to practice them with a coach.

■ Use coaching sessions as positive, developmental face time with members of your team, and sell these sessions as part of their overall professional development.

In summary, the right approach to coaching can help to create permanent changes that benefit both you and the employee. Coaching is much more than giving feedback: Perhaps most important, it is a process of helping people achieve their best, rather than catching them doing things wrong. Done well, it has many benefits including:

■ Improved transaction productivity

■ Higher customer satisfaction ratings

■ Improved morale and decreased turnover

■ A stronger, more collaborative working relationship

In much the same way that customer skills eventually become natural, in time the right coaching skills can become an innate part of who you are as a manager. In the process, you will develop a built-in competitive advantage over people who take the path of least resistance and simply criticize their team's behavior—which invariably leads to a defensive response, and often even poorer service. By using a strength-based coaching approach and applying structured communications skills to your own internal customer transactions, you will reach the goal of every leader—creating sustained, long-term performance change in the people you lead.

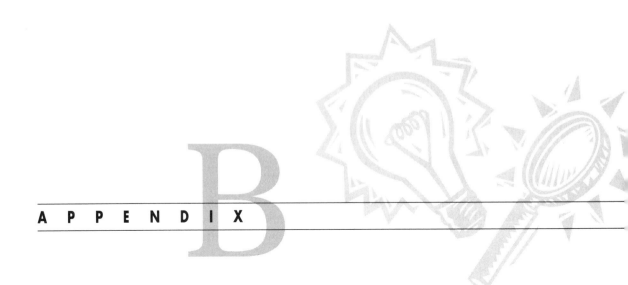

FROM CUSTOMER SERVICE TO REAL LIFE

As a trainer, do you know what my most frequent comment from students normally is after a training session? Here is a hint: It has nothing to do with their work, their customers, or even their bosses. It is this: "I can't wait to try these techniques on people at home!"

The techniques in this book go beyond mere customer skills and become human relationship skills that can affect every aspect of our lives. Customer situations are a microcosm of real life, and knowing how to manage these short relationships can translate directly to the deeper and more intimate ones that we have with other people in our lives. The same techniques that help us succeed in our service careers can also lead us to love, friendship, and smooth relationships with everyone we deal with on a daily basis.

Of course, if we treated every person in our lives exactly like a customer, it would probably make for some pretty strange marriages, friendships, and working relationships. Personal connections like these require a much broader mosaic of skills, ranging from showing intimacy to resolving conflict. At the same time, the basics of successful customer relationships form a good base from which to build and improve all of these skills. In this chapter, we will look at some examples of how to take many of the customer techniques we have learned and put them to good use in the rest of our lives.

THE CHATTY COWORKER

You are very proud of how hard you work on the floor of a local retailer. But your coworker Francine, who works alongside you, constantly talks a mile a minute. You do your best to be nice and pay attention to her, but she gabs incessantly about politics, the boss, her grandchildren, and whatever else is on her mind—to the point where it is cutting into your productivity. What should you do? ■

We spoke in Chapter 10 about using the acknowledging close technique, where you break in to the conversation, enthusiastically acknowledge the last thing that the person says, and then use binary questions to wrest control of the conversation from an overly talkative person. However, having a talkative coworker creates some interesting challenges compared with a talkative customer:

- *It never ends.* Talkative customers go away after you handle them successfully—but the talkative coworker is there with you day in and day out.

- *The stakes are higher.* A talkative customer isn't likely to go around your workplace blabbing about how he or she feels about you, but if you make your coworker feel bad about her gabfests, she just might.

- *It isn't your job.* You are being paid to serve the talkative customer, but the talkative coworker is actually taking you away from what you are being paid to do.

These issues all make this situation much more challenging than a customer transaction. But although the playing field is different, the game plan is still the same: Take control of the conversation, and steer it to a conclusion while still making the other person feel good. Here is how you might modify the basic acknowledging close technique for a coworker:

- *Prepare "conversation stoppers."* After you break in and acknowledge a customer, your goal is to get back to the business at hand. With a coworker, your goal is to change the subject, preferably to something that he or she will not discuss at length. Plan ahead of time to have binary questions that deftly move the subject into neutral territory.

■ *Talk about yourself.* Some—but not all—talkative people tend to be self-absorbed with their own issues. They are happy to go on and on as long as they have a willing ear but quickly run out of steam when someone else has the floor. If this is the case, make sure that your binary questions bring up issues in your life, and turn the tables.

■ *Steer the topic toward your work.* When a chatty coworker is part of your problem, consider making him or her part of your solution—by asking him or her to pitch in with what you are doing, in return for your continuing to hang breathlessly on every word.

■ *Use "outs" judiciously.* A great way to acknowledge a compulsive yakker is to give yourself an out that gives both of you what you want—for example, "I really want to hear about this—could we touch base for lunch today, after I finish this project?" In this way, you can actually express interest and build a good relationship while putting a lid on your talk time.

■ *Bring the issue out in the open.* Finally, we get to the big question—do you ever ask your coworker to stop talking so much? The answer is, it depends. You generally cannot change another person's basic personality—and if you can manage the situation by using good communications skills, while saving face on both sides, by all means do so. At the same time, you have the right to set appropriate boundaries that protect your own interests.

Remember that the goal of almost any human interaction is to speak to the other person's interests while getting what you want in return. In this particular case, the classic dating breakup line of "It's not you, it's me" may serve as your best approach. For example:

You: I often have a hard time concentrating, and I don't ever want you to feel like I'm not paying attention to you. Is there some kind of signal that we can work out for times when I need to focus on my work?

For example, one of my former employees used to handle interruptions by hanging a golden rope across the door of her cubicle, as a signal that she needed to be left alone. No one was singled out, and no one was personally insulted—but she had a way to get peace and quiet when she needed it. By changing her approach from a personal to a procedural one, she got what she wanted without causing any hard feelings.

Now, let's compare these approaches to human nature. In a situation like this, most of us would be tempted to simply do the obvious: Ask Ms. Blabbermouth to stop talking. But when you think logically about your own reactions when peers criticize *your* behavior, you also know the results in your heart: It can change the working relationship, often permanently. By thinking like a customer and working it in to your everyday relationships with coworkers, you open up a whole new way to get what you want while still building positive, win-win relationships.

WHEN YOUR FRIENDS HIT A SOUR NOTE

Your old friends from college are visiting your town for the first time in years. They can't wait to see you again, and since you were all such big rock music fans in school, they are particularly keen to relive old times and go to a concert with you—and therein lies the problem. Twenty years after graduation, your tastes have matured somewhat, and nowadays you and your spouse like Tony Bennett, cool jazz, and small clubs with air-conditioning and good food. Your friends, on the other hand, still like to wear tie-dyed shirts and go to crowded rock festivals—the thought of which makes you gag these days.

They just dropped you a line about how they made it a point to schedule their visit around the annual Rock and Reggae Blast, a two-day outdoor event slated to draw more than twenty thousand people, and how much they are looking forward going with you. You would rather gargle with glass shards than attend. Tomorrow, they will call you to firm up the details. What will you tell them? ∎

In an ideal world, you would simply express your preferences to other people and they would respect them. But these aren't just any other people—these are your old college buddies who were always challenging you to party with them, and never took no for an answer. But they are still great friends, and you want to show them a good time. How you handle them in this situation is a good template for any situation where other people are imposing on you, yet you want to respond graciously and preserve your friendship.

This situation has plenty in common with ones where customers ask for things that you can't do. Remember back in Chapter 7, where we learned how to use the Can-Can technique to never say no to these customers? Many of the same elements are here as well—someone wants something, you aren't comfortable providing it, and you still want to send the person away feeling good about both you and the situation.

At the same time, there are some key differences when good friends are involved instead of customers:

- *They know you.* When you make it clear to customers that something cannot be done and offer them alternatives, they aren't likely to respond with: "Aw, come on, Steve, you used to do this all the time!" Your friends, however, just might.

- *The expectations are higher.* A customer transaction takes place between relative strangers, so the expectations revolve around what they want, not you personally. A reunion with old friends, conversely, puts the spotlight squarely on you.

- *Old roles die hard.* For example, if you tended to let these people take the lead in college and allowed them to pressure you into having a good time back then, it can be all too easy for them to presume that they still know what's best for everyone.

At the same time, you have every right to change the old script and stand up for what you want, particularly with the help of some good communications skills. Here's how you might use the Can-Can to get your personal friends back on track:

- *Play up the benefits.* The first task in using the Can-Can is always to acknowledge the other person, and then find something to his or her benefit. For example, you might say, "Music sounds like a great idea—but since this is a special visit, I want you to see this town the way that only my spouse and I know it. We know some of the most incredible clubs, where they have some really hot players. How about letting us treat you to a new experience this time?"

HOW TO SPEAK LIKE A GOVERNMENT OFFICIAL

Whatever you may think of the U.S. government, the people who work in it certainly know how to disagree with each other.

I recently had the pleasure of working on a project with people in the public health sector of the federal government—people who interact with both the public and legislators on a regular basis, trying to make policy-level changes to improve our public health. In this environment, their success depends on working collaboratively with other people, including some whom they may not agree with at all. It was a delightful experience to see how these people negotiated their differences without ever losing face or even breaking a sweat. Here are some examples of how they speak compared with most people:

Most people: That idea stinks! I hate it!

Government official: That is an interesting point. I can see how you feel that way. Maybe I'm wrong about how I feel, which is another way.

Most people: Person X isn't doing a lick of work.

Government official: Person X is probably busy with a lot of other things.

Most people: Let's meet in Chicago. I hate coming to Washington.

Government official: I'd like to do whatever is convenient for everyone. The food is really great in Chicago. If people would really rather be in Washington, I understand. If we go to Chicago, we really should take in some live jazz. What do you folks think about where we should go? Chicago is one of the easiest places to fly to.

What you see here is a simple case of people expressing the same sentiments in a different way, within an overall atmosphere of great civility—even when they have strong disagreements. No doubt there are days when people are saying, "Maybe I'm wrong about how I feel" to each other with great vigor, but overall this style of communicating clearly makes it easier for people to reach consensus while preserving good feelings on all sides.

■ *Use "even though" to get specific.* If your friends don't take the hint, it's time to let them know how you feel—without uttering the word *no*, of course. The most direct way to accomplish both of these goals is to word your preferences in the form of an "even though" statement:

"Even though my last experience at a rock festival involved sitting on a soggy blanket with mud on my face, surrounded by teeming crowds, eating cold food, I do like the idea of catching some live music with you. Do you have any other ideas?"

- *Deal with the full-court press.* Of course, some people want things badly enough that they don't know when to quit. They always pressured you to join them in college, and, by golly, they're still doing it many years later. (Remember how we said in Chapter 9 that personalities don't change easily?) So, you need to know what to do when their response is something like, "But this is going to be the greatest show since Phish and the Grateful Dead, man! You just can't miss this."

    Your challenge here is to tell your friends to stop pressuring you, without openly telling them to stop pressuring you—a perfect opportunity for using the "I" technique, where you phrase your concerns exclusively in the first person:

    "I know how badly you two want to go to this festival. But whenever I've pressed people to do things they really didn't want to do, it never worked out as well as I hoped. We are really looking forward to seeing you, so is there something that we would all enjoy, perhaps after you go to the festival yourselves?"

There comes a point, of course, where your friends are not being friends, but being boors—and I will leave it as an exercise to the reader to ponder how far to accommodate boorish people in your life, even when they are old acquaintances. At the same time, the greater point is that sticking up for yourself and accommodating your friends do not always have to be mutually exclusive goals. Even when your so-called customers are pushy friends, you can still use good customer skills to stand your ground with grace and charm.

THAT *WAS* A NICE VASE

You are sitting in the den, reading the newspaper, when suddenly a loud *pop* startles you—followed by the sound of glass shattering onto the floor. Jumping up, you rush to the living room, where you see an expensive antique vase lying in little pieces on the floor—and your twin eight-year-old sons nervously peering around the corner, with dart guns in their hands. Glancing down at the floor again, you see a rubber dart among the shattered glass pieces. How do you react? ∎

Anyone who idealizes children as being sweet and innocent has probably never lived in a house full of them. Most kids are full of energy and are constantly testing boundaries, which predictably causes situations that would try anyone's patience. Moreover, communicating with them presents some unique challenges versus dealing with customers:

- *They are not the same as adults.* Children are, well . . . children—which means that you cannot always expect the same level of rational behavior, intelligent choices, or communications skills that you expect from (most) grown-ups.

- *There are issues of power and trust.* You can't normally punish a customer, but children, on the other hand, often live in fear of how their parents will react—particularly when something goes wrong. As a result, avoiding trouble can color everything that your kids say to you.

- *They are vulnerable and need your love.* You are not your customer's protector and guardian, but you are with your children. This means that the things you say to your kids have a great influence on their sense of security and self-worth.

At the same time, many of the same techniques that let you have difficult conversations with customers—such as staging and the "I" technique—can actually work equally well with your children. Let's take a look at some specific steps for the previous situation:

1. *Break the tension with an introductory statement.* When you use the staging technique with customers, you try to reduce the tension of unpleasant news by introducing it first. Things are no different in a tense situation with your own children. By choosing an introduction that lowers the anxiety level, you help open up a much more productive dialogue about a frustrating situation. Here are some examples:

   - "It looks like we've had an accident. Could you kids help me clean this up?"

   - "Did you two hurt yourselves?"

   - "It's too bad that this broke, but there are worse things than losing a vase."

Let's be honest—it is very tempting to react angrily in a situation like this. Your children should not have been this careless with expensive glassware sitting around. But you also know enough about customer psychology to realize that putting someone on the defensive usually makes people angry instead of cooperative. By choosing an emotionally neutral opening statement at this moment, you are much more likely to get what you want—namely, honesty and contrition from your children.

2. *Don't ask questions—discuss alternatives.* What are the first things that many parents do when they are confronted with an unpleasant surprise? Often, they start firing questions, like:

- "Did you kids do this?"

- "Didn't I tell you two to stay out of the living room?"

- "Now what are we going to do?"

Now, be honest with yourself—how often were those questions met by useful answers? There is a difference between gathering information and venting frustration, and understanding this difference is critical to breaking down the barriers between you and your children.

In his classic book *Between Parent and Child*, the late child psychologist Dr. Haim Ginott advises against asking questions to which you already know the answer. As an alternative, he shares a delightful anecdote about what a mother chose to say when she saw her son drawing on the wall with crayons: Getting past her initial frustration, she handed him three sheets of paper and said, "Walls are not for drawing. Paper is."[1] In this example, a similar response might be: "I want you two to have a good time playing—and if you do it in the family room or outdoors from now on, we won't have situations like this. OK?"

This is a direct analogy to the customer skill of staging—by introducing the situation, and then explaining what you want, in a way that saves face while getting your point across. By focusing on what you *want* instead of *why* they made a mistake, you stand a much better chance of creating a teaching moment that actually changes behavior—with the respect and self-esteem of your children intact.

3. *Use the "I" (was a kid once) technique.* Did you ever break something expensive when you were a child? Or do something else that really caused problems? If so, that's great! Because you now have a dandy opportunity to take this bad experience, and turn it into something really good: an opportunity to get closer to your children, at the same time that you teach them to do the right thing. When you share things that *you* did as a child, you step down from the pedestal of being a flawless grown-up, and make yourself a part of what just happened with your children.

   This technique works as well with adults as it does with children. One day, one of my senior call center employees made a mistake that completely erased the hard drive of a computer that one of our customers had shipped to us—and this customer was already known for having a hot temper. So how did we handle the situation? By pulling her aside, and having me and the customer's account representative spend at least fifteen minutes laughing and joking about all the things that *we* had messed up with customers. Then we proposed having all of us call this customer together, as a lab experiment for how to handle a difficult situation—and in the end, things quickly turned out okay with both the customer *and* the employee.

   For most of us, the relationship with your children can benefit from the same shift in perspective that helps you work with customers—looking past your own interests, and responding in ways that gain the cooperation and trust that you need to solve problems. More important, these techniques form building blocks to a much more important goal: a great relationship with your kids. This is why good parents often have a head start on the basics of working with customers—and in a very real sense, both children and customers can teach us valuable things about working with either group.

HOME (NOT SO) SWEET HOME

You and your spouse are madly in love—except when you are fighting like cats and dogs, which happens all too regularly these days. Whenever either of you brings up a concern, the other person usually feels defensive and reacts with anger and sarcasm—and then you are both off to the races, yelling and screaming at each other.

Last week, you forgot to take the garbage out—and when your spouse informed you about it by making a cutting remark, you shot back with a list of everything that your darling never got around to doing either this week. After several minutes of hurling insults at each other, you are now steaming at opposite ends of the house. What do you say when you get back together again? ■

Can customer skills turn into marital counseling? Perhaps more than you might think. But while good communications form the bedrock of any relationship, in this case they are part of a deeper set of needs on both sides. There are some important differences between situations like these and a typical customer issue:

■ *You have to participate emotionally.* This is perhaps the biggest difference between customer relationships and personal relationships. If your communications with your spouse consisted solely of good customer skills with him or her, you would probably seem pleasant, stiff, and disengaged. In an intimate conversation, by comparison, your feelings matter as much as the words that you choose.

■ *You have to deal with disagreements.* Most of us rarely need to confront a customer—but it feels very different when a loved one is criticizing you, dumping too many responsibilities on you, or ignoring your basic needs. Personal relationships, and particularly marriages, involve needs on both sides of most transactions.

■ *You are personally invested.* With customers, most of us can learn to put on a game face to hide our most personal feelings from them. It is very difficult to do the same thing constantly with loved ones, because we intimately share our lives with them, and in turn care about how they feel.

On top of all of these issues, you are dealing with a life partner who probably knows you better than anyone. With people who know you, your relationship exists on a base of past experiences—both good and bad. This means that while you can use your skills with the public to communicate better, these skills must be adapted to the needs of an intimate relationship. Some things that you might consider when you both get back together after a fight include the following:

■ *Make it about you instead of about them.* When things are at a stalemate with your partner, the "I" technique can be particularly effective in changing the course of an argument. Psychologists routinely counsel couples to use "I feel" statements, where you focus on what affects *you*, as an integral part of resolving disagreements with your partner.[2] Here are some examples of turning common barbs into effective "I" statements:

■ "You are a jerk!" becomes "I feel bad when you criticize me in public."

■ "Can't you ever do anything right?" becomes "It makes more work for me when you don't take the time to read the directions."

■ "How dare you do that!" becomes "I feel hurt when you do go back on your promises."

In arguments, we often instinctively focus on painting the other person in a bad light, to prove that we are right—which, in turn, provokes a defensive response that usually leads us both hurtling into a downward spiral. By comparison, using "I feel" statements to share your own story helps to focus the discussion on your concerns, rather than the futile quest to get the other person to admit that he or she is bad.

■ *Be curious, not furious.* You know how asking questions of angry customers helps to calm them down? Guess what—the same thing happens on the home front. Used appropriately, the right questions can help people on *both* sides of the question cool down and start to talk rationally with each other. For example:

■ "How dare you say that!" becomes "Why are you saying that?"

■ "You aren't being fair!" becomes "Tell me why you feel this way."

■ "Stop pestering me!" becomes "Do you feel this is more important?"

When you ask questions—and of course, we mean legitimate, information-gathering questions rather than pointed ones—you accomplish two important goals. First, you are showing interest, rather than shutting your partner down.

Second, you give the other person a chance to talk while directing the conversation to your concerns. By replacing displays of emotion—which are rarely effective—with questions that get issues squarely on the table, you lower the heat while moving closer toward a solution.

■ *Find points of agreement.* With customers, the Can-Can technique is all about finding common ground, by focusing on what *can* be done. In a similar way, couples can break through their disagreements more quickly by finding where they *can* agree, and building from there. This approach doesn't mean submerging your own feelings—rather, it means taking an open, mature, respect-based negotiating stance, based around acknowledging at least part of what the other person is saying.

Normally, in an argument, we do exactly the opposite of this approach: We keep finding ways to give no credit at all to the other person, which is like pouring gasoline on a fire. For example, let's consider the previous disagreement, which started over a cutting remark about taking out the garbage. In all likelihood, the argument evolved along lines like these:

Spouse: Well, I see you didn't take out the garbage, for the 453rd time! I guess you are just going to let it pile up in front of the house for the rest of our lives.

You: Look who's talking—the most laundry-challenged person on the face of the earth!

Spouse: We were talking about you, not me! Can't you ever keep up with anything in the house?

You: If you had half as many responsibilities as I do, you'd find something better to do than complain all the time.

Here both parties are talking past each other and will never reach common ground as long as they keep reacting to each other this way. Now, let's try this exchange again, but with an important difference—they each continue to express strong feelings but also give the other person credit for that part of the issue that they *can* agree with.

Spouse: Well, I see you didn't take out the garbage, for the 453rd time! I guess you are just going to let it pile up in front of the house for the rest of our lives.

You: You are right. I do forget to take out the garbage too often, and I'm sorry that it happened again. But it really bothers me when you talk to me with sarcasm and disrespect.

Spouse: You're right. I shouldn't do that. I just get so frustrated when this happens week after week. I feel so powerless when you agree to do things, and then I get back from work and they haven't happened.

In this case, neither person is giving ground on his or her own grievances—as they shouldn't—but both of them are opening the door to a rational discussion, based on their mutual needs. By giving even a little credit to the other person, while still openly expressing his or her concerns, both parties are now a lot closer to solving their problems as a team.

Intimate relationships are one area of communications skills where logic sometimes fails us. For example, noted marital psychologist John Gottman cites research showing that active-listening techniques, such as paraphrasing the other person, are actually not terribly helpful in resolving marriage conflicts.[3] (For instance, saying "I understand that you want me to stop leaving the laundry around" is far less effective than not leaving the laundry around!) Conversely, showing strong emotions, which is usually a complete no-no with customers, can be very common in solid relationships where partners care about each other. Life partners call for different approaches than customers, as well as the sensitivity to recognize these differences.

At the same time, certain communications skills are universal, even in our interactions with the person with whom we share our life. When you are angry with someone close to you, bland advice about being a nice person doesn't help—but a structured process that you both agree to follow *can* help. With a little help from your proficiency with customers, you can not only defuse difficult situations on the home front but also become even closer to the person you love.

WHEN CUSTOMER SKILLS SAVE LIVES

A very gripping example where good communications skills had a life-or-death impact played out in the suburbs of Atlanta in early 2005.

One evening, as waitress Ashley Smith returned home from buying cigarettes, she was confronted by escaped suspect Brian Nichols, who was being sought in a shooting rampage that had left his trial judge and three other people dead over the past twenty-four hours. Forcing Smith into her apartment with him, Nichols bound her and warned her that if she screamed, he would kill both of them.

Smith's reaction to this situation was very different from any other person Nichols confronted that day: *She spoke to his interests.* "I will do what you say," she told him. Calling it a miracle that he had survived thus far, she soon convinced him that "there must be a reason you are still alive."

Over the next few hours that she was held hostage, she spoke calmly to Nichols and tried to make him feel better about his situation. She read to him from the bestseller *The Purpose-Driven Life* about serving others,[4] later telling him that his own life had a purpose—and that by ministering to other inmates, "you can go to jail and save many more people than you killed." She shared pictures of her family and told him about her own husband's tragic murder. Later that morning, she even cooked him a breakfast of pancakes and eggs.

Eventually, Nichols agreed to let her leave the apartment to see her daughter, tacitly expecting her to call the authorities, and he was later captured without incident. Before she left, he told her, "You're an angel sent from God to me," and even offered to help set up the curtains in her new apartment.

By comparison, Nichols confided to Smith that one of his earlier victims was killed because "he wouldn't do what I asked him to do. He fought me, so I had to kill him." The authorities later praised Smith's cool handling of the situation, with one police officer calling it a "best-case scenario" that was the opposite of what usually happens.[5] ■

What happened here was, in a very real sense, a life-or-death version of the Can-Can technique that we discussed in Chapter 7. In a situation where most people would be excused for thinking only about themselves—in the face of a suspect who was being portrayed in the headlines as a cold, remorseless murderer—Smith took the unusual step of finding things that she *could* acknowledge (for example, that he was still alive) and *could* do (such as feed him and discuss hopeful outcomes) that spoke to *his* interests. In the process, she successfully spared both of their lives, while in a deeper sense living out a spiritual goal of treating any person—even a murder suspect—with a sense of worth and value.

Although most situations don't have stakes that are this high, cases like this underscore that the words we choose to use are one of the most powerful forces in our lives. These words can change people's moods, and change their actions. They can make us a success in our careers and our personal life. They can bring us love and intimacy. And in some cases, they can even save our lives.

POSTSCRIPT: HOW TO BE A BETTER CUSTOMER

One other question I often get asked by audiences is: "Can I use these techniques to get better service as a customer myself?" The answer is absolutely!

Of course, the dynamics of a customer transaction change considerably when you are on the other side of the counter. In a similar way to how your perception shifts from being a driver to a pedestrian, you shift gears from worrying about demanding customers to an equally strong concern about getting what you want. Instead of trying to satisfy someone, you are seeking satisfaction yourself. You are now the person with the problem, and the service person you are dealing with is your key—or your impediment—to resolving this problem.

At the same time, you and a customer service professional share one very important thing in common—you are both human. No matter how cool he or she appears on the outside, nearly every frontline person has unspoken fears every time that a customer approaches—and if you become aware of these feelings and address them, it can help you get much better service. Some of these worries include:

- Being confronted with your anger

- Appearing stupid in front of you

- Being asked to do things that he or she can't do

- Looking bad in front of his or her boss

- Falling behind on the rest of his or her work

This means that the techniques in this book can be used to your advantage to address their feelings, particularly when you are dealing with customer service people who haven't been fortunate enough to read this book! Here are some of examples of how you can use these skills in your own customer situations:

CASE 1: YOU NEED SOMEONE'S ATTENTION
Typical Customer: I have this really bad computer problem.

Using Role Reversal: You probably hate it when customers have complex problems, so I'll try to take as little of your time as possible.

CASE 2: SOMEONE DOES A POOR JOB, AND YOU HAVE TO COME BACK

Typical Customer: You messed up this repair.

Using the "I" Technique: I know how hard it is to fix these lawn mowers correctly.

CASE 3: RETURNING A DEFECTIVE PRODUCT

Typical Customer: This product stinks! It broke down after just a week. I'm really upset that you sold me such a shoddy piece of crud.

Using Staging: I want to show you what happened with this product. Most of these last for years under normal use—but this particular one cracked in half, right here, after just a week. I'd like to see if we can arrange a credit against a better-quality model.

CASE 4: MAKING THINGS RIGHT

Typical Customer: I demand a refund right now!

Using the Can-Can: I realize that you normally don't give refunds. But since this was clearly the store's fault, if you can make good on what I've paid for this, I'd be happy to consider the matter closed.

CASE 5: ASKING FOR A FAVOR

Typical Customer: Can't you upgrade me to a better hotel room than that?

Using Acknowledgment: You guys are really swamped tonight—I feel for you! I've had a long day too. If you can upgrade me, that would really be great—if not, I understand.

The common denominator in each of these situations is that you are also speaking to the interests of the person on the other side of the counter—just like good service professionals do with their customers. More important, you are using specific techniques that help you know what to say, in situations where human nature often gets the better of most of us. By bringing these skills to the table with our own customer problems, we can help things go much smoother on both sides—and get what we want much more often.

Situations like the ones in this chapter bring the core point of this book full circle: Specific communications techniques can dramatically change the outcome of almost any interaction with another person. Whether these are customer transactions; personal situations involving your coworkers, friends, children, or spouse—or even a critical, high-stakes scenario—the difference between success and failure is often nothing more than a simple choice of words. When you learn to handle customer situations well, using techniques that take the guesswork out of what to say, you are taking a big step toward improving human relationships in every other area of your life—and, in turn, reaping personal rewards that go far beyond good customer relationships.

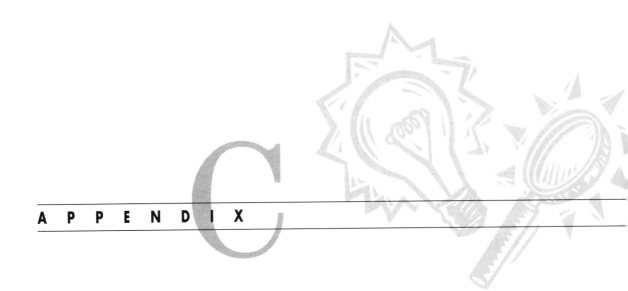

CUSTOMER SKILLS FOR GREAT CUSTOMER CONNECTIONS

This appendix is a convenient summary of the key communications skills described in this book. It follows the life cycle of a customer transaction from beginning to end and provides a summary of when to use each technique and how it works, with examples where appropriate.

I. BEFORE THE TRANSACTION STARTS

These techniques help with the important process of changing your mind-set toward a customer before a transaction even starts. This mind-set subconsciously affects your reactions toward customers as they interact with you.

Unconditional Positive Regard

Purpose: To counteract *negative expectation,* a self-protective instinct caused by presuming that a customer has ill will toward you.

How it works: First, frame your thoughts in terms of the customer's reality rather than your own. Then genuinely accept the customer's behavior for what it is, within the bounds of fairness.

E X A M P L E :

A customer is loudly comparing different products in detail with a friend. Instead of thinking "She's very picky," think "Making the right decision is very important to her."

Reframing

Purpose: To counteract *stereotyping,* where you make judgments about customers based on their outward appearance or demeanor.

How it works: Think of one unique thing that you respect about each customer, and picture it clearly in your mind.

E X A M P L E :

You see a young customer who is dressed in loud punk-rock clothes. Instead of thinking "This kid probably hates authority and has a bad attitude," think "This kid is very expressive."

Reattribution

Purpose: To counteract *personalization,* where you presume that a customer's behavior is directed at you personally.

How it works: Actively seek reasons to disprove that this customer has something personally against you, or means ill will toward you, and replace your automatic thoughts with more rational ones.

E X A M P L E :

Instead of presuming "This customer is angry at me personally," think "This person needs my assistance, and I know how to help him or her."

II. AT THE BEGINNING OF A TRANSACTION

The first thirty seconds of a transaction are a critical period during which customers form their first impressions of you, which in turn will affect their level of cooperation and teamwork with you for the rest of the transaction. The following techniques address how to create a strong, positive opening impression with customers.

The Opening Greeting

Purpose: Create an atmosphere that welcomes a customer, within the guidelines of your workplace.

How it works: Many organizations have scripted opening greetings, particularly in telephone or online service environments. If you can choose your own greeting, prepare and rehearse an opening statement fitting your personality and workplace that is:

- *Sincere*—say something you mean.

- *Appropriate*—meet the cultural norms of the customer situation.

- *Benefits the customer*—the first thing you say should offer a benefit.

EXAMPLE:

Opening greetings are as varied as the workplaces in which they are used. "Welcome, and make yourselves comfortable!" might be appropriate for a local bar and grill, while "Good evening, sir, how can I assist you?" might be more appropriate for an upscale hotel. Either way, choose something that is *sincere, culturally appropriate,* and *benefits the customer.*

First Response

Purpose: Respond to a customer's opening statement in a way that connects with the person right away and sets the stage for the rest of the transaction to go well.

How it works: First, address the customer's agenda—preferably using the person's own words. Second, acknowledge the customer's feelings, and remember that *feelings are never wrong.*

EXAMPLE:

Customer: I pulled too hard on this product I just bought and broke it.

You: I hate it when things like that happen! Let me show you some models that are sturdier.

Active Listening

Purpose: Make customers feel that you hear and understand what they are telling you.

How it works: The four key components of active listening are:

1. Showing interest and giving feedback

2. Gathering information

3. Keeping things light

4. Using eye contact and body language

EXAMPLE:

Customer: I need a new outfit to take on vacation to Bora Bora.

You: That sounds like fun—I wish I was coming along too! Tell me what the weather is like there, and I'll help you pick something out.

III. BASIC CUSTOMER COMMUNICATIONS

These techniques help you to deliver information to customers and respond to them in ways that create a much easier and smoother transaction on both sides.

Staging

Purpose: Delivering information to customers, particularly when they might not react well to this information.

How it works: Deliver information by using the following three-step process:

Step 1. Introduce what you are going to say before you say it.

Step 2. Explain what you are saying as you say it.

Step 3. Empathize with customers—whatever their response is—after you say it.

EXAMPLE:

(*Step 1: Introduce*) I have been looking over your warranty coverage.

(*Step 2: Explain*) Even though the warranty expired three months ago, we still have some other options for getting this camera fixed.

(*Step 3: Empathize*) This must be a really frustrating time of year for a camera to break down.

The *Jeopardy!* Technique

Purpose: Get customers to open up and share information with you, to show interest and gather knowledge to help them.

How it works: This technique is named after the popular game show rule to word things in the form of a question. Respond to customers with questions that are targeted, relevant, and benefit driven.

EXAMPLE:

Customer: I'm looking for a new stereo system.

You: I'll be glad to help you! Are you looking for a shelf system or a portable system?

The "I" Technique

Purpose: When customers do (or are about to do) something wrong, correct them without their losing face or feeling defensive.

How it works:

Step 1. Frame your comments in terms of yourself and not the customer; for example, "*I* know how this works, and *I'd* like to show you" instead of "*You're* doing that wrong."

Step 2. Talk about solutions that will help the customer; for example, "You will have to pay to fix this" becomes "Here are what options we have," while "You need to learn how to use this" becomes "I'd like to discuss some training programs that might interest you."

EXAMPLE:

You: Your computer crashed, and you didn't save your data? I certainly understand—I get really frustrated when I forget to save my work and lose it. Let's see what we can do to help you.

Role Reversal

Purpose: Defuse a bad customer reaction from happening in the first place by speaking from the customer's frame of reference.

How it works: Anticipate a customer's likely reaction, and then address this reaction *before* he or she responds—making it clear that you understand and acknowledge how it will affect him or her.

E X A M P L E :

Before: You'll have to wait in line over there, sir.

After: "I'll bet you had better things to do then stand in a line for twenty minutes! We'll get to you as soon as we possibly can.

IV. SHOWING RESPECT AND EMPATHY

Respect and empathy are skills, not just feelings. These techniques help you to show a genuine sense of concern for your customers in any situation.

Phrase Substitution

Purpose: To show respect for a customer's agenda.

How it works: Replace standard responses with planned, rehearsed phrases that say exactly the same thing, but are worded to be enthusiastic and responsive, and to acknowledge the customer's agenda.

E X A M P L E :

Before: That isn't my department. You'll have to talk to Sam over there.

After: I know exactly the right person for that. Sam is an expert on this, and he'll be glad to help you.

Playback

Purpose: To show empathy with a customer's feelings.

How it works: Make statements that provide customers with a playback of what they just said, worded in such a way that you demonstrate acceptance of their feelings.

E X A M P L E :

You: Because you want to fly as cheaply as possible, I have a flight for you that is $300 less than the next flight, and leaves two hours later.

V. PREVENTING AND DEFUSING CONFRONTATIONS

The vast majority of angry customer situations can be prevented, and nearly all of them can be successfully managed. These techniques help you speak to customers in ways that keep the heat from rising, and quickly defuse a difficult transaction.

The Can-Can

Purpose: Preventing or avoiding a confrontation when customers cannot get what they want.

How it works: Always respond with what you *can* acknowledge and what you *can* do. Never, ever say no—use "I wish" and "Even though" to transition to what you *can* do.

E X A M P L E S :

"We aren't open yet" becomes "We're glad you're here! I can seat you in just a few minutes."

"You can't get an appointment with Dr. Smith for three weeks" becomes "I want to get you in as soon as possible. Would March 21 work for you?"

"We can't do that" becomes "I wish we could do that. Here are some other options."

The Triple-A Approach

Purpose: Defusing customer anger when a confrontation has already started.

How it works:

Acknowledgment—acknowledge feelings and give the problem importance.

Assessment—gather facts and assess the situation.

Alternatives—set boundaries and sell alternatives.

E X A M P L E :

You: I can tell by your tone of voice that you're really frustrated about this. Can I get some information about what happened? Here are some options that we have from here.

VI. MANAGING SPECIFIC CUSTOMER PERSONALITIES

Customers have different personalities, and knowing how to recognize and communicate with them can make a noticeable difference in how well the transaction goes. Here is a summary of how to work with some of the most common customer personalities.

The Free Spirit

How to tell: These customers tend to march to their own drummer—they tend to not follow instructions and want to try things on their own.

What to do: To take good care of them, acknowledge their initiative, give them options, and ask them what they think.

EXAMPLE:
You: That's great! You're thinking very creatively about this. Here are some possibilities that I see. What are your thoughts?

The Solid Citizen

How to tell: These customers tend to want to get right down to business, with as little chitchat as possible. They have little patience for people beating around the bush.

What to do: To take good care of them and be serious, professional, and to the point.

EXAMPLE:
You: Here is a good solution for that problem.

The Thinker

How to tell: These customers are the classic know-it-all. They like to show their own expertise and want to feel that you are as competent as they are.

What to do: To take good care of them, share your knowledge of a situation, and be prepared to defend your suggestions.

E X A M P L E :
You: I've dealt with several hundred of these situations and in fact train other people on our team how to handle them. You've come to the right place.

The Feeler

How to tell: These customers want to know that you care, and nothing irritates them more than being treated like "just a number."

What to do: To take good care of them, show your concern for their situation, and respond to their feelings.

E X A M P L E :
You: This must have been really frustrating for you. I'm going to personally make sure that we take care of this.

VII. WRAPPING THINGS UP

These techniques are designed to handle "time wasters"—in other words, people whose personalities have the potential to take up large amounts of time—by using structured approaches for quickly closing the transaction and getting customer buy-in.

The Talkaholic: Using the Acknowledging Close

Purpose: Take control of the conversation when someone is talking too much.

How it works:

- Break in and *enthusiastically acknowledge* the last thing they say.

- Follow up with a *binary question* that requires a yes/no or short-statement answer.

- Continue using binary questions and take control of the conversation.

E X A M P L E :
Talkative Person: So I was on this fishing trip, and, boy, you should have seen the size of those bass, and—

You: You know, Steve, it seems like the fish are never biting when I go out there. Now, I just have a few more questions on this loan application of yours. . . .

The Strong, Silent Type: Using Feathering

Purpose: To help shy, reticent customers come out of their shell and communicate productively with you.

How it works:

- Listen carefully and intently.

- Respond with a roughly equal mix of questions, feedback, and reassurance.

- Go slowly and avoid information overload.

- Check understanding frequently.

EXAMPLE:

You: Are you sitting at your computer? Good. Now I'd like to have you click the START button in the lower left-hand corner of your screen, and tell me what you see. You are seeing a list of options? Excellent! Does one of them say "Control Panel"? That's perfect. We're doing great.

The Nonlinear Thinker: Using the Acknowledging Return

Purpose: To get a transaction with an intelligent but scattered customer back on track.

How it works:

- Acknowledge their tangents.

- Explain your position.

- Return them back on track.

- Repeat as needed.

EXAMPLE:

You: I can see why you are pressing that button—I might have guessed that too. But believe it or not, they actually put the OFF switch here on the side of the engine, over here. . . .

The Needy Novice: Setting Positive Boundaries

Purpose: To set appropriate boundaries for customers who need more help than you can reasonably provide in a customer transaction.

How it works:

- Refer them to more appropriate resources or training.

- Sell the benefits of these resources to them.

- Protect the customer's dignity.

E X A M P L E :

You: Lots of people are using computers for the first time, and I know some great training resources that can help you.

The Verbal Receipt

Purpose: Set customer expectations and set the stage to close the transaction smoothly.

How it works: Provide a proactive summary of action items from the transaction, and verify the customer's acceptance of these action items.

E X A M P L E :

You: You should be getting a replacement product sent to your home address within the next ten days. If you haven't received anything by then, please call us. Is there anything else we can help you with?

N O T E S

Chapter 1. The New Science of Customer Service

1. Joe Torre with Henry Dreher, *Joe Torre's Ground Rules for Winners* (New York: Hyperion, 1999), 7.

Chapter 2. The Inner Game of Customer Contact

1. Scott Frank and John Cohen (screenplay), *Minority Report*, Steven Spielberg, director (20th Century Fox/DreamWorks SKG, 2002).
2. "How Polite Are You?" (survey), http://surveycentral.org/survey/14853.html.
3. Susan C. Losh, "A Social Cognition Primer," Florida State University, http://syp 5105-01.fa02.fsu.edu/Guide3.html.
4. Susan C. Losh, "A Social Cognition Primer," Florida State University, http://syp 5105-01.fa02.fsu.edu/Guide3.html; Michael Shermer, *Why People Believe Weird Things*, rev. ed. (New York: Owl Books, 2002).
5. Daryl Sharp, "Jung Lexicon," *Jung Page: CG Jung, Analytical Psychology and Culture*, www.cgjungpage.org.
6. Laurie Budgar Dwek, "The Dummy Pill Cuts Both Ways; Placebos and Brain Function," *Psychology Today* (May 1, 2002).
7. Carl R. Rogers, Ph.D., *On Becoming a Person: A Therapist's View of Psychotherapy* (New York: Mariner Books, 1961), 62.
8. *Merriam-Webster Online Dictionary*, www.m-w.com/dictionary.
9. David Burns, *The Feeling Good Handbook* (New York: Plume, 1990), 111–112.

Chapter 3. The First Thirty Seconds

1. *Merriam-Webster Online Dictionary*, www.m-w.com/dictionary.
2. Carl R. Rogers, Ph.D., "The Therapeutic Relationship," in *The Carl Rogers Reader*, Howard Kirshenbaum and Valerie Land Henderson, eds. (New York: Mariner Books, 1989), 136.

3. Richard R. Terry, "What Patients Think About Their Doctors," *Osteopathic Family Physician News*, American College of Osteopathic Family Physicians (March 2003), http://www.acofp.org/member_publications/ca_0303.html; Daniel Goleman, "Working Smart," *USA Weekend* (October 2–4, 1998).

Chapter 4. Getting the Message Across

1. Morton Hunt, *The Story of Psychology* (New York: Anchor Books, 1994), 350–395.

2. Richard S. Gallagher, *Delivering Legendary Customer Service* (Central Point, Ore.: Oasis Press, 2000), 32–36.

3. Bruce E. Compas and Ian H. Gotlib, "Psychotherapy: Behavioral and Cognitive Approaches," *Introduction to Clinical Psychology: Science and Practice* (New York: McGraw-Hill, 2001), 353–384.

4. Frank Brady, *Citizen Welles* (New York: Anchor Books, 1990).

Chapter 5. Getting into Your Customer's Head

1. *Jeopardy!* (Sony Pictures Television), http://www.jeopardy.com.

2. Dr. C. George Boeree, "Albert Bandura," *Personality Theories* (online textbook), http://www.ship.edu/~cgboeree/bandura.html.

3. Garrison Keillor, "Almost Perfect" (Mr. Blue column), *Salon Magazine* (October 10, 2000).

4. Martin Buber, *I and Thou*, trans. Charles Scribner and Sons (New York: Scribner, 1970).

Chapter 7. How to (Almost) Never Say No

1. Terri Morrison and Wayne A. Conaway, "Lie to Me," *Frequent Flyer* (June 19, 2002).

2. "History," *Bal du Moulin Rouge*, www.moulinrouge.fr.

3. Graham Chapman, Eric Idle, Terry Gilliam, and Terry Jones, *The Complete Monty Python's Flying Circus: All the Words, Volume 2* (New York: Pantheon Books, 1989), 141.

4. *Love Story*, Arthur Hiller, director (Paramount, 1970).

5. Manuel J. Smith, Ph.D., *When I Say No, I Feel Guilty* (New York: Bantam Books, 1975), 104.

Chapter 8. How to Become a Human Bomb Squad

1. American Psychological Association Public Affairs, "Controlling Anger—Before It Controls You," http://www.apa.org/pubinfo/anger.html.

2. David D. Burns, M.D., *The Feeling Good Handbook*, rev. ed. (New York: Plume, 1999), 10.

Chapter 9. Managing Specific Customer Personalities

1. Morton Hunt, *The Story of Psychology* (New York: Anchor Books, 1994), 309–349; MMPI Research Project (official website), University of Minnesota, http://www1.umn.edu/mmpi/.

2. David Keirsey and Marilyn Bates, *Please Understand Me*, 5th ed. (Del Mar, Calif.: Prometheus Nemesis Book Company, 1984); "Keirsey Temperament Website," www.keirsey.com.

Chapter 10. Wrapping Things Up

1. Richard S. Gallagher, *Delivering Legendary Customer Service* (Central Point, Ore.: Oasis Press, 2000), 82–85.

2. Bill Rose, *Managing Software Support* (San Diego: Software Support Professionals Association, 1990).

Chapter 12. Pulling It All Together

1. Dale Carnegie, *How to Win Friends and Influence People*, rev. ed. (New York: Pocket Books, 1982).

Appendix A. Coaching for Peak Customer Experiences

1. A. Collins, "The Role of Computer Technology in Restructuring Schools," *Phi Delta Kappan* (1991): 73(1), 28–36; S. Daly, "The Role of a School Technology Coordinator: Changing Teachers' Attitudes and Their Use of Technology in the Classroom: A Review of the Literature" (report), *Action Research Exchange*, Valdosta State University, vol. 2, no. 1 (Summer 2003), http://chiron.valdosta .edu/are/; Brent G. Wilson, Roger Hamilton, James L. Teslow, and Thomas A. Cyr, "Teaching Methods and Technology," *ERIC Review* (Education Resources Information Center), vol. 4, no. 1 (Fall 1995): 3; Jon R. Katzenbach and Jason A. Santamaria, "Firing Up the Front Line," *Harvard Business Review* (May 1, 1999): 107; Richard Strozzi-Heckler, *In Search of the Warrior Spirit: Teaching Awareness Disciplines to the Green Berets*, 3rd ed. (Berkeley, Calif.: North Atlantic Books, 2003).

Appendix B. From Customer Service to Real Life

1. Haim G. Ginott, *Between Parent and Child: The Bestselling Classic That Revolutionized Parent-Child Communication*, rev. ed., Alice Ginott, and H. Wallace Goddard, eds. (New York: Three Rivers Press, 2003), 119.

2. Clayton E. Tucker-Ladd, Ph.D., *Psychological Self-Help* (online book), 1997, www.mentalhelp.net/psyhelp.

3. Randall C. Wyatt, Ph.D., "An Interview with John Gottman, Ph.D.," Therapist of the Month, Psychotherapy.net, 2001, www.psychotherapy.net/totm/gottman .shtml.

4. Rick Warren, *The Purpose-Driven Life: What on Earth Am I Here For?* (Grand Rapids, Mich.: Zondervan, 2002).

5. Bill Rankin and Don Plummer, "'I Believe God Brought Him to My Door': Taken Hostage in Her Home, Duluth Woman Shared Her Life, Faith," *Atlanta Journal-Constitution* (March 14, 2005); Daniel Yee, "Georgia Woman Held Hostage Describes Ordeal," Associated Press (March 14, 2005).

I N D E X

abusive situations, 122–125, 171–173

acknowledging close, 143, 146, 198–199, 223–224

acknowledging returns, 149–150, 224

acknowledgment
   in Can-Can technique, 95–96
   of customer's agenda, 77, 80
   of customer's anger, 165–166
   of customer's feelings, 56, 95–96
   of situations where you are at fault, 161–162
   in Triple-A approach, 112–114
   types of, 96

active listening, 37–44, 218
   in coaching, 189–190
   and eye contact/body language, 43–44
   gathering of information in, 41–42
   light touch in, 42–43
   in marriage conflicts, 210
   showing interest and giving feedback in, 39–41

admitting fault, 158–159, 161–162

advocate for customer, becoming, 166–167

agenda of customer
   acknowledgment of, 77, 80
   addressing, in first response, 34–35
   focusing on, 56
   respect for/response to, 76, 162–163
   and use of customer's statements, 84

agreement, finding points of, 209–210

alternatives
   in high-stakes problem solving, 163–164
   with inappropriate customer requests, 171
   with justifiably angry customers, 166–167
   in Triple-A approach, 116–118

anger
   abusiveness vs., 122–125
   causes of, 108–110
   defusing, see defusing hostile customers
   justifiable, 164–168
   as shared experience, 125

appropriateness (in opening greeting), 31

asking customers for information, 32

assessment
   questions used for, 114–116, 166
   in Triple-A approach, 114–116

attitude, 178

"attitude" school of customer service, 4–8

Bandura, Albert, 69

behavioral psychology, 1, 3
   in competitive sports, 6
   principles of, 5–6
   in transcending human nature, 8

benefits to customer
   in asking customers for information, 32
   in greeting remarks, 31

benefits to customer (*continued*)
  questions aimed toward, 65
  working to reflect, 94
Between Parent and Child (Haim Ginott),
  205
biases
  influence of, 12–13
  personality-based, 138
binary questions, 144–145, 199
blame-free atmosphere, 187
body language, in active listening, 43–44
boundaries
  crossing, 103, 124
  personal, 170–173
  positive, 151–154, 225
  setting, 103–104, 124, 151–154
Buber, Martin, 72–73
Burns, David, 25, 109

Can-Can technique, 90–105, 221
  as change in frame of reference, 104–105
  in coaching, 192, 193
  counterintuitive nature of, 91
  to deflect inappropriate customer requests,
    171
  life-or-death version of, 211
  limitations of, 102–104
  in practice, 100–102
  psychological basis for, 95
  replacing "can't" statements in, 92
  used with friends, 201–203
  what to say instead of no step in, 99–100
  what you CAN acknowledge step in, 95–96
  what you CAN do step in, 96–99
"can't" statements, replacing, 92
Carnegie, Dale, 176
catchphrases
  in first responses, 36
  in opening greeting, 31
  rewording of, 66
chatty coworkers, 198–200
chatty customers, *see* Talkaholics
children, using relationship skills with,
  203–206

closing conversations, *see* terminating trans-
    actions
closure, sense of, 34
coaching, 181–195
  benefits of, 2
  deficit-based, 184
  need for, 182
  popular image of, 182
  and service quality of organization,
    183–184
  strength-based, 184–188
  successful styles of, 6–7
  using customer skills in, 188–193
collective unconscious, 13
common ground, 96
  in empathizing, 84–85
  in staging technique, 52
communication, 45–60
  about inappropriate customer behavior,
    173
  as cause of customer conflicts, 59–60
  with children, 204
  impact of personality type on, 138
  reasons for poor quality of, 46–68
  self-protection in, 47–48
  staging technique for, 48–60
communication skills
  achieving success in, 183
  in basic customer communications,
    218–220
  at beginning of a transaction, 216–218
  for closing transactions, 223–225
  human nature vs., 3, 5
  for managing customer personalities,
    222–223
  for preventing/defusing confrontations,
    221
  for showing respect and empathy, 220
  for before a transaction starts, 215–216
competency, demonstrating, 54, 163
conflicts, communication as cause of, 59
confrontation
  avoidance of, 48, *see also* defusing hostile
    customers

with spouses, 207
and wording of remarks, 95
conversation stoppers, 198–199
courtesy, 4
criticism, lack of, 196–197
customer-focused responses, 35
customer perspective, developing, 61–74, 177
by putting things in form of questions, 62–67
with role-reversal technique, 71–73
ultimate goal of, 73–74
by using "I" technique, 67–71
customer service
attitude in, 178
"attitude" school of, 4–8
books about, 1
definition of, 3
new perspective on, 2–4
as science, 1
when you are the customer, 212–214
customer service skills, 178–179
human nature vs., *xi–xii*, 3, 5, 8, 9
value of, 2

deficit-based coaching, 184
defusing hostile customers, 107–125
and anger vs. abusiveness, 122–125
and causes of anger, 108–110
Triple-A approach for, 110–122
dignity, 3, 153–154
disrespect, 77

emotional participation (with spouse), 207
emotions, *see* feelings
empathy, 75–76, 82–88
with anticipated feelings, 87
definition of, 82
in difficult situations, 87
"playback" approach for showing, 83–88
respect vs., 82
as skill, 76, 88
in staging technique, 55–59
as technique, 57

ending customer transactions, *see* terminating transactions
enthusiasm, showing, 79
"even though" phrases, 202
expectations
for coaching, 194
of friends vs. customers, 201
expertise, showing, 41
explaining message, 53–54
eye contact, 43–44

facial language, 43
failure to execute, 109
fault, admitting, 158–159, 161–162
feathering technique, 147–148, 224
feedback
in active listening, 39–41
in coaching, 194
to improve service quality, 183
for Strong, Silent Type, 147
Feelers (personality type), 130, 134–136, 223
Feeling Good book series (David Burns), 25, 109
feelings
acknowledging, 56, 95–96
agreeing with, 36
anticipation of, 87
empathizing with, *see* empathy
and phrase substitution, 81–82
respecting, 77, 95
shared, 128
fight-or-flight response, 108
first impressions, 29–44
and active listening, 37–44
impact of, 29
key idea for, 44
and opening greeting, 30–34
when customers cause problems, 168–169
and your first response, 34–37
first responses to customers, 34–37, 217
fogging, 104
formalities
in first responses, 36
in opening greeting, 31

frame of reference, 104–105, 160–161
Free Spirits, 130–131, 222
friends, using relationship skills with,
    200–203

Ginott, Haim, 205
Gottman, John, 210
government officials, speaking like, 202
greetings, 30–34, 217

harassment, dealing with, 170–173
high-stakes problem encounters, 162–164
hostility management, *see* defusing hostile
    customers
How to Win Friends and Influence People
    (Dale Carnegie), 176
human bomb squad, *see* defusing hostile cus-
    tomers
human nature, *xi, xii*
    customer skills vs., *xi–xii*, 3, 5, 8, 9
    fundamental truths about, 185
    and self-protection, 14
    transcending, 8, 9
    and use of staging technique, 51
humor, use of, 42
    with inappropriate sexual behavior,
        171–172
    in "I" technique, 70
    when customers cause problems, 169

"I-It" relationships, 73
"I'm sorry," 101–102
inappropriate customer behavior, 170–173
information
    asking customers for, 32
    gathering, in active listening, 41–42
    providing, 54
    sharing, in staging technique, 52
information overload, 147–148
injustices, real/perceived, 109
inner game of customer contact, 11–27
    and key errors in customer encounters,
        14–15
    and mind-set toward customers, 25–26

and negative expectation, 15–19
neutral observation as basis of, 26–27
and personalization, 23–25
and science of "vibes," 12–14
and stereotyping, 19–23
interactions with customers
    behavioral psychology in, 3
    changing dynamics of, 3–6
    interactions with friends vs., 41
    key errors in, 14–15
    life cycle of, 6
    preconceived mental image of, 11, 12
interest, in active listening, 39–41
interrupting other people, 145–146
introducing message, 52–53
"I" technique, 96, 219
    with children, 206
    in coaching, 191–193
    in first responses to customer, 35
    with friends who impose, 203
    with spouses, 207–208
    steps in, 68
    in understanding customer perspective,
        67–71
"I-Thou" relationships, 73
"I understand" (use of phrase), 36–37

Jeopardy! technique, 62, 67, 219
Joe Torre's Ground Rules for Winners (Joe
    Torre), 6–7
Jung, Carl, 13, 129

Keillor, Garrison, 70
Keirsey, David, 130

learning
    from mistakes, 185–186
    psychology of, 182
learning moments, 158
"let's try this," different ways of saying, 136
life-or-death situations, skills used in,
    210–211
light touch
    in active listening, 42–43

in asking customers for information, 32

with inappropriate sexual behavior, 171–172

in "I" technique, 70

when customers cause problems, 169

limits, setting, 124

listening, *see* active listening

marriages, relationship skills in, 206–210

MBTI, *see* Myers-Briggs Type Indicator

"me first" responses, 35

mental images of customers

changing, 12

key errors in, 14–15

preconceived, 11

mind-set toward customers, *see* inner game of customer contact

Minnesota Multiphasic Personality Inventory (MMPI), 129

mistakes

admitting to, 158–159

learning from, 185–186

MMPI (Minnesota Multiphasic Personality Inventory), 129

modeling behavior, 6

in "I" technique, 69–70

learning by, 69

moments of truth, 6

moral high ground, 102–103, 167

Myers-Briggs Type Indicator (MBTI), 129–130

Needy Novices, 142, 151–154, 225

negative expectation

definition of, 14–19

unconditional positive regard vs., 16–19

neutral observation, 25–27

"nice job," different ways of saying, 137

niceness, good customer service vs., 3, 4

Nichols, Brian, 211

nocebo effect, 16, *see also* negative expectation

Nonlinear Thinkers, 142, 148–151, 224

"no," saying, *see* saying "no"

objections, anticipating/counteracting, 54

observation

basing "I" statements on, 68

neutral, 25–27

On Becoming a Person (Carl Rogers), 17

opening greetings, 30–34, 217

operant conditioning, 47

options, providing, 54

paraphrasing, 39–41, *see also* playback approach

passion for work, 41

performance

coaching and improvement in, 186

measurement of, 194

personal boundaries, 170–173

personality(-ies), 127–139

aspects of, 128–129

and attraction toward others, 128–129

benefits of understanding, 138–139

Feeler type of, 134–136

Free Spirit type of, 130–131

genuineness in expressing, 42–43

key types of, 129–130

self-perceptions of, 12

Solid Citizen type of, 131–133

tailoring phrases to, 136–138

and tendency toward anger, 110

Thinker type of, 133–134

personalization, 23–25

definition of, 15, 23

reasons for, 24–25

and reattribution, 25

by using customer's statements, 84

personal relationship skills, 197–214

with chatty coworkers, 198–200

in life-or-death situations, 210–211

in marriages, 206–210

when children misbehave, 203–206

when friends impose, 200–203

when you are the customer, 212–214

personal space management, 43–44

perspective, of customer, *see* customer perspective, developing

phrase substitution, 78–82, 220
placebo effect, 16
playback approach, 83–88, 220, *see also* par-
    aphrasing
police officers, empathy by, 87
politeness, self-views of, 12
positive boundaries approach, 151–154, 225
problems
    caused by customers, 168–170
    when you are at fault, 158–162
professionalism, 169–170
psychology
    behavioral, 1, 3, 5–6, 8
    of learning, 182

questions
    assessment, 114–116, 166
    binary, 144–145, 199
    for customers, criteria for, 64–65
    engaging customer with, 6
    ineffective phrasing of, 66
    in marriage relationships, 208–209
    in opening seconds of transactions, 41–42
    relevance of, 65
    responding with, 62–67
    for Strong, Silent Type, 147
    targeted, 64–65

reassurance, 42, 85, 147
reattribution, 25, 216
reframing, 21–23, 25, 216
relating to customer's situation, 52
relationships
    forms of, 73
    and knowledge of personality types, 138
    see also personal relationship skills
relevant questions, 65
rephrasing, 6
respect, 75–82
    and acknowledgment of customer's
        agenda, 77
    appropriate level of, 76–77
    in asking questions, 65
    definition of, 76

empathy vs., 82
    phrase substitution for showing, 78–82
    as skill, 76, 88
responsiveness, 80
Rogers, Carl
    on freedom to grow, 17
    paraphrasing in work of, 39–40
    technique developed by, 16–17
role reversal, 71–73, 219–220

safety
    in abusive situations, 124–125
    with inappropriate customer behaviors,
        172–173
saying "no"
    avoidance of, 89–90, *see also* Can-Can
        technique
    substitutions for, 99–100
science, customer service as, 1
self-deprecating statements, responding to,
    85
self-focused responses, 35
self-image (of customer), 83
self-perceptions, 12
self-protection, 13, 14, 47–48
setting boundaries, 103–104, 124
setting limits, 124
sexual harassment, 170–171
shoplifters
    Can-Can technique with, 98
    kindness in dealing with, 18
"should-y" approach to life, 109
showing interest, 39–41
silence, use of, 115
silver lining acknowledgments, 96
sincerity, 31
skills
    coaching to improve, 182
    respect and empathy as, 76, 88
    used in coaching, 188–193
Skinner, B. F., 47
smiling, 4, 43
Smith, Ashley, 211
Smith, Manuel, 104

social cognition, 13, 29
Solid Citizens, 130–133, 222
solutions, offering, 56, 58
speaking
    from customer perspective, 62
    like government officials, 202
spouses, using relationship skills with, 206–210
staging technique, 48–60, 218–219
    and causes of customer conflicts, 59–60
    with children, 204–205
    in coaching, 190–191
    empathizing step in, 55–59
    explaining message step in, 53–54
    introducing message step in, 52–53
    service professionals' experiences with, 51
    in situations where you are at fault, 159–160
    steps in, 49
stereotyping, 19–23
    causes of, 19
    definition of, 15
    of good vs. bad, 2
    and reframing, 21–23
    and social cognition, 13
strength-based coaching, 184–188
Strong, Silent Type, 142, 146–148, 224
systematic desensitization, 49

Talkaholics, 141–146, 223–224
targeted questions, 64–65
terminating transactions, 141–156
    with Needy Novices, 151–154
    with Nonlinear Thinkers, 148–151
    with the Strong, Silent Type, 146–148
    with Talkaholics, 142–146
    types of customers requiring, 141–142
    verbal receipts for, 154–156
"that would be stupid," different ways of saying, 137
Thinkers (personality type), 130, 133–134, 222–223

thinking
    effect of unconditional positive regard on, 18
    like the customer, *see* customer perspective, developing
    personalization in, 25
    reframing in, 22–23
threat assessment, 13, 14
time-consuming transactions, *see* terminating transactions
Torre, Joe, 6–7
Triple-A approach, 110–122, 221
    acknowledgment step in, 112–114
    alternatives step in, 116–118
    assessment step in, 114–116
    goal of, 111
    typical situation for, 118–122

unconditional positive regard, 16–19, 215–216
United States Marine Corps, 186
upbeat responses, 42

verbal receipts, 154–156, 225
"vibes," science of, 12–14

warm responses, 42
Welles, Orson, on hinting at scenes, 49
When I Say No, I Feel Guilty (Manuel Smith), 104
Wolpe, Joseph, 49
worst-case scenario(s), 157–174
    involving sexual harassment, 170–173
    staging technique for, 59–60
    when customer causes a problem, 168–170
    when customer is justifiably angry, 164–168
    when stakes are high, 162–164
    when you are at fault, 158–162

"you first" responses, 35

R ichard S. Gallagher is a former customer service executive who is a nationally known authority on communications skills and workplace culture. He has been described as "one of the founding fathers of modern customer support" by one of its leading professional societies. As the director of customer services for a major West Coast software start-up, Rich helped lead its growth to become a major NASDAQ firm. In addition, he has served on the management team of numerous high-growth companies.

Rich is a critically acclaimed author whose previous books include *The Soul of an Organization* and *Smile Training Isn't Enough*. As a popular corporate trainer and public speaker who specializes in the mechanics of how we interact with customers, Rich's unique approach has a track record of creating dramatic performance changes in customer contact organizations of all sizes. To learn more, visit this book's official website at www.greatcustomerconnections.com. For more information about Rich and his training and consulting programs, visit him online at www.rsgallagher.com.